MANY TONGUES,
ONE PEOPLE

Many Tongues, One People

THE MAKING OF THARU IDENTITY IN NEPAL

Arjun Guneratne

❖

CORNELL UNIVERSITY PRESS

ITHACA AND LONDON

First published 2002 by Cornell University Press
First printing, Cornell Paperbacks, 2002

Printed in the United States of America

Library of Congress Cataloging-in-Publication Data

Guneratne, Arjun, 1961–
  Many tongues, one people : the making of Tharu identity in Nepal /
Arjun Guneratne.
      p. cm.
  Includes bibliographical references and index.
  ISBN 0-8014-3912-4 (cloth : alk. paper) — ISBN 0-8014-8728-5 (pbk.
: alk. paper)
  1. Tharu (South Asian People)—Ethnic identity. I. Title.
  DS493.9.T47 G85 2002
  305.8'0095496—DC21

                                                                    2001006193

Cloth printing   10 9 8 7 6 5 4 3 2 1
Paperback printing 10 9 8 7 6 5 4 3 2 1

To the memory of my father
Upali Ananda Guneratne
and for my mother
Erica Guneratne
with love

CONTENTS

ILLUSTRATIONS

TABLES

PREFACE

This book is an account of the making of ethnic identity among culturally distinct and historically separate peoples. These peoples share an ethnonym, Tharu, and inhabit an area of the Himalayan foothills once known for its forests, swamps, and endemic malaria. This is the Tarai, which extends more than fifteen hundred kilometers from India's district of Naini Tal into Assam. Much of the Tarai lies within the borders of the modern state of Nepal, and it is with the Tharu of Nepal that this book is concerned.

Nepal is a particularly fruitful area for those interested in ethnicity, since the ethnology of Nepal readily shows the shortcomings of approaches that assume that ethnic groups are primordial. Identity in Nepal seems always to be emergent. Nancy Levine, whose important paper on the relationship of ethnic identity in Nepal to the state was an early impetus for this book, observes that "much of the writing on Nepal implies that groups such as Tamang, Limbu, Rai, and Gurung have an intrinsic and enduring ethnic identity" (1987: 74). Such views of ethnicity, writes Fredrik Barth, have produced in ethnography "a world of separate peoples, each with their culture and each organized in a society which can legitimately be isolated for description as an island to itself" (1969: 11). This outlook, Barth adds, does not address the question of the subjective human actor who creates his identity in the course of social interaction, instead of simply inheriting a given identity by reason of birth and upbringing (13–14). Over the last twenty years a large body of literature has been produced which moves away from this essentializing perspective to demonstrate the fluidity of identity formation in Nepal and its close relationship to the state—for example, Nancy Levine,

"Caste, State, and Ethnic Boundaries in Nepal"; David Holmberg, *Order in Paradox*; and an important volume edited by David Gellner, Joanna Pfaff-Czarnecka, and John Whelpton, *Nationalism and Ethnicity in a Hindu Kingdom*. This book is meant as a contribution to this literature.

I offer in this book a theoretical perspective on ethnicity that emphasizes its grounding in the political and material conditions of life. I argue against perspectives that see a shared culture or shared symbols as a necessary precondition for the emergence of shared identity. But this book is also an ethnography of the origins and activities of an ethnic (caste) association, a phenomenon about which little has been written in the ethnography of Nepal. It expands our understanding of the Tharu—particularly the Tharu elite—who are among the most numerous of Nepal's *matwāli* or liquor-drinking groups (often referred to erroneously as tribes).

This study of ethnicity is based on research conducted from November 1989 to May 1991 in a village I have called Pipariya, in the Chitwan District of Nepal. I was able to do additional research in the field in January 1997, in December 1997 and January 1998, and in March 1999. Pipariya and Chitwan were my primary field sites. I was able to accomplish what I set out to do because of the hospitality and friendship of many people in Chitwan. In particular I want to thank Satya Narayan Chaudhary and his wife Lakshmi. Satya Narayan worked for several months with me on this project before he had to return to his own studies; he introduced me to the social and cultural life of the Chitwan Tharu, interpreted for me during the first months when I was still learning the language, and over the years has transcribed endless reams of taped interviews. His house has been a home for me whenever I visited the district. I am grateful also to Indra Raj and Leela Chaudhary, Basu Dev Chaudhary and his family, Shukai Chaudhary, the Bidari family, and Dhana Raj Giri for their hospitality and friendship spanning ten years of visits to Chitwan. This book would have been impossible without the kindness that they, and other Pipariya villagers too numerous to mention here, extended to the inquisitive stranger who appeared one day on their doorstep.

Despite my focus on Chitwan, I was able to travel extensively in the Tarai. My first visit was to Kanchanpur in the far west, where I spent several days looking for a field site. I made several visits to Siraha, visiting Satya Narayan's cousin Parvati, who had married a man from that district. I made two visits to Saptari, where I stayed with Amar Lal Chaudhary. Much of what I know about the Kochila Tharu I learned from Parvati, her husband, Tulsi Prasad Chaudhary, and Amar Lal; I am grateful to all of them. I spent three days in Morang, during an important Nepal-wide Tharu convention there, and thank Sunil Kumar Biswas and his family for their hospitality. I visited Rautahat, where I was the guest of Kewal Chaudhari, and spent three days in the Tharu village of Jamuniya in Champaran District in Bihar. I returned to Nepal in 1999 to attend the jubilee of the Tharu ethnic organization known as the Tharu Kalyankarini Sabha, which took place in Hadiya village in the district of Udaypur. That visit was facilitated by Tribhuwan Chaudhary of Gallup, New Mexico (who patiently answered a flurry of last minute questions as this manuscript was being finalized), and Tilak Mahato of the Biosphere II Project in Arizona. They first brought the jubilee to my notice, and the hospitality of Lakshmi Narayan Chaudhary of Hadiya village enabled me to attend. I thank all of them.

My account of the Tharu Kalyankarini Sabha is based on interviews with many of its leading members, various publications put out by national and local Tharu organizations, and attendance at three of its meetings, including two national conventions, the first in 1991 in Biratnagar and the second in 1999 during the jubilee in Udaypur. I had the opportunity to talk informally with Tharus from different parts of Nepal at these two conventions. Having learned of the Tharu organization BASE (which is formally a nongovernmental organization but in reality a significant social movement) from the anthropologist Tom Cox, I made several visits to Dang, where I got to know Dilli Bahadur Chaudhari and saw firsthand the work of his organization during its early years. My account of BASE draws on extensive conversations with Dilli Bahadur Chaudhari and other activists during three or four visits to Dang beginning in November 1990 and on a follow-up visit in 1997. I benefited greatly from the unpublished papers that Tom Cox very generously made available.

Apart from the fieldwork, this book is also informed by archival research, some of it in Nepal in the Tribhuvan University Library and in the Kaiser Library in Kathmandu, but mostly in the India Office Library in London, carried out during the summer of 1991. I am grateful to Francis Pietersz and his family for their hospitality that summer. I have benefited also from my access to the papers of Merrill Goodall, at the Honnold Library of the Claremont Colleges in California.

The language in which this study was carried out was mostly Nepali, which I learned to speak fluently during two years of fieldwork; I also learned Chitwan Tharu, but when Chitwan Tharu was used in interviews I usually needed the help of my research assistant. I had studied Hindi during two intensive summers at the University of Wisconsin, and this knowledge proved useful in the multilingual discussions at meetings of the Tharu Kalyankarini Sabha. Interviews with some of the key figures of the Tharu Kalyankarini Sabha, including Parshu Narayan Chaudhari, Tej Narayan Panjiar, and Narendra Kumar Chaudhary, were in English; my discussions with Ramanand Prasad Singh, whom I met on several occasions, veered from Nepali to English as the mood took him. I thank all of them for making me welcome at the conclaves of the Tharu Kalyankarini Sabha. Most of my interviews with them were taped and transcribed, and I have been able to quote them verbatim in this book. Other quotes I have translated from the Nepali.

Apart from the people mentioned above, a great many others have contributed to the writing of this book (I hasten to add that the book's shortcomings are my responsibility alone). Over the years I have benefited from the critical reading, advice, and the encouragement of many. David Holmberg, Kathryn March, Katherine Bowie, and Jim Fisher have encouraged me over the years, and given me much critical feedback. David Gellner recruited me to the Sasakawa Peace Foundation's project on ethnic coexistence in Asia, which provided the initial impetus for chapter 4; I thank him and Chris McDonaugh for their critical reading of that chapter. I benefited greatly from the comments, criticisms, and all-around good advice of my thesis advisors, Barney Cohn, Terry Turner, and Hoyt Alverson. Colleagues who study Tharu society and culture (a small but growing band) have provided me with their publications and stimulated my thinking through their work: in addition to Chris McDonaugh I thank Gisèle Krauskopff, Ulrike Müller-Böker, Harald Skar, Kurt Meyer and Pamela Deuel, and the late Sigrun Ødegaard. This book has also benefited from the advice, criticisms, and general support of colleagues at Macalester College: David McCurdy, Jack Weatherford, and Anne Sutherland. Others who have helped in various ways include Shambhu Oja, Geeta Manandhar, Asif Agha, Stephen Mikesell, and Jamuna Shrestha. My students Bimbika Sijapati and Evan Acharya helped with the translations. I also thank Carol Gersmehl, Liz Hajek, Siri Eggebraten, and especially Gina Dabrowski for their help with the maps. Two reviewers for Cornell University Press and one for Cambridge University Press made very useful suggestions for improving the text, many of which I have taken to heart. I would also like to thank my copy editor at Cornell University Press, John LeRoy, for his meticulous work on the text.

My initial research was funded by a Fulbright-Hays Doctoral Dissertation Research Grant and by a grant from the Joint Committee on South Asia of the American Council of Learned Societies and the Social Science Research Council with funds provided by the William and Flora Hewlett Foundation. A doctoral dissertation research grant from the National Science Foundation paid for my return to Nepal for a second year of field-work and also funded three months of research in the India Office Library and Archives in London. I also thank the Sasakawa Peace Foundation and the International Centre for Ethnic Studies, Colombo, and Macalester College. Their financial support funded my return visits to Nepal.

My last and greatest debt is to my wife, Kate Bjork, who accompanied me to Chitwan during my second year of field work and endured with patience those times when we could not be together. She read and vigor-ously critiqued this book at various stages of its development. Many of her insights have found their way into the final text. My children, Ananda and Sara, have taken no interest at all in the question of the rela-tion of ethnicity to the state or to culture, which is probably just as well. They have given me something else to think about, and for that I thank them.

NOTE TO THE READER

Nepali and the various Tharu languages are written in the Devanagari script. In rendering Nepali and Tharu words into English, I have followed the convention in Turner's *A Comparative and Etymological Dictionary of the Nepali Language* with some modifications. Where Turner uses *c*, I use *ch* (e.g., "chaudhari"), and Turner's *ch* (indicating an aspiration) I render as *chh* (e.g., "Chhetri"). I use *s* for Turner's *s*, *ś*, and *ṣ*. Nepali and Tharu words are italicized on the first occurrence. I have pluralized them according to English conventions, by adding an *s*.

I have not used pseudonyms in this book except for my field site in Chitwan, which I have called Pipariya; the people who live in that village are also identified by pseudonyms.

Published sources consulted in Nepali or Tharu languages typically use the Nepali calendar (Bikram Sambat). I have indicated this in the text where appropriate with the abbreviation B.S. preceding the date. Otherwise, all dates refer to the Common Era.

Chapter 4 was originally commissioned for a study on ethnic coexistence in Asia funded by the Sasakawa Peace Foundation and published in *Multiculturalism: Modes of Co-existence in South and Southeast Asia* (Washington, D.C.: Sasakawa Peace Foundation, 1999). It will be reprinted in the final volume of that project edited by Darini Rajasingham Senanayake, *Multiculturalism: Cosmopolitanism, Co-existence and Conflict in Asia* (New Delhi: Sage, in press). Material in chapter 6 appeared in abbreviated form in "Modernization, the State, and the Construction of a Tharu Identity in Nepal" (1998) in the *Journal of Asian Studies* 57 (3):749–773.

MANY TONGUES,
ONE PEOPLE

❖

CHAPTER ONE

Introduction: Ethnicity and Culture

In January 1991 the Tharu Kalyankarini Sabha (Tharu Welfare Society) met in the town of Biratnagar in eastern Nepal. The organization counted among its members the elite of Tharu society—large landowners, government officials, professionals, and students—and this was their first nationwide meeting since the restoration of democratic parliamentary rule to Nepal the year before. The census later that year would record that there were 1,194,224 people sharing the ethnonym *Tharu* living in Nepal (His Majesty's Government 1999), but the Tharu elite has always decried the government figures as a gross underestimate. What struck me, however, as I listened to the speeches at the opening session of the meeting, was a phrase repeated by several speakers: "From the River Mechi to the Mahakali," they asserted, "we are all one jāt."[1]

The word *jāt* can be glossed in different ways; it means in essence "species" or "kind," and has been variously rendered by English writers as "tribe," "caste," "ethnic group," and "nation." But if indeed the Tharu were a single jāt, I wondered, as I sat listening to these speeches, why did their leaders feel it necessary to remind their audience of that fact? What did it mean to be a single unitary jāt? For while the state treated the Tharu unproblematically as a unity, with their own category in the census, they consist in reality of a great many named, historically endogamous groups sharing neither a language nor a distinctive culture that sets them apart. Here I sat in a hall surrounded by hundreds of Tharus who had come, at considerable expense and inconvenience, from as far away as seven hundred kilometers. Although they were speaking to each other in Nepali and Hindi rather than in their different Tharu languages, they had been brought to that place by their conviction that they had something in common: they were all members of a single "ethnie"—to use a term coined by Anthony Smith (1986)—in the multiethnic polity of Nepal.

This book addresses the conundrum posed by the Tharu elites' claim to ethnic unity: why people who seem to share so little in common, and who, by their own admission, considered themselves unrelated and distinct as recently as fifty years ago, have come to think of themselves as one people and have developed a sense of peoplehood through which to situate themselves in Nepal's polity.

Prior to modern times (that is, before the end of Rana rule in 1951), the Tharu of different regions did not think of themselves as all belonging to the same jāt. There was little intercourse between Tharus from different districts or regions, and perhaps little knowledge about other groups of Tharus. Ramanand Prasad Singh, a Tharu who served King Mahendra as his attorney general, remarked about the early days of the Tharu Kalyankarini Sabha, "As a matter of fact, [once] we became educated we thought of exploring for ourselves, [and] we used to hear that there [are Tharus here, and Tharus there and Tharus everywhere]. So we used to go from one district to another. . . . There was an institution called the Tharu Welfare Society, Tharu Kalyankarini, we founded [it]. And then it used to inform others about their own common origin." What Singh's words point to is that modern Tharu identity is not received from the past but has emerged from the conditions of modernity, the outcome of the organizing efforts of people whose life experiences are being transformed through modernization and state building.

Despite the critiques to which they have been subjected in the last three decades, especially since the publication in 1983 of Benedict Anderson's influential *Imagined Communities*, primordialist explanations of ethnicity—which hold in essence that contemporary ethnic identities are received, more or less unchanged, from the premodern past—continue to flourish, not only in the academy but, more pervasively (and persuasively), outside it. Ethnic conflict in the modern world is usually explained in terms of ancient hatreds, whether it involves Hutus and Tutsis in Rwanda-Burundi, Serbs and Albanians in Kosovo, Hindus and Moslems in India, or Sinhalese and Tamils in Sri Lanka. The case of ethnie formation examined here, that of the Tharu of Nepal, furnishes us with a laboratory in which the assumptions of the primordialist approach can be critically examined. But it also challenges some of the assumptions of the modernist school, particularly the notion that a common ethnicity implies a common culture—a notion that modernists and primordialists share.

I argue in this book that theories of ethnicity—whether primordialist, modernist, or instrumentalist—that stress its derivation from culture are too limited. For while theorists of ethnicity have seen some form of shared symbol as a sine qua non for the development of ethnic consciousness, the men and women who met in Biratnagar under the aegis of the Tharu Kalyankarini Sabha had only three things in common: their citizenship in Nepal, their common ethnonym, and the association of that ethnonym with a particular territory, the northernmost strip of the Indo-Gangetic plain called the Tarai. Ethnicity is contingent upon the historical circumstances in which it develops, and it is therefore not primordial and enduring but rather always changing. Although the existence of some ethnic labels can be traced back centuries—and *Tharu* is no exception[2]—what is important to the analyst is the content of those terms, the referents and the meanings that people attach to them. As Eugen Weber has shown, the category *Frenchman* did not have the same meaning in prerevolutionary France that it does today (Weber 1976). Frenchmen had to be created from Gascons, Bretons, and others through the active intervention of the state. The Nepali state did not deliberately set out to create a category called Tharu (at least so far as we can tell); but that was the effect of its policies.

Ethnicity is not primordial, nor is it simply the product of elites manipulating the consciousness of subaltern classes and inventing traditions, as some analysts seem to suggest. But as Anderson has noted, the idea of invention carries with it connotations of fabrication and falsity (Anderson 1991: 6). I share with Anderson the view of elite activity as a process of creative imagining encouraged or enabled by the changing circumstances of life. For the creative imagining of elites to resonate with the population at large (the ethnic group concerned), it must speak to the circumstances in which people find themselves. Ethnicity is the outcome of specific historical processes that shape a society's experience. Elites act to interpret and give voice to this experience. And very often these processes throw up leaders whose views are at odds with those of the old leadership. This seems to have been the case with the young Tharu men who founded the Tharu Kalyankarini Sabha, whose then radical ideas diverged from the more conservative views of their elders. The same divergence is repeated today with the rise of the Tharu social movement known as BASE (Backward Society Education), whose enormously successful grassroots organizing is seen by some members of the Tharu elite as threatening.

This book examines the shaping of ethnic consciousness as it emerges from the intersection of social and historical processes. The catalysts of Tharu ethnic consolidation were the changes in Nepal over the last fifty years: the collapse of the Rana dictatorship in 1951, the institution of a limited form of participatory politics, the impact of modernization, the effort to create a modern bureaucratic state, and the extension of rights and privileges of citizenship as opposed to subjecthood. The emergence of a Tharu ethnic consciousness was made possible in part by the spread of modern communications, which brought into contact communities once separated by vast tracts of jungle. Tharus had closer links to peoples and places north and south of them than they had to other Tharus to the east and west. Even as late as the early 1990s, the easiest form of ground transportation to the far-western districts of Kailali and Kanchanpur from other areas of the Nepal Tarai was through India.

The rapid social transformation brought about through the economic development of the Tarai is centrally important in shaping Tharu ethnic consciousness. For many Tharus it has resulted in the erosion of the relative autonomy they had enjoyed in the sphere of production, leaving them with much less land if not landless. Of crucial significance is the demographic shift that has taken place as a substantial proportion of the country's population moved from the hills to the fertile lowlands of the Tarai following the malaria eradication projects of the 1950s. At the same time, land reform introduced as part of the post-1951 modernization sought to give the tenants of the state (the largest tenurial category in premodern Nepal) property rights in the land they cultivated. But this system of private property relations, whose implications many ordinary Tharu tenant farmers appear not to have understood (Guneratne 1996; Pandey 1987: 11), led to their exploitation at the hands of some immigrants and to the loss of the land they had acquired. Throughout the Tarai and especially in the west, Tharus have lost control of land either through outright fraud or through indebtedness. In the western Tarai, many of them have been reduced to the status of bonded labor. The demographic transformation also meant that the expansive land frontier, which had once been a central factor governing the relationship of the state to its labor, was closed off. The option traditionally favored by the Tharu, that of moving elsewhere in the face of exploitation and oppression, was no longer viable. The malaria eradication project and land reform redefined the relationship between Tharus and hill people, usually to the detriment of the former. As Lionel Caplan puts it with reference to the Limbu of the eastern hills of Nepal, "Cultural identity becomes political identity in the context of the confrontation over...land" (Caplan 1967: 113). This situation is aggravated because the bearers of the dominant cultural tradition (the Brahman and Chhetri immigrants from the hills who have settled in the Tarai) collectively wield superior political and economic power. The Nepalese anthropologist D. R. Dahal remarks, "If the talk these days is of human rights, then the Tharus deserve special treatment among all the Tarai groups" (1992: 18). To understand the roots of Tharu ethnic consciousness, we must understand what these changes have meant and how they have affected Tharu identity.

Education has also been important, both the education that the children of elite Tharus received in India and, after the demise of the Rana state, the education that became available to Tharus with the establishment of a national school system. In the early years such schools were few and far between, but they provided a context in which Tharus from different parts of the Tarai could meet and interact. Many members of the Tharu elite first met one another in schools established during the fifties and the sixties. The school in Birganj, for example, educated many members of the Tharu elite in Chitwan, Bara, Parsa, and Rautahat districts. Singh's phrase "once we became educated..." is significant, for the Rana state had little interest in the construction of schools, and mass public education had to await the demise of that regime in 1951. The founders of the Tharu Kalyankarini Sabha were educated in schools in India. The schools that were later established in Nepal were (and at college and university level continue to be) the incubators not only of new ideas but of new relationships, as young men from different regions of the Tarai encountered others who shared their ethnonym but not their culture and language. These differences became matters that had to be negotiated and explained, and through that process of interpretation, new forms of consciousness came into being. Narendra Chaudhary, who was president of the Tharu Kalyankarini Sabha when I met and interviewed him in 1997, put the matter well: "This is what we ourselves are in confusion [about].... If they are...Tharus, we shouldn't be Tharus, [yet] we are. This is what strikes me all the time. Our culture is different, our dress is different, everything, you see. But we are all Tharus. So now we assume that we are all one."

While the encounter between Tharus and hill people has served to "Nepalize" the Tharu population in districts such as Chitwan,[3] it has also sharpened the sense Tharus have of being a distinct people. The changes that took place after the collapse of Rana rule in the 1950s—the opening up of the Tarai, the building of schools and roads, and the development of participatory politics, however limited in scope—made possible the emergence of a national Tharu elite that established itself in Kathmandu while retaining its ties to Tharu villages, communities, and regions. The development of ethnic consciousness among Tharus is particularly interesting because the different Tharu groups have little in common culturally except their common ethnonym. As a consequence of socioeconomic changes initiated primarily through the activities of the state, the boundaries (in Fredrik Barth's [1969] sense) between these groups are being dissolved. The Tharu are now well advanced in constituting themselves as a single ethnic entity, whose components are beginning to interlink, at least at the elite level, through relations of marriage. This is a significant departure from historical practice.

Like Leo Despres (1984) and Joan Vincent (1974), I treat ethnicity as "a mask of confrontation"; an ethnic consciousness exists only in opposition to other ethnicities against which it defines itself. Tharu ethnic identity is defined in contrast to that of the hill people, primarily immigrants of the dominant Brahman-Chhetri castes. Although an important factor shaping Tharu consciousness has been the impact of immigrant hill people on Tharu communities and subsistence, it is important to note that Tharus have been subordinated to hill states for centuries. While these hill states used Tharu labor to derive a surplus from the Tarai, the Tharu retained a great deal of autonomy over local affairs, as well as control over the factors of production.

Thus the sharpening and political articulation of Tharu ethnic identity is a result of a complex of factors, of which the state is one; there is a certain irony in this, because the Nepal government during the era of *panchāyat* rule laid great stress on a policy of "national integration." But if Tharu ethnic identity, in the sense of a politically self-aware identity "for itself," is partially an outcome of the state's own activities, I should add that Tharus in Chitwan and elsewhere are also conscious of themselves as members of a wider Nepali polity. To be Tharu does not contradict being Nepali; indeed a Tharu is reminded of that as soon as he crosses the border into India. The two identities do not exist in tension, which is what makes the Tharu case an ethnic rather than a nationalist phenomenon.

The Organization of the Argument

In this book I contend that it is primarily the energy and motivation of Tharu elites—large landowners, schoolteachers, university students, and professionals—that has led to the refashioning of the Tharu as a single ethnic group in modern Nepal. While there is undoubtedly an instrumental aspect to this, the actions of elites are also motivated by their belief that they have discovered a commonality of which they were previously ignorant, and which is indexed by the shared ethnonym. The label itself has become reified, and the question for Tharus becomes one of how to explain their differences, not their unity. The Tharu solution is to posit an original unity and then argue that underdeveloped conditions in the Tarai, especially its infrastructure, left them ignorant about their ethnic kin and produced the cultural and linguistic variation that one sees today.

My own status as a non-Tharu social scientist leads me to a different starting point, however, one that requires an explanation for the ethnic unity that Tharus claim throughout the Tarai. The problem here is that of the "imagined community," to use Anderson's well-worn phrase. The imagined community is an entity larger than a village (although Anderson seems to think even a village might be one) because its members "will never know most of their fellow-members, meet them, or even hear of them" (1991: 6). The notion is undoubtedly applicable to the ethnic group that the Tharu Kalyankarini Sabha is seeking to shape, but the degree to which smaller, more localized ethnic units are imagined in the same way is open to argument. Thus, for example, the Tharu of Chitwan, an endogamous group that in the 1950s numbered not more than twenty-five thousand people, did not have to imagine their kinship with one another; they were already bound by a network of affinal and consanguineal kinship that extended throughout the valley. A unity that is structured in this way is, in my view, very different from an "imagined community" where such linkages are absent; its existence poses a conundrum that the anthropological tradition stemming from Durkheim sought to address. That is, how do societies overcome their inherent contradictions and tensions to maintain conformity and cohesion? What makes societies solidary? The problem that this book seeks to answer is a different one: What forces lead people who have no historic linkages to each other to constitute themselves as a single ethnic unity? How (and why) is this sort of social and cultural contract negotiated?

In the remainder of this introduction I shall take up the question of the relationship of ethnicity to culture. But first let me begin with an overview of chapters to come. In chapter 2, I discuss the territorial basis of Tharu ethnic identity, that is, their self-identification as the aboriginal people of the Tarai, and I describe and compare the most important of the different Tharu groups that inhabit the region. The Tarai region was and continues to be of significant political and economic importance to the

Nepali state. It has a large population of recent Indian migrants whose political loyalties are, in the eyes of Nepal's ruling class, suspect. The region is a mainstay of Nepal's agricultural and industrial economy and a source of land for land-hungry hill people. The foundation on which Tharu elites are attempting to shape an ethnic identity is the common position that Tharus occupy in the political economy of the Indo-Nepal border. This position is related to the crucial role they have historically performed in the division of labor, to their relationship to the states that have to some degree controlled or defined their social systems, and to their close identification with a region (the Tarai) associated—in the popular imagination of non-Tharus (British, Nepalis, Indians)—with malaria.

In chapter 3, I examine two approaches that states take to multiethnic polities: the integrative and the plural. I discuss there the role of the nineteenth-century state in organizing identity through the creation of a national caste system (the plural approach) and the role of the twentieth-century state in seeking to de-emphasize the social and cultural distinctiveness enshrined in nineteenth-century legislation in order to create a Nepali identity in the name of "national integration."

In the anthropological literature on India, and in the writings of colonial officials, Tharus have been placed in the tribal category, in contrast to Hindu caste society. The category *tribe* is of little analytic utility with respect to the Tharu; as I show in chapter 3, the range of attributes displayed by different Tharu groups is so great that some groups resemble "tribes" while others look more like castes. The concepts of tribe and caste originate in the marginal status of the first with respect to the second; both are translations of a single native term, *jāt,* that does not distinguish between social groups in the manner implied in the English glosses.

Chapter 3 also critiques the way South Asian societies have been idealistically interpreted in terms of caste ideology. I suggest that caste systems are structured through the exercise of power and the control of resources, and that in the absence of polities committed to upholding the principle of caste, caste systems decompose into systems of ethnic stratification that can no longer be plausibly accounted for in terms of the concepts of purity, pollution, and the like. Caste is closely bound up with the exercise of power. Because caste, as a legitimate way to organize society and to structure intergroup relations, is no longer sanctioned at the level of the state in both Nepal and India, caste systems are being replaced by systems of ethnic stratification that result in very different forms of interaction between groups. The transformation in the nature of state power, and of the aims for which it is wielded, help to account for the reorientation of Tharu consciousness from the local to the national stage.

These interethnic relations are explored in detail in chapter 4, where I compare the experience of Tharus in two inner Tarai valleys, those of Dang and Chitwan, following the successful implementation of the Malaria Eradication Project, which allowed hill immigrants in search of land to move into both valleys. While Nepal has escaped much of the violent interethnic conflict that characterizes many parts of South Asia, it is by no means a land of ethnic harmony; Dang Valley has seen a "low-intensity" ethnic conflict between high-caste immigrants and Tharus, often centering on disputes over land. In Chitwan, however, despite the loss of land by Tharus to high-caste immigrants (although on a much smaller scale than occurred in Dang), there has been no interethnic violence, and relations between the various ethnic groups are reasonably amicable. In Chitwan social conditions for Tharus are not as oppressive as in Dang. In western Dang the vast majority of Tharus have lost their land to immigrants from the hills, and a great many were also forced into bonded labor. The class structure there corresponds fairly closely to the ethnic structure: high-caste landlords dominate a largely landless Tharu peasantry. Dang has produced, in the Tharu social movement called BASE, the only significant alternative to the Tharu Kalyankarini Sabha, although it is confined to the western districts of the Tarai. And unlike the Tharu Kalyankarini Sabha, BASE is a genuinely grassroots organization that has bettered the lives of some of the poorest segments of Tharu society. In Chitwan, Tharus lost much less land than in Dang; large Tharu landowners are still found in most villages; and there is no discernible correlation between class and ethnicity or caste.

Chapter 5 deals with the part played by the Tharu elite in fostering and shaping a sense of peoplehood. The principal agents of ethnic identity formation are elites, and their activities are typically located in ethnic organizations of various kinds. A given society may have several elite groups whose interests and philosophies are at cross-purposes; or an elite may be divided on the question of what constitutes the essence of the identity it seeks to promote. In this chapter and the next, I discuss the role of the Tharu Kalyankarini Sabha and other Tharu organizations in promoting an ethnic consciousness. The focus in chapter 5 is on the origins of the Sabha and its organization, and I provide brief biographies of some of its principal spokesmen at the national level.

In chapter 6, I discuss the cultural work of the Sabha: the public meetings, the activism regarding the language issue, the reshaping of marriage relations, and other ways in which Tharu identity is being remade. I also examine some of the tensions, both within the organization and between the Sabha and ordinary villagers. Thus, with reference to my field site, Pipariya, I discuss how the Sabha attempts to realize its leadership role at village level and how ordinary Tharus view its activities. I describe the Sabha's controversial resolution of an elopement case, which enabled me to perceive some of the class division and class consciousness that are usually obscured by the common ethnic identity uniting rich and poor against hill immigrants. The last chapter sums up my argument and places it in the wider theoretical perspective of how we understand the concept of culture.

ETHNICITY, SOCIETY, AND CULTURE

The general argument I make in this book is that contrary to the assumptions of many scholars, a common ethnic identity does not have to be predicated on a shared culture. Anthony Smith proposes six features of an ethnie: it has (1) a collective name, (2) a common myth of descent, (3) a shared history, (4) a distinctive shared culture, (5) a specific territory and (6) a sense of solidarity (Smith 1986). With respect to this typology, Tharus can be said to possess only features 1, 5, and (to some degree, particularly with respect to the consciousness of elites) 6. What the Tharu ethnic category lacks is a common myth of descent, a shared history, and a distinctive shared culture. With respect to shared culture, Smith writes, "Members of an ethnie are similar and alike in those cultural traits in which they are dissimilar from non-members" (26). But with respect to the cultural traits enumerated by Smith,[4] the Tharu differ as much among themselves as they do from non-Tharus. And some Tharu groups have more in common with non-Tharus with respect to these traits than they do with others with whom they claim an ethnic kinship.

Ethnic identity is not measured by checking off items in a list; it is relational and processual, and like any ethnic phenomenon it must be understood in its historical context. It is infinitely malleable and changeable, unlike the concept of caste, which has built into it (despite ethnographic evidence to the contrary) the connotation of rigidity or inflexibility. Paul Brass has urged that attention be paid to the question of the *formation* of group identity; the question for him is one more of process rather than structure (Brass 1974: 48). Ethnicity, like nationalism, is about "the production of ideologies of peoplehood" (Fox 1990: 3). The emphasis in that phrase, following on this understanding of ethnicity as processual, is clearly on production.

Ethnic groups and ethnicities are thus not fixed phenomena but are constantly being created and re-created anew; objective realities such as differences of language, territory, religion, and custom are transformed into the basis of a subjective consciousness or self-awareness. The study of ethnic identity is therefore historical in scope, even though ethnicity usually presents itself to us as a fait accompli. The Tharu case is noteworthy because the pan-Tharu identity discussed in this book is not yet an accomplished fact; we are able to go backstage and watch it come into being.

An ethnic identity, like other identities, is constituted through social contact; it must define itself dialectically in relation to other ethnicities (cf. Barth 1969; Despres 1984; Eriksen 1993). It serves to constitute them, just as they serve to constitute it. The force that propels the development of ethnic consciousness and identity is political. Ethnicity emerges in a political field that structures, in unequal terms, different cultural communities engaged in a competition for resources (see Comaroff 1987: 307). It expands or narrows as circumstances make necessary or possible; Tharu identity formation in modern Nepal is an instance of expansion.

That ethnicity can encompass a hierarchy of identities is well known. In other words, ethnicities can be differentiated into sub-ethnicities, with no necessary contradiction between the dominant category and the subordinate one. The culture of the primary group (the kin group, for example) can articulate, or be made to articulate, with the culture of other social groups in a hierarchy of identities. Such a system of identities is defined in opposition to hierarchies formed by social groups whose cultures are less compatible or, in Gellnerian terms, are more entropy-resistant.[5] But even here, identities that are incompatible at a lower level can arrive at a synthesis at a higher one; thus, in Chitwan, Brahman and Tharu are opposed identities, but Brahman and Tharu are both subsumed under the identity of Nepali. Similarly, American nationalism subsumes the deep-rooted conflictual relationship between whites and blacks in American society.

Although it might be banal to say that smaller ethnic units nest within larger ones (the metaphor sometimes invoked is that of a babushka doll), this hierarchization of ethnicity is often ignored or taken for granted in discussions of the topic. The notion of "inter-nestingness" (admittedly an awkward term) implies that the superordinate level encompasses more than one subordinate level or identity. Why the inferior levels (which may in fact define their particular identities in opposition to each other) should unite in a higher ethnic synthesis is not often asked.

At its most basic, ethnicity is a local identity based on the endogamous group. Tharu society in Chitwan, for example, is small enough and territorially concentrated enough to define itself on the basis of a kinship network and face-to-face interaction. Chitwan Tharus are historically structured as an endogamous unit; they are aware of the boundaries of this unit, which is for the most part congruent with a territory, i.e., the Chitwan Valley. Chitwan Tharu identity is thus a received one. Its structure, in terms of relations of kinship between villages and households, is fairly well known to its members. In this respect it resembles what has been called, in the ethnography of North India, a *jāti;* and is an identity taken for granted. It becomes a *self-conscious* identity when it enters into struggle over resources with other, similarly distinct groups with which it has neither a history nor the possibility of kinship. In this sense, kinship, whether real or fictive, is a basic building block of ethnic identity; the "imagined community" is the most abstract level of a hierarchy of identities based on the principle of real or supposed kinship.

Tharu identity in Nepal exists at two significant levels. The first level, as I suggested above, is a local one; it is an identity that is well established, deeply rooted, and structured through intermarriage. The second, more encompassing level of identity is fluid, constantly in the process of being refashioned; it is a self-reflexive identity that objectifies its "being in the world." My argument in this book refers to this second level. Social and political elites in the various culturally distinct communities that comprise the Tharu might have confined their activity to emphasizing their identity at the local level. Instead, they threw their energy into organizing a meta-identity, a sense of common peoplehood that would bring their communities closer together. This notion, that of a Tharuness shared with people from remote districts with whom one has no history of a relationship of any sort, must be inculcated through various material and symbolic acts (I discuss these in chapter 6). When an ethnic group encounters another with which it competes, and which it cannot assimilate, then processes of social reproduction normally taken for granted and therefore unquestioned are likely to become the object of self-conscious awareness, because they now appear as only one of a number of possibilities. This is the movement, in Bourdieu's terms (1977a: 169), from doxa to orthodoxy. Ethnic identity belongs in the domain of the latter, for its social processes can no longer be understood simply as natural processes, the normal way of the world. The once unquestioned aspects of one's culture then become the focus of argument, debate, discussion, and objectification generally, an essential dynamic in the creation of an ethnic boundary.

Ethnicity is shaped by state formation and economic development or modernization (cf. Gellner 1983; Glazer and Moynihan 1975). It is salient in political contexts because it is a form of identity that competes with others, such as class, in organizing groups to compete for resources. As such, ethnicity is a response to the process of cultural and economic transformation that has been termed modernization, and it is a close cousin to nationalism, into which it has the potential to evolve (cf. Eriksen 1993; Gellner 1983). As early as 1969, a prominent member of Nepal's national elite summed up modernization's fissiparous potential in the following terms:

> For though in the long run transport and communications, education and awakening tend to bind the diverse people of a country into a nation, the first effect of awakening is of group consciousness: consciousness of belonging to a caste, clan, tribe or village.... [U]nless a country conducts its process of economic development with a careful eye to its sociological effects, the immediate consciousness of particularity may prove too much for a nation. (Rana 1969: 7)

Terence Turner has discussed the transformation in the social consciousness of the Amazonian Kayapo from an unreflective, accepted cosmology to a basis for political action and self-representation in a multiethnic social system. In Turner's words, culture, in its ethnic context, "served to define [the Kayapo] as an 'ethnic group' distinct from and opposed to the dominant group" (Turner 1991: 294). Ethnicity is not coterminous with culture; rather it is a self-reflective, self-conscious understanding of it, which becomes salient under specific historical circumstances. Furthermore, a particular ethnic identity may subsume many different cultural identities, which is the case among the Tharu. Our task is to delineate the circumstances through which a cultural group (or set of groups) reconstitutes itself as an ethnic group.

An ethnic group is not simply a cultural group; it is a cultural group that is self-consciously aware of its culture, a group for whom its culture—or some aspect of it—has become an object and a symbol of its separate identity. Objectively speaking, ethnic consciousness does not require any great degree of cultural distinctiveness, but it does require that the members of a given ethnic group believe in their cultural distinctiveness. In this usage, culture is quite different from the unselfconscious process of social reproduction that characterizes pre-ethnic groups. Of the Kayapo, for example, Turner has remarked, "The cosmological terms in which [the] traditional Kayapo view of the social world [was] cast left no room for a consciousness of the structure of this integral process of social production as itself a social product. It was, rather, seen as the natural structure of the cosmos" (Turner 1991: 295). Or as Ernest Gellner puts it, "In the old days it made no sense to ask whether the peasants loved their own culture: they took it for granted, like the air they breathed, and were not conscious of either" (1983: 61). From being a "natural" (unquestioned) aspect of one's existence, culture becomes reified through reflection and objectification of certain practices and key symbols. It is only when culture becomes politically relevant that ethnic or national identity is fashioned.

Although there is cultural content in ethnic identity, an ethnic group is not necessarily coterminous with a specific cultural group. An ethnic label may simply be a classification applied by outsiders or by the state to a collectivity to facilitate interaction. In Nepal, for instance, the label *Tamang* was invented by the state to classify a collectivity of diverse peoples lacking a uniform culture, social structure, or language; its creation laid the basis for the emergence of an ethnic identity structured around it (Levine 1987: 73; Holmberg 1989). An ethnic label may also be adopted by the people themselves for the same purpose, as in the case of *Magar* (Fisher 1986: 3; cf. Levine 1987). Because certain ethnic labels were imbued with a certain prestige or value, people began to adopt them as a way of laying claim to or partaking in that status; they became in fact a summation of status (Fisher 1986: 3).

Approaches to Understanding Ethnicity

The concept of ethnicity has been applied in a variety of ways in the study of cultural differences and social interaction. These approaches can be divided into two broad categories. On the one hand are those who believe that ethnicity is primordial and natural; important proponents of this view include John Armstrong (1982), Walker Connor (1978), Edward Shils (1957), Anthony Smith (1986), and Pierre Van den Berghe (1981). On the other, ethnicity is viewed as being historically contingent, relational, and shaped by the material and social forces of the time (Comaroff 1987; Eriksen 1993).

The term *ethnicity* was first used by the sociologist David Riesman in 1953 (Glazer and Moynihan 1975: 1), but Shils appears to have been the first to posit that it referred to a form of primordial identity (Thompson 1989: 7). The primordialist position is based on the assumption that "a group identity is an indispensable aspect of a person's personal identity" and, following from this, that ethnic attachments are the most natural kind of group affiliation (55–56).

The idea of primordiality may be understood in two ways. It may be an essential identity, defined by the metaphor of blood: an ethnic group consists of people who are of one blood and whose essential biological unity is expressed in a common culture that has remained fundamentally unchanged through the centuries. This is the view held for example by Shils (1957) and Harold Isaacs (1989). It should not need reiterating, however, that cultures are not immutable. There is no necessary relationship between any given culture—as a system of values, beliefs, and practices—and the genetic endowment of those whose way of being is shaped by it. Cultures change and become the basis for the creation of different social formations—which may, under certain conditions, become ethnic groups. The primordialist approach cannot satisfactorily explain the fluidity of ethnic identity, its ability to metamorphose into something new.[6]

What is primordial about ethnicity is not a particular cultural content or a particular label but the fact that human beings have always organized themselves into groups defined in opposition to other groups. There is nothing in nature, nor for that matter in culture, that specifies what kind of group that should be, how large it is, how extensive, or how inclusive. The social group that has the individual's primary allegiance can vary from the immediate kin group to the nation. The primary group for most of human history was the kin group and, perhaps, the network of such groups established through marriage. Beyond these groups, which are small enough for direct contact among their members, the community can only be imagined. The more broad-based a particular social identity becomes, and the more it cuts across other allegiances and identities, the less likely it is to have developed in an organic, unreflective manner. On the contrary, allegiance to a particular identity that is preeminent or apical in a system of inter-nesting identities comes about only when human beings actively promote their own interpretations of their community experience and contest those of others. Their activities are a response to, or emerge from, and are validated by specific historical conditions. In Nepal, the historical conditions that have led in modern times to the emergence of a pan-Tharu ethnic unity could just as well have resulted in the intensification of regional Tharu identities to the exclusion of the pan-Tharu one. For instance, the Kochila Tharu of the Birganj area (the modern districts of Bara, Parsa, and Rautahat), whose elites took the lead in founding the Tharu Welfare Society, could have simply confined their ethnic activism to their own region and its villages; they share a common language (Bhojpuri Tharu), they are substantially Hinduized, and they share many of the features that theorists of ethnicity have come to expect as characteristic of an ethnic group. Instead, the Kochila Tharu elite sought to build links to ethnic communities, particularly in the far west of the country, with which it had nothing in common culturally except a shared ethnonym. The ideas and vision of the social groups and individuals who provide leadership is clearly of central importance to the formation of identity. Although the consciousness of most Tharus—who may be landless bonded laborers or small peasants—may be intensified by their experience of the state's praxis, there is nothing intrinsic to that experience that would lead them to forge ties to Tharus living in other parts of the country. It is their social and political elites who interpret those experiences in ways that encompass others sharing their ethnonym.

Among the Tharu of Nepal, ethnic identity is, on the one hand, purely local (the identity of a particular Tharu group in a particular region, which defines itself in contrast to the other ethnic groups in that area) and, on the other, a collective consciousness of the various different groups in the Tarai calling themselves "Tharu," a consciousness that defines itself vis-à-vis other ethnic groups in a multiethnic state. This consciousness is generated as particular Tharu groups establish relations (political, marital) with others of their category, a process that structures them as self-conscious groups. The endogamous group is taken for granted by its members as the natural, self-evident unit of social reproduction; its members do not reflect on it. In contrast, if a group is to dissolve its boundaries and amalgamate with other groups in order to shape a new unit of social reproduction (as Tharu elites have done), it can do so only when the group itself, as a cultural entity, rises into the self-awareness of its members as an object to be discussed and thought about. The local Tharu group becomes conscious of its cultural distinctiveness when it is brought into a close, competitive, and conflictual relationship with a larger, better organized, and culturally different population that threatens its ability to reproduce itself in the "natural" way; it is this threat that makes it self-conscious and engenders an ethnic consciousness. Praxis is no longer "self-evident" but must be rationalized and even defended because the presence of a politically and culturally dominant ethnie subjects one's habitus (Bourdieu 1977a) to a daily interrogation. Because all such Tharu groups, occupying as they do a structurally similar space in the political economy of the state, share a similar experience and the same ethnonym or ethnic category, they have both a subjective and an objective basis on which to form alliances and engender the next level of ethnic identity formation.

The situation described here is analogous to the expansion of caste categories in India, which took place when local caste groups began to establish political and social relations with other such groups with which they had formerly had no contact. That became possible only with the demise of the premodern states, which had integrated society vertically in caste hierarchies reinforced and maintained by royal power. The dissolution of that power permitted castes to establish links with other castes that had formerly been integrated along the same lines in other polities. For reasons that will become clear, ethnic identity cannot be assimilated to caste in this situation; castes, however, are being transformed into ethnic groups. (I return to this point in chapter 3.)

The other set of approaches to the analysis of ethnicity can be subsumed under the rubric of social-historical: they emphasize the contingent nature of ethnicity. This approach is exemplified in the work of Brass (1974, 1991), John Comaroff (1987), Thomas Eriksen (1993), and, in relation to nationalism, Anderson (1991) and Gellner (1983). Brass in particular and John Breuilly (1982) have emphasized the extent to which ethnic identity is created through the purposeful activities of dominant classes or elites. Elite consciousness is a precondition for mass ethnic consciousness; elite consciousness lends color, form, and direction to the subjective beliefs of the mass of people. As Brass puts it with reference to the vehicles of elite organizing, political organizations and voluntary associations do not arise spontaneously, reflecting the demands of a "natural" ethnic group. They often precede the existence of a widespread sense of group identity, and they play a critical role in shaping it (Brass 1974: 38).

This does not mean that elites are simply able to manipulate popular consciousness at will. For elites to succeed in shaping a common consciousness among groups, or a feeling of cultural solidarity, there must exist some symbol, some reason, that makes their constituency receptive to the idea. Sometimes, even when the symbol is well defined and serves to distinguish a particular group, it fails to be effective and the elite project is rejected. The Maithili movement in North Bihar described by Brass (1974) is one such case.

The Maithili movement was a political project led by the Maithili-speaking Brahman-Kayastha caste elite in North Bihar to have Maithili recognized as one of the national languages of India and, ultimately, to demarcate a separate Maithili-language state in the Indian Union. This effort failed because Maithili speakers have different social identities, of which the linguistic is by no means the most important. The Yadavs, for example, a significant component of Maithili speakers in North Bihar, form a politically important caste category throughout northern India and have organized themselves on that basis. Since Maithili speakers used a colloquial idiom that was closer to the Hindi of their neighbors than to the Maithili of the Maithili-speaking elite, they identified the Maithili language with the Brahman and Kayastha elite that promoted the movement. Unlike the Yadavs, the Brahmans and Kayasthas had no social alliances with others of their caste categories outside the Maithili-speaking area. Nor is the failure of the Brahmans to mobilize mass support due to a lack of political involvement on the part of the masses; Brass points out that Maithili speakers have the highest rate of participation in electoral politics in Bihar. The Maithili-speaking elite was competing with the elites of the socially inferior castes they wished to mobilize, to define the issues of political relevance. Mithila is the poorest part of Bihar, and intercaste relations there are among the most violent. Maithili-speaking Biharis were more effectively mobilized along issues arising out of this situation than they were by the elitist, and in their view irrelevant, demands of the dominant Brahman and Kayastha castes. The symbol of the Maithili language itself (the most plausible symbol around which to organize an imagined Maithili ethnicity) proved to be inadequate for two reasons: it lacked the force to draw the different Maithili-speaking peoples together on the basis of a common ethnicity, and it lacked sufficient definition and clarity to constitute a boundary that would separate them from other groups.

The point is that although elites are the principal agents through which ethnic and nationalist consciousness may be shaped, there must first be something to shape. The mere existence of a shared symbol does not draw people together; conversely the lack of such a symbol does not necessarily militate against the creation of ethnic unity.[7] Elite groups which strive to organize their communities into ethnic groups must have some basis on which to do so. There must be some political or social issue that people find relevant to their experience and on the basis of which they may be mobilized; when people imagine communities, they do so based on something and in response to something. That something must be sufficiently powerful to subordinate all other issues. Where Tharus are concerned, it is access to and control of land.

Barth criticizes "objective" approaches to ethnicity because they leave unaddressed the question of ethnic boundaries and their maintenance. As a consequence of this theoretical omission, these approaches lead to the production of "a world of separate peoples, each with their culture and each organized in a society which can legitimately be isolated for description as an island to itself" (Barth 1969: 11). South Asian ethnography is no exception. James Fisher observes of anthropologists studying Nepal in the decades after it was opened to foreign scholars that they assumed that "the relevant units for study are either tribes or villages, both of which are conceived of as separate, independent, fragmented entities" (Fisher 1985: 106). As a consequence, little attempt was made to fit these village studies into a broader perspective, or to explore the relationship of these "little communities" to the developing Nepali state. In the last couple of decades, however, the ethnography of Nepal, reflecting a general shift in anthropological concerns, has moved away from the parochial conceptualization of discrete and self-sufficient cultures isolated in their own locales. Nancy Levine (1987), for example, has related processes of ethnic transformation and ethnic labeling to the policies of the centralizing Nepali state. Andras Höfer has noted that the term *Rai* originally referred to the heads of local descent groups among the contemporary population labeled with the ethnonym *Rai*, which is, he says, "an artificial designation of recent origin under which a great number of more or less endogamous local groups with considerable varying dialects are subsumed" (Höfer 1979: 142). More recently David Holmberg has pointed to the recent ethnogenesis of the Tamang (Holmberg 1989). William Fisher (1987) has analyzed Thakali ethnicity along the same lines. This book builds on this reconceptualization of the nature of Nepali society and the relationship among the various elements of its population. I shall show that Tharu ethnic identity in Nepal is itself contingent upon the praxis of the state and upon the relationships that Tharus have established with other ethnic groups, particularly the hill people who have settled in the Tarai in recent years.

In summary, we cannot treat ethnicity as something primordial or enduring. Ethnicity, like nationalism, is socially constructed out of pre-existing cultural orders, and social and political elites are significant actors in this process. Not all of the potentially infinite number of symbols available will be used in this construction; some will be more salient. The effectiveness of the symbol is determined by the extent to which it can, first, speak to the population whose identity it essentializes and, second, establish a boundary demarcating that population. The attempt, for example, by Tamil nationalists in Sri Lanka to include all Tamil-speaking people as belonging to the ethnic (or national) category of Tamil failed because of the refusal of Muslim Tamil speakers to count themselves in. For these Muslims, the essence of their identity was rooted in religion, not language. But even where a common symbol does not exist in an objective sense, it can be creatively imagined. For the Tharu, we shall see, such a symbol is language. But before we discuss the material and symbolic production of the Tharu ethnic category, we need to understand the relationship that the people sharing that ethnonym have to a particular territory, the Tarai, and to each other. We need also to understand the political context in which that production takes place. That is the work of the following two chapters.

CHAPTER TWO

The Tharu and the Tarai

The various ethnic groups subsumed under the shared ethnonym Tharu inhabit the region of Nepal known as the Tarai, of which they account themselves the aboriginal inhabitants. This also is the way outsiders perceive them. The Tharu are thus identified and grouped together by their attachment to a particular region and an associated way of life. The Tarai is also a region of particular significance. On the one hand, it is the interface between the distinctive Himalayan culture area and that of the Indo-Gangetic plain. Politically, the Tarai has been a zone of transition between the power of the hill rajas, always insignificant until the rise of the House of Gorkha, and the imperial states that ruled the plains of India. It was the bulwark that protected those rajas from the attention of their more powerful lowland neighbors. The Tarai has also been a refuge: for criminals, for political refugees, and in recent times, for Sikh militants from the Punjab. But the most powerful symbol of the Tarai, and one that has attached to the Tharu as an attribute of their identity, is malaria, to which the native inhabitants are thought immune.

The word *tarai* refers to that strip of the Indo-Gangetic plain that abuts the foothills of the Himalaya and stretches over two thousand kilometers from the district of Naini Tal in northwestern Uttar Pradesh to Arunachal Pradesh in India's far eastern corner. The meaning of the word, according to Frederick Gaige, who cites various unspecified Hindi and Urdu sources, is "land at the foot of mountains, often wet and swampy land" (Gaige 1975: 2). This strip varies from a few kilometers in breadth to about fifty-three kilometers at its broadest. It was heavily forested until modern times, the dominant species being sal (*Shorea robusta*). By the end of the nineteenth century, although still substantial, this forest had been reduced to a fraction of its former extent. Today, only a remnant survives, mostly along the western portion of the Indo-Nepal border. The greatest extent of the surviving Tarai forests is in Nepal's westernmost Tarai districts of Kanchanpur, Kailali, Banke, and Bardiya.

C. G. Trevor and E. A. Smythies, the authors of a manual on forest management for the Forest Department of British India, considered it likely that large areas of the sal forest of northern India had been cleared and cultivated in very ancient times. They believed this process ceased with the decline of Buddhism. "Once a *sal* forest has been effectively cleared for cultivation a very long period would have to elapse before such cultivation would revert to *sal* forest, although it would quickly relapse into waste with scattered miscellaneous trees and shrubs" (Trevor and Smythies 1923: 3). Lumbini, where the Buddha was born, is located in the Tarai, and so are numerous other places associated with Buddhism. This has relevance for the contemporary representation of Tharu identity, for leading Tharu intellectuals argue that the Buddha was a Tharu (I discuss this in chapter 6). The region was in decline by the fourth century A.D., and the vast expanses of forest that characterized it when the British arrived had taken hold by the seventh century. From being an important and vital part of the civilization of northern India, the Tarai became marginal to the economy and affairs of the Gangetic states until close to the modern era, although it was always important to the adjacent hill states.

The Tarai is characteristically swampy and marshy, with forests of sal trees interspersed with tracts of tall grassland over fifteen feet high. The land slopes gently away to the south and east from the Himalayan foothills, which are variously known as the Siwaliks or the Churia. The transitional region between the hills and the plains proper is known as the Bhabar, a zone of alluvial fans composed of highly porous gravels, rocks, and sands washed down from the hills. In places these hills diverge from the main mountain range, the Mahabharat, which lies behind them. The valleys that result are known as *dūns*, and are referred to as the Inner Tarai, or, in Nepali, *bhitri mades,* as opposed to the Tarai, which is *mades.*

Rivers originating in the mountains and flowing south to unite with the Ganges drain this northern extremity of the Gangetic Plain. In the dry season, these rivers are reduced to sluggish trickles meandering between vast expanses of hot sand, which sometimes exceed a kilometer or two in width. During the monsoon, they become wild torrents that make travel in the Tarai difficult and sometimes impossible. This, plus the dense forests that existed well into this century, discouraged extensive contacts among the various Tharu groups prior to modern times.

MALARIA

The defining attribute of the Tarai is malaria. The hill people feared it, and if they went into the lowlands or the Inner Tarai valleys such as Chitwan or Dang, it was during the day only. To spend a night in the Tarai was thought to tempt death. One British observer, who likened the region to the Roman Campagna under the Alban Hills because of the malaria, wrote, "Plainsmen and *paharis* [hill people] generally die if they sleep in the Terai before November 1 or after June 1" (Webber 1902: 197). Endemic malaria discouraged extensive immigration into the region from other areas of northern India, although such immigration did take place, particularly in the latter half of the nineteenth century. That and the inhospitable summer climate of the Tarai kept the hill people out as well. British travelers to Kathmandu would cross the Tarai from their entry point at Raxaul as quickly as possible, to get into the hills before nightfall and the onset of the aul (from *aulo*, malaria). The Tarai became a place of mystery and danger that was better avoided. By extension, perhaps, some of this mystery attached itself to the few human groups that lived there. Plains people, according to nineteenth-century British sources, believed Tharu women to be adept at witchcraft and avoided contact with the Tharu (cf. Crooke 1896: 405; Alexander 1881: 358). The Reverend S. Knowles, a British missionary in Gonda during the latter half of the nineteenth century, reported that "the forest officer...had the greatest difficulty in getting carpenters and masons to come out and build his house; because they were afraid of Thâru *tona!*"—that is, the power of the evil eye (1889: 215).

There is also a widespread belief, prevalent even today, that Tharus are immune to malaria, or perhaps less susceptible than most to its ravages. Although this belief is routinely repeated in the ethnographic literature of nineteenth-century British India, not everyone subscribed to it. Sir Joseph Fayrer, himself a physician, observed that although the Tharu were said to be immune to the disease, "the appearance of many of them belied it" (Fayrer 1900: 119; he refers to a meeting with Tharus in 1855). Orfeur Cavenagh observed of them, "The Tharus are the denizens of the

Terai, and are said not to suffer from the deadly malaria, they are how-ever sickly-looking men, and although from their being acclimatized, the poison may not work actively or rather speedily upon their frames, it is evident that their constitutions are debilitated and undermined from its effects, and their lives are, I believe, of short duration" (1851: 94). Another observer wrote of the Tharu, "They live in a particularly sub-merged tract where, from the unwholesome climate, they are the victims of fever and ague and other diseases."[1]

Recent medical research appears to confirm popular belief in the (rela-tive) immunity of Tharus to malaria. L. Terrenato and his colleagues analyzed the records of the Nepal Malaria Eradication Organization and discovered that the incidence of malaria in Tharus is substantially lower (at least a sixfold difference) than among hill people. They con-clude that "the historical data" and their epidemiological findings pro-vide evidence "for a very substantial and peculiar ability of the Tharu people to resist mortality and morbidity from malaria" (Terrenato et al. 1988: 9). They discard cultural explanations for this—for example, that Tharus are better protected against mosquito bites or that their diet might contain some antimalarial substance—as unsatisfactory. They conclude that the most plausible explanation is that "Tharus have a genetically determined resistance factor which may or may not be one of those already known" (10). G. Modiano and colleagues (1991; cited in Shafey 1997: 34) subsequently discovered that the Tharu had "developed a hemoglobin variant, alpha-thalassemia, which allowed them to survive the malaria hyperendemicity of the lowland jungle." Hill people and the people of the Gangetic plains do not have this genetic adaptation, which "disrupts the invasion and multiplication of *Plasmodium* parasites" (Shafey 1997: 34).

Mark Weiss and Alan Mann attribute the spread of malaria to the clearing of forest land for agriculture. They add, "The mosquito that car-ries the parasite has little chance of breeding in a tropical rain forest; although its breeding sites are highly diversified, it cannot reproduce in shaded, salty, or polluted water" (1990: 491). Continued cultivation makes the ground impervious to water, and coupled with poor drainage, this results in the creation of breeding grounds for mosquitoes. While it is beyond the scope of this book to investigate this further, the agricul-tural activities of the Tharu themselves may have helped to perpetuate the incidence of malaria. The Tarai, however, is an area that is naturally wet and marshy, and it is equally possible that these natural ecological conditions favored its establishment.

Malaria took a heavy toll of human life, and the fear it evoked not only among the peasantry but also in the hearts of British administrators and travelers is not surprising. In Nepal, just before the implementation of the malaria eradication program, there were thirty-five thousand deaths annually from the disease in the Tarai (Elliott 1959: 72). The Maharajganj *tahsil* in northern Gorakhpur, which borders Nepal, was said to be the most unhealthy part of that district (*District Gazetteer of the United Provinces* 1925). Deaths by "fever" in Gorakhpur accounted for 84 percent of the mortality in 1920–21 and 62.4 percent of deaths in the following year. Further east, in the densely populated district of Champaran, where the demand for land was high, only the malarial dūn valley of Chigwan remained poorly settled and left almost entirely to the settlements of Tharus (Hunter 1877: 221). The Morang, in eastern Nepal and Sikkim, was similarly renowned for its fevers and general unhealthiness.

The Nepal Tarai

The Tarai region of Nepal comprises 15 percent of the country's total land area (Gaige 1975: xv). According to the 1991 census, it is home to 46.7 percent of the country's population (His Majesty's Government 1993a: ii). From the Mechi to the Mahakali River, it is almost nine hundred kilometers long. During the late eighteenth century, the period of the East India Company's initial expansion, the Tarai region was largely a wilderness and marginal to the economy of northern India. It was more important to the hill rajas, however, and when their principalities were annexed to the House of Gorkha, the Tarai came to be essential to the economic viability of the Nepalese state.[2] It became so essential that when threatened with the loss of all their Tarai possessions by the treaty of Segauli, which concluded the Anglo-Nepal War, the Nepalese threatened to continue fighting rather than surrender it.[3]

The Tarai can be divided into two zones, the Outer Tarai or Tarai proper and the Inner Tarai (see map 1). The outer Tarai is an extension of the Indo-Gangetic plain, which slopes up gently along its northern rim into the foothills of the Himalaya. No geographical barriers hinder communication between this region and the border districts of India; the political boundary is demarcated by stone pillars erected at intervals. The Inner Tarai consists of the dūn valleys lying between the Mahabharat and the Siwaliks. Chitwan is by far the most important of these Inner Tarai dūn valleys; others include Dang-Deokhuri and Surkhet in the west and Udaypur in the east.

The Outer Tarai of Nepal can be further subdivided into three separate regions on the basis of history and geography. The four westernmost districts of Kanchanpur, Kailali, Bardiya, and Banke comprise an area once known as the Naya Muluk. These districts have the least developed infrastructure of the Nepal Tarai. Kanchanpur, for example, lacked in 1989 an all-weather road linking it to Kathmandu and the rest of the country. Although a road of sorts existed to connect Kanchanpur to Nepalganj in Banke (the western Tarai's principal commercial town) in 1989, when I first visited the far west, it could only be negotiated in the dry season, due to lack of bridges over the huge seasonal rivers of the western Tarai. The journey was arduous even by Nepalese standards. Those Nepalese who traveled to the region preferred to cross the border at Nepalganj into India and take the train west, to reenter Nepal at Mahendranagar, the district capital of Kanchanpur. I took the easy route and flew in from Kathmandu. The Naya Muluk contains the bulk of what remains of Tarai forest, although these are under threat, as hill people move into the area from the mountains immediately to the north.

Not all of the Tarai falls within Nepal's jurisdiction. The Tarai south of the Siwaliks, adjacent to the district of Dang-Deokhuri, is a part of India. The area between Dang-Deokhuri and the Inner Tarai districts of Nawalparasi and Chitwan formerly comprised part of the principality of the old Butwal Raja and is now divided between the districts of Kapilavastu and Rupandehi. The Buddha's birthplace, Lumbini, is located in Rupandehi. The Tarai east of the Gandak River and immediately south of Chitwan is included within the boundaries of the district of West Champaran in India.

The entire eastern Tarai, however, from the Bagmati to the Mechi, belongs to Nepal. Politically and economically, this is the most important part of the Tarai region. From west to east, it comprises eleven districts: Parsa, Bara, Rautahat, Sarlahi, Mahottari, Dhanusha, Siraha, Saptari, Sunsari, Morang, and Jhapa. In part, this importance is due to historical factors. Nepal lost the western Tarai districts of the Naya Muluk to the East India Company following the Anglo-Nepal War of 1814–16 and did not recover them until 1860. During that period, those districts were transferred by the British to the Kingdom of Awadh (Oudh) in repayment of debt, and this area was and remains the most backward economically of Nepal's Tarai districts. The Butwal Tarai, smaller than the eastern districts, yielded less revenue than the broad, well-populated, and fertile plains east of the Bagmati River.

Until modern times, districts were classified according to criteria of revenue, population, and strategic importance, with A class districts

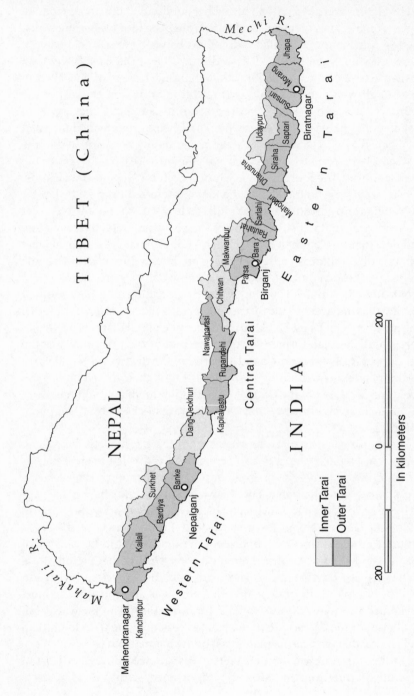

Map 1. *The Tarai districts of Nepal and the principal Tarai towns*

Table 1. Classification and selected statistics of Tarai districts in Nepal, 1959

District	Population[a]	Area (sq. miles)	Administrative Headquarters
Class A districts			
Bara, Parsa, Rautahat	514,556	1388	Birganj
Saptari and Siraha	431,599	912	Rajbiraj
Mahottari and Sarlahi	700,000	1200	Jaleswar
Morang	228,946	1080	Biratnagar
Class B districts			
Kailali and Kanchanpur	100,000	1400	Trinagar
Banke and Bardiya	150,000	800	Nepalgunj
Class C districts			
Dang and Deokhuri	150,000	1100	Ghorahi
Chitwan and Nawalpur	150,000	1100	

Source: Nepal Trading Corporation 1959: 163.

[a] The population figures for all Class A districts except Mahottari and Sarlahi are based on the 1952 census. The figures for Class B and Class C districts are obviously estimates.

being the most important and C class districts the least (Elliott 1959: 69). In the Tarai, the eastern districts (Bara, Parsa, Rautahat, Saptari, Siraha, Mahottari, Sarlahi, and Morang)[4] were all Class A districts. The least important were the districts of Dang-Deokhuri, Chitwan, and Nawalpur (Nawalpur has since been divided into three districts: Rupandehi, Kapilavastu, and Nawal Parasi). Most Class C districts are Inner Tarai valleys. Class B districts in the Tarai included Kailali-Kanchanpur, Banke, and Bardiya (i.e., the Naya Muluk). Outside of the Kathmandu Valley, the three largest towns in Nepal in 1959 were all in the eastern Tarai. The largest Tarai town was Birgunj, in the district of Bara, with a population of 10,037; the others were Biratnagar in Morang (population 8,060) and Janakpur in Dhanusha (population 7,027) (Elliott 1959: 48).

The eastern portion of the Nepal Tarai, which stretches four hundred kilometers east of the Gandak River, is economically and politically the most important area in Nepal next to Kathmandu. The area around the large eastern town of Biratnagar is the most highly developed area of the Tarai and is "said to have been cleared from jungle only within the last 100 years or less" (Takaya 1977: 64). The development of the Morang, once swampy and malarial, dates back to the end of the nineteenth century. It is today one of the most densely populated areas of the

Tarai. Apart from the Tharu and other native Tarai peoples, much of this population is descended from Indian immigrants who have settled in the region over the past 150 years.

Indian Immigration into the Nepal Tarai

While the Tarai was of considerable economic importance to the Nepalese state, being the source from which much of its revenues were derived, it suffered from a shortage of labor throughout the nineteenth century and the first half of the twentieth. In order to maximize agricultural production and increase the revenue, the state pursued an official policy, beginning in 1768, of encouraging immigration from the adjacent districts of India (Dahal 1983: 1; Regmi 1978: 139–148). Durga Ojha 1983 believes that these measures were initially unsuccessful, but as the nineteenth century progressed, immigration undoubtedly increased significantly. Even so, during the first half of the nineteenth century, much of the Tarai, including the eastern and central areas, remained under heavy forest. According to Ludwig Stiller (1976; cited by Dahal 1983: 2), the Great Famine of 1769–70 in Bihar brought many peasants into the Tarai, and similar calamities in India in the century that followed added to the Tarai population. The extent of immigration in the last half of the century was very high (Dahal 1983: 3). The 1911 census of the United Provinces, for example, estimated the emigration into the adjacent Tarai districts of Nepal at about 150,000 (Blunt 1912: 48). In the period 1911–21, an estimated 40,000 people migrated from Gorakhpur District into the Nepal Tarai (53).[5] Champaran, Muzafferpur, and Dharbanga, which border on Nepal's eastern Tarai, were all densely populated, and the agrarian system was characterized by low wages and high rents. The region was susceptible to natural disasters and bore the brunt of the failure of rains in North Bihar and Bengal. North Bihar suffered famines in 1874, 1891, and 1896–97 (*Imperial Gazetteer of India* 1908: 283). These were the "push" factors that complemented the relatively easy terms offered by the Rana state in order to attract tenants (for a discussion, see Regmi 1978).

By the early 1960s, this immigration was curtailed for two reasons. First, the control of the incidence of malaria in the Tarai, and various laws and regulations governing the control and development of land, encouraged the migration of hill Nepalese into the Tarai. Second, for reasons having to do with the definition of a Nepalese national identity and the suspicion with which the post-Rana state regarded Nepalese of Indian origin, the state restricted immigration.

The revenue that the Nepalese state derived from the Tarai came from four sources: first and most important, land revenue paid by cultivators; second, duties imposed on the felling, sale, and export of timber to British India; third, sale of elephants; and last, fees paid by herdsmen who brought their cattle from India to graze on Tarai pasture during the dry season. In 1834, Brian Houghton Hodgson, the British Resident in Kathmandu, estimated the Tarai revenue from these four sources at almost a million rupees (table 2). In the mid-nineteenth century, another British observer estimated the Tarai revenue in Nepal at almost two million rupees (20 lakhs) (Cavenagh 1851: 71). The doubling of the revenue must be attributed to the absolute expansion of cultivated lands, which was made possible by increased immigration from India.

The economy of the Nepal Tarai, particularly in the east, was, and is, based on the cultivation of rice, and the production of cash crops such as oil seeds (mustard), jute, and sugarcane. During the nineteenth century, the Nepal Tarai became a major source of grain for the northern districts of India. According to Yoshikazu Takaya, the region, unlike the Ganges Valley, has only recently been developed for rice cultivation (1977: 64). Most of the rice imported into Purnea District during the early nineteenth century came from the eastern Tarai (Buchanan 1928: 556); a major part of all exports from Nepal to Purnea was grain.

Another source of revenue was the grazing fees levied on cattle brought into the Tarai during the dry season from British India. Francis Buchanan recorded that the greater part of the cattle stock in Purnea District was sent to the Nepal Morang during the dry season (Buchanan 1928: 415). The Sikkim Morang also had enormous herds of cattle grazing there, from seven to ten thousand head according to one observer (Campbell 1851: 7), but this territory did not fall within the boundaries of the Nepalese state.

Table 2. Sources and estimated amount of revenue
in the Nepal Tarai in rupees, 1834

Land revenue	600,000
Timber	300,000
Elephants and ivory	71,000
Pasturage and sundries	20,000
Total	991,000

Source: Oldfield 1974: 305.

The government also derived revenue from the capture of wild elephants. All elephants were held to belong to the king and were common in the Tarai forests until the twentieth century, although wild populations have virtually disappeared from Nepal today. Gisèle Krauskopff writes that elephants "were one of the treasures of the... Tarai, royal emblems, symbols of status and an important currency between kings and their overlords in the pre-unification period" (2000: 43). Captured elephants were valued at about Rs 300 each in the mid-nineteenth century. According to William Kirkpatrick, two or three hundred elephants were captured every year around the Koshi River at the end of the eighteenth century (Kirkpatrick 1811: 17). At least two hundred elephants were captured in Nepal in 1850, for an expenditure to the state of about Rs 10,000 (Cavenagh 1851: 72). These elephants were inspected by Jang Bahadur, and those he discarded (because they did not have good tufts to their tails) were sold (Egerton 1852: 249). This source of revenue could not be sustained, however; by the end of the nineteenth century, Nepal was turning to British India to meet its need for elephants. In the winter of 1892–93, for instance, the Nepal government sought and was granted permission to carry out a *kheda* (elephant hunt) in Kumaun. The Nepalese were allowed twenty-five elephants free of royalty and were charged a hundred rupees for every elephant over that number.[6]

Timber and grain continued to dominate exports from the Tarai to India throughout the nineteenth and much of the twentieth century, and were instrumental in boosting the balance of trade in Nepal's favor. Nepal was an important source of timber for British India; the expansion of the Indian railway network heightened the demand for Nepalese timber and acted as a catalyst for further development of the Tarai. The extension of the Indian rail network to the Indo-Nepal border spurred the development of towns in the Nepal Tarai across the border from the Indian rail heads (e.g., Nepalganj, Bhairawa, and Birganj), which functioned as entrepôts for commerce. Apart from the use of timber for railway sleepers, Nepalese lumber was used for bridges and large buildings, for tea boxes, and for fuel in the large cities (*Imperial Gazetteer of India* 1908: 259). The timber would be floated down the great rivers that drain the Tarai, the Sarda, the Rapti, the Gandak, and further east, the Bagmati and the Kosi, to entrepôts in Kanpur, and sometimes as far south as Calcutta.

Tharus played an important role in all these enterprises. They were the principal source of labor, in agriculture and in other areas, although, as the nineteenth century progressed and Indian immigration into the

Tarai increased, they came to comprise a relatively smaller proportion of the labor force. Local Tharu elites were also the intermediaries between the state and this economy: they served as revenue collectors and even as middlemen in contracting for timber.[7]

The last part of the nineteenth century saw the development of rail transport in northern India, and inevitably this had an impact on the Nepal Tarai. The northern Indian market became accessible to raw materials from the Tarai such as rocks (for construction) and timber, and agricultural development was enhanced. The earliest government-sponsored settlement projects were apparently in Morang and Nepalganj in 1883 and 1897; their primary purpose was the extraction of high-revenue-yielding timber, the cleared land then being allotted to individual settlers (Regmi 1978: 142). We can only speculate on the impact of all this activity on the Tharu. It is probable that any impact was limited, due to the relatively small scale on which immigrant colonization of the Tarai took place before the malaria eradication campaign.

From 1951 to 1960 conditions were created that encouraged the rapid settlement of the Tarai, on a scale hitherto unparalleled. These were the overthrow of the Rana regime in 1951, a land reform that brought almost all land under state control,[8] the abolishing of corvée labor, and the protection of tenancy rights under the law (Ojha 1983: 27). In addition, a successful malaria eradication campaign was carried out from 1958 to the end of the 1960s. Considerable foreign aid has flowed into Nepal since the overthrow of the Ranas, and much of it has been concentrated on the development of the Tarai. The last two factors, and the deteriorating environment in the hills, have prompted large-scale immigration of hill people into the Tarai. Many Tharus, particularly in the West, have historically retreated into the forest to avoid contact with settlers; even today, there is movement of Tharus into the western Tarai, where extensive tracts of forest remain. But these forests are steadily being cleared. Thus, while the settlement of the Tarai by outsiders is not a new phenomenon, what is new is the scale on which it has taken place and the extremely rapid changes it has wrought. The influx has been too great for the government to handle; indeed, much settlement has been illegal, unplanned, and haphazard (Ojha 1983: 32–33).[9]

The foregoing discussion indicates that the Tarai was not as isolated a region as it is sometimes made out to be; it was and continues to be a focus of particular interest to the government of Nepal. The state has always been interested in bringing more Tarai land under cultivation to increase state revenues. Before the land reform of the 1950s, land was also made available under various forms of tenure to state officers and bureaucrats in lieu of salaries (Regmi 1978). To the best of my knowledge, excepting the recent work of Gisèle Krauskopff and Pamela Meyer (2000) nothing has been published that deals specifically with state policy toward the Tharu, who were an important source of agricultural labor in the Tarai.

Tribe, Caste, and Ethnic Group

The basis of Tharu ethnic identity in contemporary times arises from the fact that the various groups identified by this ethnonym have historically shared a common relationship to both the hill society and the plains society that sandwich them. All Tharu groups fit into a division of labor based on the particular ecology of the Tarai. Since the beginning of the nineteenth century and the political unification of Nepal, most of those classified as Tharu—with the exception of the Rana Tharu of Naini Tal District and the Tharu of Champaran, as well as small populations in adjacent Indian districts (mostly extensions of Nepalese populations)— have been included in a common field of political and social action (the state of Nepal) that has shaped the way they relate to each other and to outsiders. All of those called Tharu in Nepal share a common subordinate status in the social structure of the Nepalese state. This status was formalized in the *Muluki Ain* of 1854, which placed the Tharu in the category of the enslaveable *matwāli* castes (the third in a fivefold hierarchy). Tharus share, to varying degrees, the experience of discrimination and exploitation at the hands of hill castes to whom they have lost land since the malaria eradication program of the 1950s. This combination of pressures has been a major factor in the shaping of the contemporary Tharu identity, and this process has been given force and direction by the activity of Tharu elites.

The Tharu are a frontier people and the Tarai a frontier region. As a people who have been politically marginal to the centers of state power which ruled them, Tharus have been of low status. Their marginality was expressed by the term *tribe* applied to them by later colonial administrators of British India and used even today by some social scientists.[10] The concept of tribe has legal status in modern India, where it is the basis for a form of "compensatory discrimination"—the phrase is Galanter's (1989)—intended to redress previous inequities. The analytical utility of this term in the South Asian context is a matter of ongoing debate (Bailey 1961; Atal 1963; Sinha 1973; Sharma 1978; Singh 1985; Béteille 1986;

Caplan 1990). It has been pointed out that "tribe" has no precise analog in South Asian languages; the Western concepts of caste, tribe, nation, and ethnic group are all subsumed under the term *jāt,* which connotes "sort" or "kind."[11] The nearest concept to the Western notion of tribe is the indigenous concept of *ādivāsi,* which is often used as a synonym for tribe. Its convergence with the Western concept arises from the fact that the people to whom these terms are applied occupy the frontiers of, or enclaves within, larger, more complex polities. Other indigenous terms whose usage parallels that of "tribe" are *jangli* (of the jungle; usually a derogatory term used by people of high caste) and *banavāsi* (dwellers in the forest).

The notion of tribe as it developed among ethnographers and British officials during the nineteenth century was based on a number of assumptions, which contrasted tribe and caste. Tribes were defined as peoples ecologically isolated from Indian civilization (i.e., the complex polities of the Muslim and Hindu states). Internally they were economically more primitive and socially less complex, in that the tribe subsisted on hunting and gathering or shifting cultivation in place of settled agriculture and was organized on the basis of equality rather than hierarchy. As a moral order also, it was considered to be less developed than that of Hindu caste society (Caplan 1990: 129–130). In essence, the tribe supposedly represented the more primitive and less civilized ancestors of the Hindu castes, which were themselves tribal once, before "emerging into a civilization of greater organized range and scope" (Marriott 1955: 188). Andre Béteille represents the distinction thus: "Tribal society is homogeneous, undifferentiated and unstratified; Hindu society is heterogeneous, differentiated and stratified" (1986: 311).

The opposition of "tribal" society to Hindu society in this way, however, has very limited utility because "tribes" have been integral parts of Indian civilization for millennia. That they have lived in ecologically marginal or ecologically well-defined regions (forests or forested plateaus, for example) does not necessarily mean that they have been isolated from or uninfluenced by the wider society of India. Tribe and caste form a whole; in terms of the attributes of these two categories, there are castes that are tribelike, and tribes that are castelike; the categories are fluid and flow into one another. At other points in his paper, in fact, Béteille seems to recognize this. Other authors, notably Ghurye, reject the caste-tribal dichotomy altogether; Ghurye holds that tribes "are best described as Backward Hindus" (1980: 20).

The idea that isolation from Hindu society is one of the defining features of the tribe must be understood in a strictly relative sense; castes and tribes have had relations with each other for millennia, and the values of Hindu civilization have influenced tribes to varying degrees. As Béteille puts it, "in India tribes have always been in transition [to caste], at least since the beginning of recorded history" (1986: 298). Tribes have lived in the shadow of that civilization; they have been aware of it and its values, but so long as they were not transformed by the values or the form of social organization that the civilization favored, they remained a "tribe" (i.e., a group autonomous of a Hindu polity). Again, the difference between caste and tribe is one of degree; one is either more or less tribelike or castelike depending on how many of these attributes one possesses. This ambiguity was not a problem for premodern states because they did not necessarily make the distinction between the two categories; the *Muluki Ain* for example, simply uses the category *jāt*. But it is a matter of considerable concern and immense political importance for the modern state, which demands clear-cut definitions. Tribe and caste in India are legal categories which carry with them benefits and disadvantages in terms of access to state resources. Because such definitions are not sociologically possible, the Indian state's use of the category has been arbitrary. The status of the Tharu of Champaran and their demands, first to be excluded from the legal category of Scheduled Tribe and now to be included within it, is a case in point.[12]

In terms of the distinction between caste and tribe commonly made by ethnographers of South Asia, the category *Tharu* is both tribelike and castelike. Although not quite ecologically isolated, they are closely identified with an ecologically distinct region. Yet, over the last few centuries at least, they have come increasingly under the control of sources of power external to their immediate societies, and have been assimilated, in varying degrees, to complex, hierarchically structured social systems. The continuum between the categories of tribe and caste is replicated within the category *Tharu* itself. As one moves from west to east along the Tarai, one encounters, among the various groups collectively referred to by this ethnonym, a decreasing incidence of tribelike features and an increasing degree of castelike social organization. In western Nepal, the Tharu live in their own villages, in which there is a very low incidence of multiethnic settlement. In the eastern Tarai, however, there has been a steady immigration of Indians throughout the nineteenth century and the early part of the twentieth. This has had two consequences. The Tharu of this part of the Tarai (from Bara to beyond Saptari) came to live in multicaste villages and have become more extensively sanskritized than Tharus to the west. They may have come also to resemble a dominant caste at the apex of a *jajmāni* system. I quote from an interview (in English) with Ramanand Prasad Singh, former attorney general of Nepal, who is a Tharu from Saptari:

> We had a Brahmin teacher or the village schoolmaster... there were some oil men [Teli caste] who had settled on our land and we permitted them to stay there. We used to get our oil seeds pressed by them, and the whole village used to pay a certain amount to the oil people pressers, that was the system. So they used to press oil for a whole village and every household used to pay them something in kind, paddy and all those things, so they were getting from the whole village. Similar was the case with the barber, and then these menial castes like Chamars and Doms, they used to take away the dead animals.... As a matter of fact, I've never known the Tharus... to skin animals or do other things that you see the menial castes in India and elsewhere do. We were almost an agricultural caste, community, we had no other obligation than agriculture.

Unfortunately, there are no studies I know of that describe the social organization of the villages of the eastern Tarai. But Ramanand Singh's description of a village in Saptari more than fifty years ago, and some historical evidence (Krauskopff and Meyer 2000), strongly suggest that Tharus in the eastern Tarai resembled what M. N. Srinivas called a dominant caste. It is very probable, for reasons that will become clear below, that a handful of Tharu households (those that had the status of *jimidārs*, a status transmuted over time into that of large landlord, particularly in the eastern Tarai) dominated the village, and that all other Tharus shared an economically subordinate status not much different from that of the dependent service castes.

The distinction between the concepts of tribe and caste carries with it the notion that while castes are hierarchically ordered, the tribe is not. This distinction poses difficulties if we are to think of the Tharu as a tribe. At the most obvious level, the Tharu consist of a number of named groups localized in particular territories from which, typically, they derive their name. But within each local territory, there is a hierarchy of Tharu groups; the one most closely associated with the territory is the dominant (and usually numerically preponderant) one. The lesser endogamous groups typically are very small and very marginal to the category as whole. And although all Tharu and Tharu-like groups are cultivators, they are characterized by a certain degree of occupational specialization. In Chitwan, for example, the Tharu Bote (who are regarded by the dominant Rajput Tharu as inferior in status) specialize in fishing and operating river ferry services, and the Mar-

A Tharu musician sings at a religious ceremony, Chitwan

daniya are barbers. While the different Tharu groups within a local area have traditionally been ordered in a hierarchy of statuses linked to notions of purity and pollution, it is the official policy of the Tharu Kalyankarini Sabha today to assert the equality of all Tharu groups and to make no invidious distinction among them. In Chitwan certainly, little heed is paid to these distinctions except among members of an older generation.

The local hierarchy of Tharu groups in Chitwan consists of four or five named endogamous groups. Of these groups, the numerically and economically dominant one, which calls itself Rajput Tharu considers itself to be superior to the others, which it regards as polluting (but not untouchable). Young Tharus in Chitwan, however, do not pay much attention to these distinctions. At the very bottom of this hierarchy are the Musaher, who speak the same language as their Tharu neighbors (an Indo-European dialect influenced by Bhojpuri) and share many of the same customs and practices. Other Tharus do not consider them as belonging in the same category as themselves, however; that is, the Musaher are not "Tharus," although in terms of their attributes they have many things in common. The Musaher are considered by Tharus to be untouchable. In Sunsari District, the dominant Tharu group is the Kochila. While the Kochila are widely distributed throughout the eastern Tarai, smaller, endogamous groups of Tharus live among them. The Rautar, for instance, are found only in six or seven villages, while the Rajghariya inhabit about nine villages in the southern part of Sunsari. Both groups are said to differ from each other in both dress and language. Another small group, the Bhatgamiya, are found in a few villages in Sunsari and Morang.[13]

In Nepal where almost half the population has been described as tribal, the various culturally and linguistically separate populations were integrated into one statewide system of hierarchically ranked jāt. These populations are better described by the term *ethnic group* than by *tribe*. As Höfer defines it, the ethnic group is a minority which is "conscious of a solidarity due to a (mostly mythical) common ancestry and of sharing specific linguistic and cultural phenomena. In the main, this identity is expressed by an ethnonym, often 'covering' a certain local or regional range of dialectal and/or cultural features. . . . This identity is relational, that is, it is the outcome of an interplay between self-assessment and outside-assessment" (Höfer 1979: 47).

Castes are ethnic groups within a single society whose relations to each other are ordered in terms of a particular ideology of purity and pollution. I argue in the next chapter that to talk meaningfully about caste one must be able to show that this ideology informs the social relations. Where a caste system exists, ethnic groups can be absorbed into it as new castes (which would account for the way so-called tribal groups have been incorporated into the caste system over the centuries). An ethnic category can itself be internally organized into castes. A good example would be the Newars of the Kathmandu Valley, but the different Newar castes are so culturally diverse as to represent different eth-

Kochila Tharu woman, Siraha. A common custom among Tharu women throughout the Tarai (and among women of some other ethnic groups in Nepal and adjacent districts in India) is to tattoo their forearms and calves. Young Tharu women in Chitwan are increasingly reluctant to be tattooed.

nicities. What is crucial is the relational nature of ethnic identity: it is defined in relation to other ethnic groups. Geographical isolation, primitive agriculture, and the system of relations which determine the individual's access to land and the other various attributes of the "tribal" are irrelevant. The concept of ethnic group brings us closer to the indigenous concept of jāt; like a jāt, it is an inter-nesting category that can exist at a number of levels, each of which includes the next. Thus, in Chitwan, the Bantar Tharu are a jāt, and so are the Rajput Tharu, and these two categories are significant in the local society of Chitwan. As far as outsiders are concerned, however, they and all other Tharus elsewhere in the Tarai belong to the single category *Tharu*. While at the local level, different Tharu jāt are meaningful only in relation to each other, as in the example just cited, at a higher level of organization, what matters is that one is Tharu in relation to non-Tharus. The same is true with respect to Tharus from different regions. A Tharu from Chitwan is unlikely to be familiar with the social divisions in the Tharu society of the eastern Tarai and will place people in that region in an undifferentiated category, Kochila.

The origin of the Tharu as an ethnic category, like the origins of some other ethnic or "caste" categories of northern India such as the Gujar,[14] arises from their occupation as herdsmen and cultivators of a particularly difficult ecological and occupational niche. Tharus are considered (and consider themselves to be) the indigenous inhabitants of the formerly malarial Tarai jungle, a region in which other people were reluctant to settle. The Tharu kept large herds of cattle, cultivated rice in little clearings in the jungle, and, to varying degrees depending on local conditions, practiced a form of swidden agriculture. They are also, as Krauskopff (1999) has noted, people who are much given to fishing, with traps and nets. As a source of labor power, they were the pivotal inhabitants of a region that, while peripheral to India, was (and is) of vital economic and strategic importance to the Nepalese state. The term *boksā*, which is the ethnonym of a group very similar to the Tharu occupying portions of the Naini Tal Tarai in India, has the meaning in Hindi of "witch" or "sorcerer." In Chitwan, Tharus refer to witches as *daini*; the term in Nepali is *boksi*. Plains people are said to have believed that the Tharu and the Boksa were adept at witchcraft and therefore avoided them.

Nineteenth-century British descriptions of the native population of the Western Tarai indicate the fluidity and imprecision of the category *Tharu*. They also indicate that the different components of the Tharu population probably thought of each other in the same way that they thought of other ethnic groups that were not Tharu: as different, bounded entities related to them in a hierarchical way. H. M. Elliott, for example, says about the Tharu of the far-western Tarai: "interspersed with [the Tharu, i.e., the Rana Tharu of Naini Tal and Kanchanpur] are other tribes, who are generally called Tharus, but who are quite distinct, such as Gaharwar.... These never intermarry or eat with the Tharus.... others, again, as Dangras [Dangaura Tharu?], are looked down on as a lower caste by the Tharus" (Elliott 1869: 316). Almost a hundred years later, an Indian census official noted that Rana Tharu and Dangaura Tharu in Kheri and Gonda did not intermarry (Sharma 1965: 5); even their wedding seasons differed, the Rana Tharu arranging their marriages in Magh (December–January), the Dangauras in Phagun (February–March).

There is no consensus on the etymology of *Tharu*. As I noted earlier, this ethnic label, referring to a "people of very black colour and flat-nosed like the Turks" living at the foot of the Himalayas, was known to

Al Beruni in the eleventh century. Krauskopff notes that "terms such as Tharu or Boksa seem to refer more to an area of habitat and the idea one had of its inhabitants than to a specific tribe" (1989: 33; my translation). She points out that in Taranatha's history of Buddhism (which dates to 1608), reference is made to the district of Champaran in Bihar in Tibetan as *mtha'ru-y brgyud*. The term *mtha'ru* refers to the people (*-y* being the genitive), while *brgyud* may be glossed as the borderland, frontier, buffer zone, or land in between. A literal translation of the term might be "the Tharu frontier" or "the Tharu region" or "the frontier region where the Tharu live."[15] It is possible that the term *Tharu* came to be used to describe the unstable and marginal population occupying the Tarai, a frontier region for both the hill principalities of Nepal and the kingdoms of the Gangetic plain. *Tharu* and *Boksa*, as Krauskopff suggests, may simply connote the qualities attributed to people living in a landscape characterized as necessarily peripheral by its remoteness and malignity to human occupation. It is possible that *Tharu*, like *Magar* for certain groups of hill people, perhaps originally an ethnic label for one particular local population, came to be a status summation for the various peripheral aboriginal groups that occupied the Tarai.

Whatever the provenance of the term, by the turn of the twentieth century there was a well-established ethnic category called *Tharu* in the Tarai, encompassing several population groups, large and small, which had little in common in a cultural sense that might have served to distinguish them collectively from non-Tharu groups in the region. The cultural differences among Tharu groups were at least as great as the differences between any given Tharu community and those not included under the rubric *Tharu*. Conversely, in some parts of the Tarai, particularly in the east, Tharus have relatively more in common culturally with non-Tharus (such as a common language and ritual practice) than they do with others sharing that ethnonym.

One factor that distinguishes the category *Tharu* in an objective sense is its close association with the Tarai; settlements of people identified by this ethnonym are not to be found outside this region. This also helps explain why certain populations inhabiting the Tarai were not included within this category; they are not exclusively Tarai people. In the Inner Tarai district of Chitwan in central Nepal, for example, there are communities of an ethnic group known as the Darai. They live among the Tharu, speak the local Tharu language as their "native" language, and practice many of the rituals of their Tharu neighbors. Culturally, the Darai are more like the Tharu of Chitwan than the Tharu of Chitwan are like, for example, the Rana Tharu of Kanchanpur. They are not, however, considered to be Tharu; among other things, they are not exclusively identified with the Tarai, for Darai communities are also found in the lower hills. The Musaher furnish another example. Like the Darai, they have many cultural features, including language, in common with their Tharu neighbors. In one British colonial account they are listed as a Tharu group (Crooke 1896, 385–387), but Chitwan Tharus emphatically deny any ethnic connection to the Musaher. The Musaher are a caste category found throughout northern Uttar Pradesh and Bihar, and are immigrants into the Tarai. In Chitwan, their origins are comparatively recent, going back only a few generations, and they maintain close contact with their kin across the border. In addition, they are an untouchable caste; quite apart from the prejudices of Tharus regarding this matter, they would also have been beyond the pale in terms of the old legal code.

On the eastern periphery of the Tarai is another group, the Mech, who, like the Buxas, are thought by outsiders to be immune to malaria and to be indigenous to the regions they occupy. The Mech are described by William Crooke (1896: 380) as being similar to the Tharu in habits and features. Neither they, however, nor the Boksas, are considered by Nepalese Tharus to be Tharu. The Mech are a very marginal group in Nepal, numbering only 938 in the 1961 census (Grimes 2001). This ethnic group is a segment of the Bodos of Assam; they are known to have once spoken a Tibeto-Burman language, although today most speak Bengali. They probably derive their name from their occupation of the region eastward of the Mechi River, the eastern border of the Nepal Tarai. The crucial structural point is that the Mech of Nepal are only a small fragment of a much larger category in Bengal and Assam that is quite distinct from the Tharu.

The curious case of the Rajbansi pose some problems for the argument I have made above, however. The Rajbansi, numbering 85,558 by language in the 1991 census (His Majesty's Government 1993b) and 82,177 by ethnicity (His Majesty's Government 1999), are an ethnic group living in the districts of Jhapa and Morang in the eastern Tarai. But over 2.2 million Rajbansis live in India (where they are classified as a Scheduled Caste) and there is also a small population in Bangladesh (Grimes 2001). Despite this large presence outside Nepal, the Rajbansi were considered by some Tharus in the Tharu Kalyankarini Sabha to be Tharu and were in fact represented in the organization despite the fact that they have a different ethnic label. Narendra Chaudhary is one of those who rejects the idea that the Rajbansi could be Tharu; one reason for his view apparently is that they speak a different language, Bangla. A Rajbansi, however—Chaitulal Chaudhari Rajbansi—used to be a member of the central committee of the Tharu Kalyankarini Sabha and was chairman of the Sabha's Morang district committee. The Rajbansi withdrew from the Sabha in B.S. 2036 (around 1979) and now form their own organization.

Amar Lal Chaudhary, who told me this, observed, "The Tharus of Morang are called Lampuchiya Tharu and their customs are very different from the customs of Rajbansis. Rajbansis don't farm pigs. They are just like the Saptariya Tharu." Elaborating, he added that their language, marriage practices, customs, and folk songs were just like those of the Kochila Tharu of Saptari. What was more, he claimed, Rajbansis and Saptariya Tharus had always intermarried. This was not true of relations between the Rajbansi and the Lampuchiya Tharu of Morang, however. I was not able to discover why the Rajbansi had withdrawn and was not able to follow the matter up with any Rajbansis themselves, but what is clear from this account is that the Tharu were once willing to accept them as fellow Tharus.

DISTRIBUTION OF THE THARU IN THE TARAI

The Tharu consist of a number of historically endogamous groups, differing from each other in language and cultural practices and in the extent of their cultural assimilation into Hindu caste society. Each group is localized in a particular area, and some groups are referred to by a term derived from the name of their area: thus, the Dangaura are so called because the main center of their population is the Dang Valley. Given the current state of research, it is difficult to enumerate all the subcategories of the ethnonym *Tharu*, some of which consist of no more than a few thousand individuals. The Bharatiya Tharu Kalyan Maha Sangh, based in Champaran, Bihar, a sister organization of the Tharu Kalyankarini Sabha of Nepal, cites the following Tharu subgroups in its constitution, describing them as *upajāti* (sub-jāti): Rautar, Garwaliya, Gaurihar, Chitawaniya, Bantar, Lampochha, Khawash, Mahawat, Dangawariya, Kaishanaut, Kochila, Kat Khalla, Mahirwot, Marachwar, Mardaniya, Kanphata, and Katahariya.[16] Of these groups, the major ones in Nepal are the Chitwaniya, Lampochha (Lampuchuwa, Lampuchiya), Dangawariya (Dangaura), Kochila, and the Katahariya. Chitwaniya, as the name implies, refers to those Tharus who live in Chitwan. As I mentioned, however, the Tharu of Chitwan do not all belong to the same endogamous group. The Rana Tharu of the Naini Tal Tarai in the far west are omitted from this list, but are included in the membership of the Tharu Kalyankarini Sabha in Nepal.

A member of the central committee of the Tharu Kalyankarini Sabha provided me with the following list of the principal groups: Morangiya (districts of Morang and Sunsari), Kochila (numerically the largest category, living in the districts from the Koshi River to Birganj), and Dangaura (the second largest group, found from the Dang Valley westward to Kanchanpur). The Tharu of Chitwan and Nawalpur, according to my source, are related to the next category, the Katharya (or Katahariya), and finally, in the extreme west, are the Rana Tharu of Kanchanpur. The same informant also mentioned the Lampuchuwa, who he said were found in Parsa, but the same term is applied to the Tharu in the Morang District, several hundred kilometers to the east. I met no Tharu who could enumerate all the various categories encompassed by this ethnonym. Instead, there is reasonably good knowledge among members of the elite of the principal categories (Rana, Katharya, Dangaura, Chitwaniya-Nawalpuria, and Kochila) and of the various minor groups that occur in their own district.

The most detailed account of the distribution of Tharus throughout the Tarai, on the basis of available research, is by Krauskopff (1989: 28–34). The westernmost endogamous subgroup of Tharus is that of the Rana Tharu, who occupy lands from Naini Tal in western Uttar Pradesh to Kailali in Nepal. From Kailali eastward to Gorakhpur and the Central Tarai are settlements of the Katharya Tharu. According to Krauskopff, the Katharyas are divided into two "mutually exclusive" subgroups, the Pachala and the Purbya. The former are found in Kailali and Banke and in adjacent Tarai areas of the districts of Lakhimpur-Kheri, Bahraich, and Gonda (Maheshwari, Singh, and Saha 1981: 1), while the latter inhabit what used to be known as the Butwal Tarai (the modern districts of Kapilavastu, Rupandehi, and Nawal Parasi) (Krauskopff 1989: 28). Krauskopff notes that although the Rana Tharu and the Katharyas are two separate groups, they share certain cultural features in women's dress and domestic architecture. Map 2 shows the approximate distribution of the principal Tharu subgroups in the Tarai. Table 3, drawing on the 1991 census of the Tharu population by ethnicity, shows its distribution in the four main divisions of the Tarai used in this book.

The best-described Tharu group is the Dangaura, whose original homeland is said to be the valley of Dang in Nepal and the adjacent valley of Deokhuri. Communities of Dangaura are also found in Gonda and Bahraich in India, as well as throughout the former Naya Muluk (the Nepal Tarai districts from Kanchanpur to Bardiya). As many as six thousand Dangauras have left Dang in the last thirty or forty years, migrating west into Banke and Bardiya to escape the exploitation of Brahman-

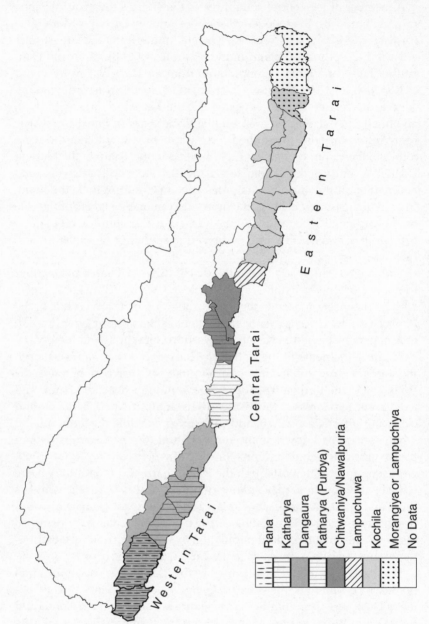

Rana

Katharya

Dangaura

Katharya (Purbya)

Chitwaniya/Nawalpuria

Lampuchuwa

Kochila

Morangiya or Lampuchiya

No Data

Western Tarai

Central Tarai

E a s t e r n   T a r a i

Map 2. *Distribution of the principal Tharu subgroups by district*

Table 3. Numerical distribution of the Tharu population in the four major divisions of the Tarai

	N	%
Western Tarai [a]	476363	39.89
Inner Tarai [b]	180276	15.10
Central Tarai [c]	173006	14.49
Eastern Tarai [d]	356342	29.84
Rest of Nepal	8237	0.69

Source: His Majesty's Government 1999

Note: See Map 1 for the breakdown of these divisions by district.

[a] The Western Tarai districts include Kanchanpur, Kailali, Banke, and Bardiya; the major Tharu subgroups here include the Rana, the (western) Katharya, and the Dangaura.

[b] The Inner Tarai districts include Surkhet, Dang-Deukhuri, Chitwan, Makwanpur, and Udaypur. In Surkhet and Dang-Deukhuri the major Tharu subgroup present is the Dangaura; in Chitwan, the Chitwaniya; and in Udaypur, the Kochila. I have no information on Makwanpur, where in any case the Tharu population numbers only a few hundred according to the 1991 census.

[c] The Central Tarai districts include Kapilavastu, Rupandehi, and Nawalparasi; the major Tharu subgroup present is the (eastern) Katharya; the Tharu population in Nawalparasi also includes the Chitwaniya.

[d] The Eastern Tarai includes all the Outer Tarai districts from Parsa to Jhapa. The major subgroups present are the Lampuchuwa (Parsa only), the Kochila, and the Morangiya (Sunsari, Morang, and Jhapa). The Morangiya are also referred to as the Lampuchiya, but are a separate group from those of Parsa.

Chhetri landlords in their home villages in Dang (Cox 1990a, 1990b; cf. also Bista 1969 and Krauskopff 1989: 66).

With the exception of significant populations in Naini Tal and Champaran, almost all the Tharu groups live in Nepal. They are, however, grossly undercounted in the Nepali census, whose categories are based on languages and not on ethnic self-identification. While Tharus in the west claim to speak Tharu *bhāsā* (Tharu language), in the east they are recorded as speakers of Maithili or Bhojpuri. This suggests the extent to which linguistic assimilation may have occurred in this area of intensive Indian settlement. The different Tharu dialects spoken in the Tarai are Indo-European in origin but to varying degrees mutually unintelligible; Tharus from different areas of the Tarai find it easier to communicate with each other in Nepali and Hindi. Although estimates of the Tharu population in Nepal based on census returns have varied from 3 percent to over 5 percent (5.4 percent in the 1991 census as enumerated by language), the actual figure of those who would identify themselves as being of the Tharu jāt is higher (6.5 percent in the 1991 census; similar figures are not available for the earlier censuses).

In the following districts of the eastern Tarai, the Tharu population is virtually nonexistent according to the 1971 census (table 7): Bara, Parsa, and Rautahat (overwhelmingly Bhojpuri-speaking areas); and Siraha, Sarlahi, Saptari, and Udaypur (Maithili-speaking). Thus, for example, the 1971 census recorded only 17 "Tharu speakers" in Siraha; ten years later, that population had increased to 3,541 (still a gross underestimate of those ethnically Tharu). Significantly, as the 1991 census figures show, the population describing itself as ethnically Tharu is almost twice the size of that describing its mother tongue as Tharu (table 7). The phenomenal increase in the numbers between 1971 and 1991 must be attributed to the increase in political self-awareness: identity *for* itself as opposed to identity *in* itself. These omissions in the census lead even so acute an observer as Krauskopff to overlook the large Bhojpuri-speaking Tharu population in Bara, Parsa, and Rautahat (see Krauskopff 1989: 29). These eastern Tarai districts are the heartland of the Tharu Kalyankarini Sabha, which was founded by Tharu elites from this particular region (see map 1). But because language is equated with ethnicity in this context, the ethnic category *Tharu* is considerably undercounted, a matter of some concern to these elites. (I discuss this further in chapter 6.) A more accurate picture of the relative proportion of the people sharing this ethnonym is given in the 1991 census, which enumerates people by ethnicity as well as language (table 7).

In the east, the Tharu share significant cultural symbols with the population of the Tarai as a whole: they speak the same languages, dress in the same sorts of clothes, share many rituals and live in multicaste villages. In the west, particularly in Dang-Deokhuri and the former Naya Muluk, the Tharu are more distinctively set apart from the rest of the population, which is primarily of hill origin and Nepali-speaking. They dress differently, they eat differently, they pray differently, and their villages are not multiethnic the way they are in the east. Those members of other ethnic groups who live among them are of recent origin, hill people who have moved into the Tarai after the eradication of malaria. It is the image of the Tharu in the far west that has come to represent Tharus as a whole; the large population of Tharus in the eastern Tarai is often overlooked.

On the Origins of the Dangaura

Circumstantial evidence suggests that the Tharu of Dang have an ethnically mixed origin, and have developed through absorbing people from other groups.[17] The primary data in support of this hypothesis comes from anthropological descriptions of the Dangaura Tharu lineage group known

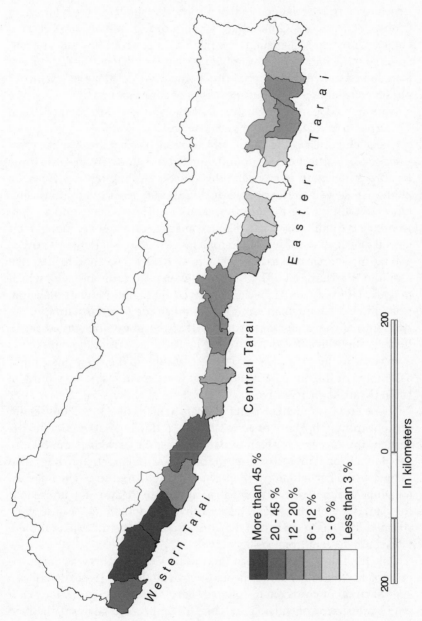

Map 3. Density of the Tharu in the Tarai districts, showing percentages of the population reporting Tharu ethnicity in 1991 (His Majesty's Government 1999)

More than 45 %

20 - 45 %

12 - 20 %

6 - 12 %

3 - 6 %

Less than 3 %

Western Tarai

Central Tarai

Eastern Tarai

In kilometers

200   0   200

as the *gotyār* (Krauskopff 1989: 123–135; McDonaugh 1984; Rajaure 1981: 166–172). The gotyār is patrilineal and exogamous, and serves primarily to structure marriage relations. In that respect, it is similar to the *kul* (clan) of Chitwan Tharus (see Guneratne 1994) but differs in that each gotyār is named. Christian McDonaugh compiled a list of about fifty such names. Some of these names refer simply to particular villages, while fourteen were linked to deities or special ritual practices (McDonaugh 1984: 104). But several names refer to outsider castes or ethnic groups from which the gotyārs are said to have originated. These gotyārs and their reputed origin is referred to by all three authors cited above.

One such gotyār is the Dahit, which traces its origin to Ahirs, a caste category of cattle herders found throughout northern India. Drone Rajaure writes with reference to this gotyār, "Dahi [yogurt]...was the main dish served to the people during the *pat lena* (integration) ceremony for converting the Ahir ancestors into Tharu caste and so they were called Dahit" (1981: 166). Krauskopff gives another account of their legend of origin: an Ahir worked for a household of the Ratgaiya gotyār, and his master decided to marry him to a Tharu woman and to integrate him into the Tharu jāt. (The Ratgaiyas were also cattle herders, which may explain why an Ahir was employed by them.) Now at the ritual feast, the pat lenā, which would accomplish the transformation of the Ahir into a Tharu, custom required that the guests be served meat. Instead, the Ahir offered yogurt that he had made from the milk of his own cows to the men present. Because of this, so the story goes, those assembled at the pat lenā decided that henceforth his name would be Dahit (Krauskopff 1989: 126).

There are a number of other gotyārs which, like the Dahit, claim descent from non-Tharu ancestors. In the following list of gotyārs, the caste of the ancestor is given in parentheses: the Cwakha Dom (Dom), the Babhan or Baman (Brahman), Satgaiyar (Newar), and Raji, also known as the Pachaldangya (Raji) (McDonaugh 1984: 104). The Rajis are an ethnic group of western Nepal; according to Rajaure, the household (or clan) deity of this gotyār, Jagarnatthya (Jagannathya), "is also worshipped by Rajis" (1981: 167). Rajaure also mentions the Magarahthen, who claim descent from a Magar (168).

Only the Tharu of the western Tarai acknowledge in this way the possibility of an ethnically heterogeneous origin. Harald Skar (1999) describes a special ritual of conversion in Rana Tharu society known as the *panth* which transforms outsiders into Rana; this appears to be normally done when a non-Rana man or woman marries into the community (see also Hasan 1993). Skar notes that hill people, including high-caste people, have become Rana in this way by marrying Rana women, "presumably to get access to land" (Skar 1999: 183). The panth ritual involves a feast given by the person who is to be adopted into the community. The feast is attended by the most important Rana Tharu men (presumably the jim-idārs and other large landowners), who signify their assent by accepting food and water from the hand of the candidate. Tharus with whom I discussed this matter in both Siraha and Chitwan insisted, however, that a man of another jāt cannot be incorporated into the Tharu community. In Chitwan, however, a woman could be made into a Tharu, provided she was of clean caste. A woman of another caste or ethnic group who forms a marital alliance (through elopement) with a Tharu may be "transformed" into a Tharu via the extension of the principle by which a Tharu woman is incorporated into her husband's kul, or clan. A man's jāt, on the other hand, in the view of Chitwan Tharus, is immutable. The Dangaura and Rana concept of jāt appears more fluid.

Here is how Rajaure explains the ethnically heterogeneous origins that these clan names seem to indicate:

> Informants in Rautgaon and Baibang villages…maintained that when in the old days the forested Dang valley was being opened for agriculture, some Tharu nobles like Mohlal and Raghunath (ancestors of some of the Tharu families of Dhanaura and Baibang villages) were granted certain rights (by royal decrees) to assimilate or adopt (*pat lena*) people into Tharu society. In those days there was a shortage of manpower for farm work since normally no person, other than a Tharu, dared to stay in that malarial valley. Persons who "became" Tharus, according to the informants, were encouraged to clear and cultivate some of the forest land in their vicinity. Thus an immigrant from outside, of whatever caste or ethnic background, once converted and settled there became a bonafide Tharu by deed as well as by 'caste', preserving the remembrance of his original caste or ethnic identity in his Tharu clan name. (Rajaure 1981: 171)

The foregoing account suggests that *Tharu* may be an ethnic category with a wide recruitment from other categories. If so, the Tharu would by no means be unusual. Holmberg writes, "Tamang can incorporate non-Tamang into their fold over a period of time—a practice that is true of the Sherpa as well" (Holmberg 1989: 14; on the Sherpa, see Oppitz 1974). The Chhetri have been increased by the offspring of female hypergamous unions between Brahman men and women from castes and ethnic groups of other status, who have been classified as Chhetri (Fürer-Haimendorf 1966: 19–20). Anne de Sales (1993) has described the ethnogenesis of an entirely new ethnic group, the Chantel of Dhaulagiri from the flotsam and jetsam of a number of ethnic groups collectively engaged in copper mining in the Himalaya. "Miscegenation," as Christoph von Fürer-Haimendorf puts it, "must be considered a permanent and accepted feature of the Nepalese caste system" (1966: 20). Such miscegenation, as both Höfer's (1979) and Sharma's (1977: 285–289) analyses of the *Muluki Ain* make clear, took place within legally defined bounds; outside these bounds, miscegenation was negatively sanctioned. The physical diversity of Tharus tends to confirm the heterogeneity of marriage. In complexion they range from fair to very dark. In appearance there are those who, with their high cheekbones and narrow eyes, would pass muster as a Gurung or Magar, while others resemble more closely the Indo-European–speaking population of the Gangetic plain.

Many Tharus claim descent from Rajput refugees of the siege of Chitor. Claims of Rajput ancestry are common in origin myths of caste and ethnic groups of inferior status throughout northern India (Sinha 1962). Some Tharu intellectuals in Nepal claim an ancestry that is even more elevated. They assert that, as the aboriginal or ādivāsi inhabitants of the Tarai, they are of the same ethnic stock as Gautama Buddha, who was born as a prince in the Nepal Tarai in what is now Rupandehi. Such speculation about Tharu origins assumes that a primordial identity has continued through time.

The State and the Tharu Elite in Premodern Nepal

The Tharu landed gentry who founded the Tharu Kalyankarini Sabha during the waning years of Rana rule derived their position and their power from the close relationship they had developed with the state as its revenue-collecting intermediaries. Earlier I noted that the Tharu were an important source of labor for the hill rajas as they sought to raise revenue from the Tarai. In addition, however, the hill states, including Rana Nepal, depended on the Tharu elite to recruit and organize labor, clear and cultivate new land, and collect the taxes that made the Tarai so vitally necessary for their economies.

The revenue-collecting system in the Tarai varied in complexity over time and space. There is no room in this book to examine its intricacies, nor is it necessary for the argument I make.[18] Some broad general features should be noted, however. The basic unit of revenue collection was a village or group of hamlets known as a *maujā*, and the official placed in charge of it was referred to as a jimidār. A jimidār was essentially an agricultural entrepreneur who undertook the responsibility of recruiting labor, cultivating the land, and paying a fixed amount of revenue to the state. He was permitted to keep anything he could raise above this amount, and he was also entitled to land free of tax for his own use, along with free (corvée) labor to cultivate it. But as my own research in Chitwan indicates, not only was a jimidār a revenue-collecting official and an entrepreneur, he also exercised juridical power; for example, he ensured that marriage did not cross the bounds of jāt. He was also a ritual specialist who was responsible for the worship of the village gods (Guneratne 1996).

A number of maujās were grouped into a *pragannā*, which came within the purview of an official called a *chaudhari*. Both jimidārs and chaudharis were usually recruited from the local Tharu village elite, for hill men were reluctant to stay year round in the Tarai for fear of malaria. Krauskopff notes that the Tharu were "the best pioneer cultivators of the barren and forested...Tarai lands" (2000: 31). There is some evidence to suggest that in the pre-unification period, these local Tharu leaders, acting as intermediaries for the small hill principalities, probably enjoyed a high degree of autonomy in return for providing service to their overlord (see Krauskopff 2000: 31). This relationship steadily changed with the unification of Nepal and the increasing bureaucratization of the Rana State. By the time of the malaria eradication program of the 1950s, the Tharu elite had been largely reduced to the status of revenue functionaries answerable to district governors (*subbas*).

This relationship of the Tharu elite to the state has been clarified in an important new book that examines and contextualizes fifty royal edicts issued between 1726 and 1971 (Krauskopff and Meyer 2000). Almost all were made to Tharu chiefs in a number of Tarai districts. These edicts, known as *lāl mohars* (red seal documents) were collected by Tej Narayan Panjiar, a Tharu intellectual and historian from Udaypur. They trace the relationship of the Tharu elite to the state over a period of 250 years. Panjiar is himself an important figure in Tharu ethnic activism, and strong ethnic pride has been one of the motivating forces behind this labor of love (Krauskopff 2000: 25). Thus he writes in his own preface to the documents, "Intellectuals and scholars in Nepal have not published much on the Tharu; some who have done so have tended to put this community down" (Panjiar 2000: 49). In his view, the documents he has collected over a twenty-year period counteract the dismissive and patronizing attitude toward the contribution of the Tharu to Nepali history, which he sees some prominent Nepali historians as holding.

Twenty-one of these documents were collected from one household in the Saptari District, and trace the history of a single family's relationship to the state from 1726 to 1843. In 1726, Mahipati Sen, who ruled over a kingdom called Vijayapur in the southeastern corner of modern Nepal, which included the modern district of Saptari, issued a *syāhā mohar* (a black seal document) to Ranapal Chaudhari. The edict reaffirmed a privilege granted earlier to Ranapal Chaudhari of keeping all the revenues from Patna village for himself. This was presumably Ranapal's compensation for overseeing the cultivation of Tarai lands in this area and thereby raising revenue for this small hill principality. Patna village remained in the control of this family for well over a century from this date, and the same family continued as revenue collectors in the Khalisa pragannā in Saptari in which it was located.

The next document in the collection is from 1776 and concerns Hem Chaudhari, who is probably a descendant of the aforementioned Ranapal Chaudhari. The king in this case, however, is Pratap Singh Shah of the House of Gorkha: "To show your loyalty to Makwanpur[19] after our victory over him, you fled to Muglan [India]. When summoned by our district official (*subba*), you returned to your homeland, kneeling before us. We therefore bestow upon you the post of village revenue collector (*jimidar*) on the land on which you lived before" (Krauskopff and Shrestha 2000: 118).

Control of Tarai land served no purpose without the labor to cultivate it and produce revenue, and here the Shah king recognizes the importance of the local Tharu chief in organizing that cultivation. Hem Chaudhari is also respectfully addressed in this edict with the honorific *shri*, for the first and last time in this collection of documents. Many of the edicts in this collection refer to peasants who have fled to avoid excessive taxation, and some are appeals to Tharu jimidārs and their followers who have decamped to India to return and cultivate their lands as before. There are altogether six edicts issued to Hem Chaudhari between 1776 and 1787, and another six issued between 1800 and 1806 to, or concerning, his son, Madhuram Chaudhari, who had succeeded to his authority. Eight more edicts were issued to Madhuram's sons between 1817 and 1843.

One of these edicts, from the court of Girvana Yudha Bikram Shah to Madhuram Chaudhari, notes, "We have come to know through Jaya Mangal Upadhyaya of the service that you have rendered to us. In the past your father Hem Chaudhari served us well and his administration was prudent." The document is cited as an example of the good relations this Tharu leader established with the royal court (Krauskopff and

Shrestha 2000: 131). Good relations with the court were necessary to maintain one's position, as it was the king's prerogative to reappoint the officials who had served his predecessor. These documents show that one Tharu family, descendants of Ranapal Singh who had served the Sen kings in his day, continued to serve the new Shah rulers after unification and, despite some vagaries of fortune, were able to maintain themselves in the royal favor for at least 117 years.

This series of edicts also document the steady streamlining of the revenue administration, the effect of which was to reduce the autonomy of the local Tharu chief. Krauskopff (2000: 31–35) plausibly argues that in the early eighteenth century the Tharu chief resembled in his relationship to the hill raja a "little king" enjoying a great deal of autonomy in return for regular payment of revenue. But by the nineteenth century the chief had been absorbed into a centralized and clearly defined system of revenue collection, answering to a higher authority, a subba. By 1835, Hem Chaudhari's descendant, Gambhira Chaudhari, is being instructed to bring in cultivators from India to work his birtā[20] lands, and the edict lays out the tax schedule for a ten-year period as well. Tharu labor is clearly no longer adequate to the task of agricultural expansion, and the edict in fact enjoins him not to use tenant farmers from already assessed land, which would only undermine existing production. Another edict gives another member of this family permission to cut timber, transport it, and pay taxes at a reduced rate; the Tharu elite were not only agricultural entrepreneurs and revenue officials, they also engaged in trade (Krauskopff and Meyer 2000: 134–135).

Revenue collection was not the only responsibility given to local Tharu leaders. The Tarai, as I already noted, held extensive forests, and it was populated by wild beasts and evil spirits, both of which posed a threat to its successful development. The state took an active interest in protecting its interests from these threats, and the Panjiar collection contains a number of edicts issued to Tharu shamans (known in Chitwan as gurau). One, issued to Vidyapati Dhami of Udaypur District in 1842 gives him the responsibility of protecting the villagers "from the threat of tigers, elephants and bears." He is told to "perform the functions of the dhami, collect the usual dhami taxes and live on them" (Krauskopff and Meyer 2000: 140). An edict issued to a gurau in Chitwan in 1807 enjoins him to "cultivate and make the land populous and protect the people from the threats of elephant, tigers, evil spirits, disease and epidemics" (Krauskopff and Meyer 2000: 160).[21]

To sum up, the Tharu were far from being a "tribal" people living on the margins of settled Hindu civilization, although that is how colonial ethnog-

A Tharu jimidār in Chitwan performs a puja at the bramathān or village shrine. Offerings are made to the village god on behalf of the whole village on the night of the full moon and the new moon, but this is the traditional prerogative of the jimidār. The soft-drink bottle holds homemade liquor, a necessary part of specifically Tharu rituals of worship.

raphers and their twentieth-century intellectual descendants have tended to see them. They were a farming people who were an integral part of states large and small. Although the Tarai may have been unimportant to the Gangetic states, it was essential to the economies of the hill principalities to its north; and the Tharu, as the most significant population willing or able to inhabit and cultivate it, were essential to those economies as well. The Tharu were not simply labor, they played an essential and important role in making the administration of the Tarai possible.

The Tharu in British India

Despite their small numbers in British India, the Tharu loom large in the imagination of British officials in the border districts of Uttar Pradesh and Bihar. Nineteenth-century British colonial administrators continually stressed the importance of Tharus to the cultivation of the Tarai, and they were prepared to make concessions to encourage them to remain. The Tharu not only were cultivators but, from the British point of view, also provided labor for the reserves that were established for what remained of the Tarai forests. This labor would have been difficult to procure otherwise because of the reluctance of other people to settle in the area. The small Tharu population in Kheri District in Uttar Pradesh, for example, appears to have been encouraged to settle there for that reason; their settlements were not organized as revenue villages but were under the jurisdiction of the Forest Department (Sharma 1965). British officialdom's view of the Tharu appears to have been on the whole favorable, because they had the reputation of being not only good cultivators but also good tenants. Thus A. Wyatt, officiating revenue surveyor for Sarun District (before Champaran District was carved from it) noted "they are an honest sort of people, and are proverbial in the regularity of their payments" (n.d.: 11; probably pre-1857). W. W. Hunter observed in similar vein, "They are first-rate cultivators. . . . Those who have dealings with them say they are far more upright and honest than the ordinary Champaran rayat" (Hunter 1877: 245).

An early mention of the Tharu is found in Walter Hamilton's account of British India (1820), a predecessor of the prolific series of handbooks or gazetteers that were to be published later in the century. (He reproduces essentially the same account in his *East India Gazetteer,* published in 1828). This account, detailing an incident that involved Tharus during the Anglo-Nepal War of 1814–16, takes up approximately one-third of the space devoted to an account of the Gorakhpur District; the remainder of the entry is a description of the district's geography. This incident is referred to again in Alan Swinton's account of Gorakhpur (1862[?]: 1). What this early account and other British perspectives throughout the nineteenth and early twentieth centuries indicate is the importance of the Tharu to the economy of the Tarai. Their labor was considered irreplaceable, both because of their own peculiarities (their reputed immunity to malaria) and because the ecological conditions of the Tarai discouraged others from settling there.

Hamilton's accounts describe the strategy followed by the East India Company's forces to deny to the Nepalese military operating in the Tarai of Butwal (and ultimately to the Nepalese state) the fruit of the region's agricultural production. This was to be accomplished in two ways: first, by laying waste the territory and, second, by persuading the population to relocate in British territory, thus permanently denying their labor to the Nepalese. The population concerned was Tharu:

> With a view ... to injure the resources drawn by the enemy from the low lands to the utmost practicable extent, Major-General Wood suggested ... removing the class of persons inhabiting the forests of Bootwul, denominated Tharoos, to a greater distance from the hills. ... [He] issued a proclamation, explanatory of the measure, to the Tharoos. ... An arrangement is accordingly in progress for settling the Tharoos and others in a more southerly tract in Goruckpore, by assigning to them a provision in the waste lands of that district, by which means the enemy will be precluded from deriving any benefit from the low lands in that quarter in the event of a second campaign.[22]

To judge from Hamilton's account, it appears that the Tharu were themselves content with the arrangement. Indeed, they objected to being given new land too close to the hills, where they might be subject to the attack of their old masters. In the event, about two thousand of them were eventually settled in British territory (Hamilton 1820: 356).

Tharus were clearly prepared to move on if pressed too far, either by the demands of revenue or by the pressure placed on them by new settlers. W. C. Benett observed of Tharus in Gonda, "They are very shy and must be treated with great consideration, or they will migrate into Nepal" (1878: 102); H. R. Nevill noted that the numbers of Tharus in that same district had steadily decreased because of emigration into Nepal (1905: 71); A. W. Cruickshank recorded the tendency of Tharus to abandon their farms in the face of encroachment by other settlers into areas they had opened up for cultivation (1891: 68), and C. J. Stevenson-Moore noted the nomadic tendency of Tharus in Champaran (1900: 17).

These sources also describe the Tharu as "first-rate cultivators" and the possessors of "large herds and granaries" (Hunter 1877: 245). They are characterized as the pioneers of cultivation in the Tarai, paving the way for future settlers. The Tharu propensity for agriculture is taken to be an inherent quality of Tharus wherever they may be found in the Tarai (Benett 1878: 102; Blyth 1892: 2; *Gazetteer of the Province of Oudh* 1877: 1:506). They are also described as great hunters, but recent research by Krauskopff suggests that, as far as Dangaura Tharus are concerned (i.e., those who live in the Dang Valley in Nepal), this view is highly exaggerated. They are, as she puts it, "a people who are peasants above all else" (Krauskopff 1987: 41).

Many British officials also saw the Tharu as being hardworking and relatively prosperous when compared to other cultivators, a perception which also predisposed them to look favorably on this ethnic group. Hunter, contrasting the Tharu to other peasant cultivators in Champaran, whose poverty he attributed to avidity of moneylenders, the improvidence of the people, and the impact of drought, floods, and malaria, wrote:

> To this general rule of poverty, however, the Tharus form a marked exception. They cultivate with great care the *tarai* lands in the north of Ramnagar, which are naturally fertile; and their general prudence and foresight have raised them far above all other castes in Champaran. During the famine of 1874, not one of them came to the relief works; and they then asserted that they had sufficient rice in store for six months' consumption. (Hunter 1877: 257)

Stevenson-Moore, the settlement officer in Champaran at the end of the nineteenth century, agreed that "the Tharus...are probably the most prosperous cultivators in Champaran" and noted that "[they] are well off and support themselves in season of famine" (Stevenson-Moore 1900: 168, 17). He observed that the average Tharu landholding in Champaran was 9.3 acres compared to a district average of 3.9 acres (168). The Tharu, however, comprised only 1.5 percent of the total population of the district and were concentrated in its most insalubrious, least desirable, and consequently least populated part. The population of the Champaran Tarai, lying immediately to the south of Chitwan, consisted almost entirely of Tharus (Hunter 1877: 296; Stevenson-Moore 1900: 3; Wyatt n.d.: 11).

The British authorities were aware that the Tharu had the option of crossing the border into Nepal, and were prepared on many occasions to make concessions to keep them in India. One such instance is recorded in the *India and Bengal Despatches* of 1851. A local *zamindār* (landlord) had claimed as his hereditary possession a tract of land (the *talukā* of Namikmutta in Pilibhit District) for which a community of Tharus had made a separate revenue settlement with the settlement officer. The Board of Revenue of the East India Company held against the zamindār in the matter, on the grounds that his right had never been acknowledged. Furthermore,

The settlement...was made by Mr. Robinson with a community of Tha-roos who are stated to be the only people capable of residing in that par-ticular part of the country on account of its extreme insalubrity. The arrangement was satisfactory to the Tharoos, and was, in the opinion of the Board, likely to conduce to clearing and populating a part of the coun-try which it had not only been found hitherto impossible to improve, but which had been in a state of continual deterioration, and as the people in question...had expressed the desire to undertake the cultivation of the Tract at their own risk, and made all their arrangements for mutual assis-tance and self government, the Board were of opinion that they ought not to be cramped in their undertaking by any official control.[23]

From Gonda comes another instance of how some at least in the colo-nial bureaucracy offered Tharus an incentive to remain in British terri-tory. The agent of the large and important Balrampur estate in the north of the district recommended to the government that Tharus be exempted from paying fees for grazing their cattle in state forests and be allowed to freely obtain wood from the forest. Earlier, in 1878, Benett had noted that the Tharu in Gonda (presumably the same community referred to here, as the Tharu population in the district was small and settled on the Balrampur estate) had had a belt of forest reserved for their use so that they could exercise their customary rights in wild pro-duce without being subject to interference on the part of forest officials (Benett 1878: 102). The deputy commissioner for Bahraich District sup-ported the recommendation, on the grounds that otherwise the Tharu would go across the border into Nepal. He observed further, "They are of great assistance to the Forest Department in putting out fires and without such concessions it would be impossible to keep them con-tented."[24] H. W. Gibson, the deputy commissioner in Bahraich, wrote as follows to his counterpart in Gonda to support the Balrampur agent's recommendation:

They live in a particularly submerged tract where, from the unwholesome climate, they are the victims of fever and ague and other diseases, their cattle suffer, and their crops are ravaged by wild beasts. Warmth and shel-ter are doubly needed here both for man and cattle; also special induce-ments to keep the tenants. These reasons apply to the Tharus with greater force. These simple, truth-loving people have brethren in close proximity across the border, and if hard pressed could easily, and would, change masters. They should be encouraged to remain.[25]

However, both the deputy commissioner for Gonda and Eardley Wilmot, the conservator of forests in Oudh, were not convinced by their arguments. The deputy commissioner felt that making things easy for the tenantry (i.e., the Tharu) would only cause them to "increase and multiply to the detriment of forest conservancy," while Eardley Wilmot was of the opinion that it was unnecessary to make an exception for Tharus as "they are more wealthy than other cultivators" and concessions to keep them as tenants should be made at the landlord's expense, not that of government.[26] In the event, no exemptions were made for Tharus, and rates for forest produce were fixed at half the market rate.

In Gonda also, the British gave the Tharu a special dispensation to distill liquor for their own consumption under an order issued by the commissioner in 1856. When, in 1896, an attempt was made to withdraw this privilege, it was met with considerable opposition by the Tharu, who threatened to leave the country if their privileges were not restored. The regulation was never enforced. Nevill suggests that the liquor was essential to enable the Tharu to survive malaria, and comments that their threat to leave "was a powerful one, for without the Tharu there would be great difficulty in working the forests and much land would go out of cultivation; moreover, the tendency to migrate is already far too strong, as their decreasing numbers testify" (Nevill 1905: 128).

These examples all attest to the significance the British placed on the Tharu as a source of labor in areas which other communities were averse to settling because of the unhealthy conditions. More generally, Tharus were identified as the quintessential people of the Tarai: immune to malaria and given to nomadism and retreat in the face of pressure. The British considered all Tharus to be of one tribe, and the writings of the more ethnographically minded of nineteenth century officials and others are full of attempts to classify the different groups and subgroups and determine their relations to each other.

While equally detailed records for the relationship of Tharus to the Nepal state are not available, we have seen earlier that Tharus were important for the Tarai economy on the other side of the border. As late as the first half of the twentieth century, large landowners in the far-western Tarai district of Kanchanpur were encouraging Tharus from Dang to settle in the district to provide them with labor.[27] Much of the Tarai was already under Nepalese jurisdiction, however, and the state had less to fear from wholesale decampment by Tharus. Even so, as we have seen, the principal limiting factor in the attempts made by the state to develop the economic resources of the Tarai was the acute shortage of labor. Until the creation of modern Nepal, most of the Tarai was parceled up between the adjoining hill principalities, and such revenues as they paid were paid to these hill rajas. Such areas, for the most part, were cultivated by Tharus, and their chaudharis and *mahatons* (village headmen) acted as intermediaries between them and these hill rajas (see Krauskopff 1990).

Apart from their importance as cultivators, Tharus were also employed by the state for work in the elephant stables as *mahuts* and *panits* (elephant drivers of different ranks). Tharus also specialized in the capture of wild elephants (Northey and Morris 1928: 140; Smith 1852, vol. 1). The Tharu were also employed as dak runners (message carriers) and as fellers of timber. Finally, they provided labor to clear roads and campsites for the immense hunting expeditions organized by the Ranas in Chitwan and other parts of the Tarai.

The Tharu, who lived in settlements scattered throughout the length of the Tarai, and on whose labor depended a large proportion of the revenue that could be extracted from it, came to be closely identified with the region itself. Judging by the reports of belief in Tharu witchcraft on the part of the local Indian peasantry, some of the mystery of the region appears to have transferred to the people who lived there. The Tharu, whatever the particular endogamous group to which they belonged, were people of the frontier. They were seminomadic cultivators, often on the periphery of control by outside forces (more true of Indian conditions than those of Nepal), and occupying a territory that (it was believed) others could not safely occupy. There was of course a great deal of Indian emigration into the Tarai. But outsiders ventured into the Tarai only under unusual or unendurable circumstances, such as famine in India's border districts and the attractive terms offered by the Nepal government. Despite the ready availability of land, the Tarai was not the focus of a land rush prior to the malaria eradication, nor do Tharus articulate a consciousness of being the victims of such a land rush before that significant event. Rather, the Tharu elite in the eastern Tarai themselves served as revenue collectors (jimidārs and chaudharis) and were thus generally in a position of authority over the new immigrants. And not all the Tarai was equally malarial (Skerry, Moran, and Calavan 1991); the most virulent and endemic malaria appears to have been found in the *dūn* valleys (the Inner Tarai) and in the forests of the Bhabar that separated the cultivated fields of the Outer Tarai in the east from the hills.

All Tharus, whatever their culture or language or location, occupied the same well-defined position in the structure of social relations in this border area. Whatever the objective cultural differences between these groups, this uniformity enabled both the British and the Nepalese state to treat the Tharu as a single group, to conflate their particularities into a single general category. The Nepal state enshrined this category in the *Muluki Ain*, relegating "Tharu" to the lowest rung of the pure castes, that of enslaveable liquor drinkers (*matwāli*); the British, assuming that the Tharu were one people, expended a great deal of energy attempting to unravel their social divisions, and in the process hopelessly confused lineage, clan, and endogamous divisions. I turn next to how the state has contributed to the emergence of a Tharu identity.

CHAPTER THREE

Ethnicity and the Nepali State

We have seen that two elements feed into the dynamic of ethnic identity formation. One is the presence of a contrasting group against which identity can be defined, generally on the basis of preexisting affiliations. The other is the role played by elites in shaping or manipulating that identity: transforming an identity in itself into an identity for itself, that is, an identity on the basis of which one may engage in political action broadly defined. There is one other important element involved in this dynamic: the state. On the one hand, ethnicity provides a collective identity on the basis of which a group can assert itself vis-à-vis the state. On the other, the policies followed by the state with respect to the various social groups under its control plays an important role in structuring the way they relate to one another as well as to the state. This point is illustrated by the case of the Rana Tharu and their relationship to a neighboring ethnic group known as the Buxa.[1]

The Rana Tharu of the far-western Tarai are an endogamous population that straddle the border between Nepal's Kanchanpur District and the adjacent district of Naini Tal in Uttar Pradesh. Naini Tal has the largest Tharu population in India outside Champaran. But not all Rana Tharu in India accept the label *Tharu*. S. K. Srivastava, who produced the first monograph on any Tharu group (1958), noted that five of the twelve clans (*kurie* or *gotra*) into which the Rana Tharu population in India was divided, reconstituted themselves as an endogamous group, began to sanskritize, and took to calling themselves Rana Thakur. The term *Thakur* is a claim to Ksatriya status; the Rana Thakurs, according to Sri-

A Rana Tharu couple, Kanchanpur

vastava, consider it derogatory to be addressed as Tharu and deny that
they are of that ethnic category. On the other hand, members of the Rana
Tharu elite in Nepal are members of the Tharu Kalyankarini Sabha, and
consider themselves to be, and are considered by other Nepali Tharus as
being, members of the Tharu ethnic category. The explanation for this
lies in the fact that a political border separates the two populations and
relates them differently to their respective states.

Further west is another ethnic group, the Buxa, who are not unlike their Rana Tharu neighbors. They are also inhabitants of the Tarai and share the features associated with the Tharu. The first comprehensive account of the Buxa, that of J. L. Stewart, was published in 1865. His description is based on a visit made to two areas of Buxa settlement in the winter of 1862–63, Bijnour and the Patli *dūn*. Like the Tharu, the Buxa are supposedly immune to malaria; and like the Tharu, they are (or were) seminomadic, never staying more than a few years in a given spot before moving on. Stewart adds that Tharus (the reference here is to the Rana Tharu) share many features with the Buxa, as well as a common dialect of Western Hindi (Hasan 1979: 24), but neither group acknowledges any relationship to the other. What is interesting, however, is that the Buxa of Bijnour acknowledged as "Buxa" those who live further to the west, in Dehra dūn, but the Buxa of the Patli dūn insisted to Stewart that those people were Tharu, not Buxa (Stewart 1865: 149).

The Buxa and their Rana Tharu neighbors share a significant symbol: their myths posit a common origin. According to Amir Hasan, the Buxa claim that they and the Tharu are both descended from the two sons of a Rajput chief named Jagatdeo; in a Rana Tharu myth, they and the Buxa are descended from unions between the women of a Rajput royal household and their low-caste servants. When the Rajput chief was defeated in war, the women fled into the forest accompanied by their servants, with whom they formed unions. The Tharu claim descent from those who married their Chamar servants; the Buxa are descended from the unions between Rajput women and their Sais (?) servants (Hasan 1979: 20–21). Another Buxa myth attributes their origin to members of seven different castes who merged their identity after taking refuge in the Tarai: Thakur, Jat, Teli, Julaha, Bania, Nai, and Chamar (22). Furthermore, although formal arranged marriages do not take place between these two groups, there are numerous elopements in the region where the geographical distribution of the two peoples overlaps in the Naini Tal Tarai. In short, there are more ties, cultural, linguistic, and territorial, linking the Buxa to the Rana Tharu than there are linking the Rana Tharu to the Tharu of Chitwan or Dang. If the boundaries of Nepal had extended further west to encompass the Rana Tharu of Naini Tal and the Buxa (as indeed, once it did), it is possible that both might have been included within the Tharu category that is being shaped today.

The key to this difference in the formation of ethnic boundaries between the Tharu / Buxa in India and among the Tharu in Nepal lies in the way that the states of India and Nepal structure their relationship to subordinate and marginal populations. Both Buxa and Rana Tharus in India are Scheduled Tribes. The Indian state has chosen to recognize the historical disabilities under which certain segments of its population—the Scheduled Castes and the Scheduled Tribes—have suffered, and to pursue policies of "compensatory discrimination" (Galanter 1989) designed to benefit those sections of society. Both the Buxa and the Rana Tharu are listed as Scheduled Tribes in the Indian constitution, a status that entitles them to special protection and benefits in education and government service. Thus, given their historical separateness, there is no particular reason why the Rana Tharu and the Buxa should redefine their ethnicity; given their minuscule numbers in the population of Uttar Pradesh, they would gain nothing that they do not already possess. As members of Scheduled Tribes, their elites have access to opportunities in government service and education irrespective of the particularity of their ethnic affiliation. In relationship to the state, what is important is not whether one is Tharu or Buxa but whether one is a member of a Scheduled Tribe. There is no necessary reason why cultural similarity, even so potent a shared symbol as a myth of common descent, should result in a common ethnicity.

In Champaran, the Tharu were initially classified as a Scheduled Tribe in the Census of 1941. However, the Champaran Tharu, being heavily sanskritized, objected to the status, which they considered demeaning, and at their own request were removed from the list (Diwakar 1959: 84–85; Roy Choudhuri 1952: 248). They presumably realized their error, for in 1991, more than fifty years later, the primary political objective of the Bharatiya Tharu Kalyan Maha Sangh (the caste association of the Tharu of Champaran) was to be listed once again as a Scheduled Tribe. The remainder of the Tharu population in India, populations of not more than a few thousand or a few hundred scattered throughout India's Tarai districts, are merely extensions of the Nepali groups.

A similar situation does not exist in Nepal. The Nepali state has not created any special privileges for its own "tribal" population on the lines of the Indian model and is opposed to doing so. Nevertheless, the Tharu elite demands of government that they be accorded the same treatment as a Scheduled Tribe in India: that positions be reserved for them in government service and education. It makes a difference in the relationship of ethnic groups to the state in Nepal whether one is a member of a large ethnic community or a small and marginal one. Numerically, the Tharu loom much larger in the Nepali polity than the Tharu do in either Bihar or Uttar Pradesh, and larger still in the population of the Tarai; the calculus of numbers is thus an argument that supports the reconfiguration of the ethnic boundary in Nepal. And the Tharu, I should note, are very conscious of this calculus, although their estimate of their population is probably exaggerated.

Tharus believe, with some justification, as I shall discuss in chapter 6, that they have been undercounted in the census. They also believe, with less justification, that they form a greater proportion of Nepal's population than they actually do. The following paragraph, reproduced from my fieldnotes, is a summary of opinions held by a young college-educated Tharu man in Chitwan on the role of Tharus in Nepali society and their relative numerical status in the population:

> Ninety-five percent of the people in Nepal are farmers. The most populous districts in Nepal are in the Tarai and this is where most of the farmers live. Except for Kathmandu and Pokhara, the mountain districts are sparsely populated. The majority of people in the Tarai are Tharus, so about 50 percent of farmers in Nepal are Tharus. To develop Nepal, the farmers must become developed, which means the Tharu must become developed. But the Tharu are the most backward group, behind Brahmans, Chhetris, Magars, and Gurungs. At the same time it is difficult to develop the Tharu community because it is not united. If a Tharu gets rich, there are others who want to drag him down. Everyone has different ideas and opinions and therefore won't unite.

Other Tharus make similar claims. For example, Narendra Chaudhary, the president of the Tharu Kalyankarini Sabha, asserted,

> Because you see, the biggest number in this country...is the Tharu. Almost...40 percent of the total population in the Tarai are Tharus. So definitely it is bigger than any community. But they are showing that the Brahmans are the highest, then comes the Chhetris, then comes Newars, others, and then only Tharus. Whereas my belief is that Tharus should come in number one. Not only in the Tarai, in totality. [He begins to list various districts here, giving his estimates on the numbers of Tharus in each.] In Kailali...more than 70 percent Tharus. Bardiya, 70 percent Tharus. Now comes Banke, Banke also 60 percent; then comes Dang, total is 70–80 percent Tharus, you see? Likewise Tharus up to Chitwan, Parsa District, they are more than 70 percent Tharus in those districts. Then comes Bara, now 60 percent; Rautahat, 11 percent, very few; then comes Sarlahi, 30 percent; Siraha, 25 percent; Saptari, then again 50 percent; Sunsari, more than 60 percent; Morang, that also 60 percent, see?

These assertions may be compared to the official census figures given in table 7.

Mahesh Chaudhari, a member of the Tharu intelligentsia from Dang, in a mimeographed article on the undercounting of Tharus in the census (in which he examines the figures from the 1971 census reproduced in table 7), estimated the Tharu population in Nepal somewhat more conservatively at two million (Chaudhari n.d.). Even this is exaggerated, because it would require that almost the entire Maithili- and Bhojpuri-speaking population be ethnically Tharu, which is not the case. But in general, Tharus share the belief that they are a numerically significant proportion of the Nepali population. Sometimes this can lead to the perception that they have been politically slighted. Immediately following the 1990 People's Movement,[2] for example, the interim government that was supervising the run-up to the multiparty elections permitted the broadcasting of the news on Radio Nepal in Newari and Hindi, a political concession to two important sections of the population, the Kathmandu valley Newars, and Tarai people of plains origin. A Tharu villager in Dang (not of elite status) complained to me that this was showing disrespect to Tharus; why, he demanded, did the government not also broadcast the news in "Tharu," seeing that Tharus were such a large proportion of the national population? As it turned out, the government eventually did (see chapter 6).

In Nepal, a country in which no single ethnic group enjoys a clear majority, the Tharu appear to be (at least according to the 1991 census) among the more numerous of the many so-called tribal groups and are a significant part of the population in a vitally important part of the country (among the matwāli groups, only the Magar, with 7.24 percent of the population, outnumber the Tharu). The system of reservations guaranteed by the Indian Constitution already provides the Tharu and Buxa in India (in principle) the benefits that the Tharu in Nepal are demanding of the government. Their status as Scheduled Tribes is politically more significant than their particular local ethnic identities; the same is not true for the Nepali Tharu. The conjunction of forces, historical and contemporary, that has propelled the different Tharu communities in Nepal into fashioning a pan-Tharu identity do not exist across the border. The greater the proportion of Tharus in the total population, the more significant becomes the Tharu Kalyankarini Sabha (or its leaders), which claims to speak on their behalf.

In India, some Rana Tharu can describe themselves as Thakurs, act the way they imagine Thakurs act, and still be a Scheduled Tribe with all the benefits that might accrue to this legal status; in Nepal, they can claim to be Thakur only to the extent that it does not interfere with their ability to establish alliances with other Tharu groups and present a united Tharu front to the state and to non-Tharus. If there had been no Rana Tharu population within Nepal, that particular subgroup might not have been included within the Tharu category at all, at least as far as Nepali Tharus were concerned. If claiming to be Thakur becomes a barrier to common identity with other Tharus (and as far as I know that has not happened in Nepal), the calculus of numbers will serve to marginalize the Rana Tharu even further. It is not surprising then that Tharu identity is more important to Rana Tharu in Nepal than the claims to Thakurness of some of their brethren across the border.

Tharu unity in the Nepal Tarai derives from the incorporation of all these groups within the borders of a particular state. Tharu ethnic identity is formed not on the basis of shared cultural features (it would be difficult to find any cultural practices or symbols which are exclusively in the domain of the Tharu and of no other) but in terms of a particular structural relationship to the state. Whether Nepali Tharus see Tarai people across the border in India as sharing in a Tharu ethnicity depends on the particular historical circumstances. There are no Buxa in Nepal, therefore they fall outside of the limits of Tharuness. The Tharu of Naini Tal belong because they are of the same group as the Rana Tharu of Kanchanpur. The Tharu of Champaran have historical ties to those of adjacent Chitwan, with whom they intermarry, and with whom they have much in common. They are therefore considered to be Tharus as well, just as those members of Nepali Tharu groups who have settled in villages in India are accepted as Tharus without difficulty.

The comparison with India clearly indicates the importance of the state to the configuration of ethnic identity. In Nepal, sociocultural groups with much less in common than the Rana Tharu and the Buxa have claimed a common identity; in India, in contrast, analogous social groups have failed to do so, for the reasons I have suggested. The Buxas fall completely outside the domain of Tharuness. While both the Rana Tharu Parishad and the Bharatiya Tharu Kalyan Maha Sangh send representatives to the biennial conventions of the Tharu Kalyankarini Sabha in Nepal, they nevertheless maintain separate ethnic organizations with different aims in India. That is because they are separated not only by an extensive territory, but also by two different jurisdictions, Uttar Pradesh and Bihar. The remainder of this chapter is devoted to a consideration of the role of the state in Nepal that has contributed to a different outcome for Tharus there.

An influential approach to the relationship between a state and a multiethnic society, first put forward by J. S. Furnivall with reference to colonial Burma and subsequently applied by M. G. Smith to the Caribbean, is
the theory of the plural society. Plural societies are held to be colonial
creations, and "ethnicity tends to be articulated as group competition"
(Eriksen 1993: 14). Furnivall argued that Burmese society under colonial
rule was characterized by a number of different ethnic groups—Burmese,
Chinese, Indian, and European—distinct and separate from each other in
language, culture, and occupation and with little in common. They were
held together in one society only by the power exercised by the colonial
administration (Furnivall 1956). Plural society theorists see certain multiethnic states as being composed of a hierarchy of social segments each of
which constitutes a society with its own culture. These segments are kept
together because their position in the hierarchy and their relationship to
other segments of the society is enforced or regulated by the state. This
approach has been subject to much criticism; its general usefulness as a
model for describing multiethnic societies has been questioned by Brass
and by R. T. Smith, and the latter has shown that it is an inadequate
model of Caribbean society (Brass 1985; Smith 1966).

There are two problems with the Furnivall–M. G. Smith model of the
plural society. The first is its failure to adequately account for internal
class stratification within separate, culturally defined social segments.
Plural society theory tends to treat culture as being a static phenomenon,
but the maintenance of cultural distinctiveness and separateness (or, on
the other hand, assimilation to a dominant culture) is itself the outcome
of a dialectic between the dominant elite (or the dominant ethnic group)
in the society and the various classes in the subordinate social groups.
Ethnic groups constitute each other through their interactions. In spite of
this caveat, Nepal in the nineteenth and early twentieth centuries can
usefully be understood within the rubric of plural society theory in that
the state played a central role in organizing ethnic difference and in
maintaining ethnic boundaries.

The second problem with the theory of plural society is the assumption that ethnic groups are closed systems. Although the ethnic groups
of Nepal differ in cultural practices and language, they also have much
in common and have participated for centuries in a common field of
social and political action. The people of the middle hills in particular
(that is, of the Mahabharat range) have all been subject to or influenced
by Hindu-dominated polities since before the rise of the house of

Gorkha. Nepal under the Ranas was a multiethnic society whose separate segments were organized according to the principles of the Hindu caste system in a hierarchy defined, enforced, and maintained by the state. These groups, however, were not isolated from one another but were linked by a dense web of interrelationships.

Brass notes that state policy in multiethnic states takes two forms. One is integrative and seeks to assimilate the entire population of a state to a common identity. The other is pluralistic (used here in a sense somewhat different from the Furnivall-Smith thesis) and, recognizing the fact of multiethnicity, concedes to these groups various rights and privileges. These approaches, Brass adds, can either be liberal or authoritarian, and multiethnic states can follow mixed strategies (Brass 1974: 10–11). Nepal has followed both, but at two very clearly demarcated periods in its history. The Rana state, in Brass's terms, was pluralistic.

The Nepali state was the principal agent in the structuring and reifying of caste relations, caste ideology, and caste behavior during the nineteenth and early twentieth centuries. Caste ideology and caste relations in Nepal have changed as a consequence of the policies followed by the state toward its people, policies that reflect the abiding concerns of the national elite. Since the time of the first Nepali king, Prithvi Narayan Shah, these policies have focused on the problem of how to define Nepal as a distinctive polity vis-à-vis its giant neighbor to the south. The state's solution in modern times has been to promote hill culture and the Nepali language as the unifying symbols of that identity, while at the same time treating the plains culture and languages as alien. The immigration of hill people into the Tarai in recent years with the active encouragement of the state in part reflects this policy.

The Tarai has been historically the least distinctively "Nepali" region of the country; until recently, much of its population had closer social and linguistic ties to the population across the border in India than to Nepalese from the hills. Apart from the Tharu and some other smaller groups, the Tarai was inhabited primarily by immigrants from India who had crossed the border in the nineteenth and early twentieth centuries in search of land and to escape the consequences of floods, famines, and other disasters in Bihar and Uttar Pradesh. They had been encouraged by the Nepali state, which had failed to persuade hill people, because of the prevalence of malaria,[3] to voluntarily settle the Tarai. The descendants of these immigrants do not generally speak Nepali, and maintain close social and cultural ties with their kin across the border. The principal languages of the Tarai were Maithili, Bhojpuri, and Awadhi; despite the extensive immigration into the region by Nepali speakers, they remain the dominant languages in many areas, particularly in the east.[4] Hindi is also widely spoken in the Tarai. Encouraging the immigration of Nepali speakers into this region, whose political loyalty to the state was suspect, was a policy pursued by the state to "culturally stabilize" the border (Elder et al. 1976: 29; Gaige 1975: 12, 23).

Prior to the creation of modern Nepal, a process that began in the mid-eighteenth century, its territory consisted of a large number of petty states and autonomous principalities. One of their number, the kingdom of Gorkha, north and west of Kathmandu, rose to preeminence during this period. Under its ruler, Prithvi Narayan Shah, the Gorkha state began a period of political expansion and military conquest, which culminated in 1769 when the cities of the Kathmandu valley fell to its armies. This is generally treated as the founding date for the modern state of Nepal. Territorial expansion continued until 1816, when the newly unified state of Nepal was confined within its present boundaries by the British East India Company, which had established itself as the dominant power on the Gangetic plain. Following the Gorkha conquest, participation in the political life of the new kingdom was confined initially to the Brahman and Chhetri families in the following of the king, Prithvi Narayan Shah, who moved his capital from Gorkha to Kathmandu (Regmi 1978: 19). Subsequently, participation in government was extended to other influential high-caste families (Rose and Fisher 1970: 18). The state in Nepal, including the administrative service, the army, the police, and members of parliament, is dominated by members of the high castes: Brahmans, Thakuris, and Chhetris (Blaikie, Cameron, and Seddon 1980: 95–98; Hoftun, Raeper, and Whelpton 1999: 246). Of Nepal's trained work force, 70–80 percent consist of Brahmans, Chhetris, and Newars, except in the police and the army; and a survey carried out by Tribhuvan University of the total enrollment in higher education found that 45 percent of students were Brahman, 20 percent Chhetri, and 19 percent Newar (Malla 1992: 23). The leadership of the major political parties are also overwhelmingly dominated by these three ethnic groups. Until the post-1951 period, Nepal had very little in the way either of a native bourgeoisie or a working class. The state ruled over an overwhelmingly agrarian economy.[5]

The system of rule that prevailed in Nepal until modern times has been characterized by Rishikesh Shaha as a patrimonial system, which he defines as an exercise of authority characterized by peremptory command (*hukumi sāsan*) (Shaha 1982: 10). The state was an absolute monarchy to which all land belonged. According to Richard Burghart, "the king saw himself as a landlord . . . who classified exhaustively and exclusively his tracts of land according to tenurial categories and then assigned, bestowed, licensed, or auctioned the rights and duties over these tracts of land to his subjects" (1984: 103). Because land was held at the pleasure of the ruler, there was a constant turnover in ownership (meaning, in this context, holding land from the state under different forms of tenure), which precluded the growth of a powerful landed nobility strong enough to challenge the king (Shaha 1982: 11). Given the absolute nature of royal power, the political elite (drawn from the ranks of the landowning nobility) were defined in terms of their proximity to the king's person (24). From the perspective of interethnic relations in Nepal, what is salient is that the landowning nobility, the bureaucracy, and the higher ranks of the military were all drawn from the dominant Brahman, Chhetri, and Thakuri castes of the hills.

From 1847 to 1951 the state was the instrument not of a ruling class but of a ruling clan. In 1846 real political power passed into the hands of the Ranas, a clan of the Chhetri caste, which governed for the next hundred years through hereditary prime ministers, the Shah dynasty being relegated to figurehead status. The Ranas treated the country, in essence, as their personal estate. The basis of their support was their secure control of the military; the senior officer corps was (and remains) mostly Rana. All their potential rivals among the pre-Rana nobility were ruthlessly persecuted; other members of these rival families were co-opted by being made into minor functionaries of government. According to Bhuwan Joshi and Leo Rose, "only a few non-Rana elements rose to positions of authority within the government during the period of Rana rule" (Joshi and Rose 1966: 38). The Nepali state immediately prior to the modern period therefore was an instrument, not of a ruling landed class or a bourgeoisie, but of a clan:

> The Rana political system was an undisguised military despotism of the ruling faction within the Rana family over the King and the people of the country.... [The] main domestic preoccupation [of the government] was the exploitation of the country's resources in order to enhance the personal wealth of the Rana ruler and his family. No distinction was made between the personal treasury of the Rana ruler and the treasury of the government; any government revenue in excess of administrative expenses was pocketed by the Rana ruler as private income.... As a system accountable neither to the king nor to the people, the Rana regime functioned as an autochthonous system...and served only the interests of a handful of Ranas and their ubiquitous non-Rana adherents. (Joshi and Rose 1966: 38–39)

Perhaps the most important artifact of Rana rule was the *Muluki Ain* of 1854, a legal code that attempted to organize the population of the Nepali state along Hindu principles of social organization. The *Muluki Ain* was a codification—but also a reification and homogenization—of existing customs, usages, and practices, particularly those that governed the relations among caste/ethnic groups. The central principle of the *Muluki Ain* was ascribed status (Höfer 1979: 39). Although the code went through a number of editions until it was finally abolished in 1963, the provisions concerning caste hierarchy underwent no significant revision. The caste hierarchy codified in the *Muluki Ain* is, as I noted earlier, similar in some ways to Furnivall's conception of a plural society in that culturally distinct and primarily endogamous populations were organized into a hierarchy enforced by the state; where it differs is that these groups, for the most part, had well-defined relations with each other that structured them as a common society. It was plural in the sense that the state organized the population on the basis of its cultural diversity.

Nepal is, culturally and linguistically, a very heterogeneous state. Much of its diverse population has been assimilated by the state since the nineteenth century into a number of named categories, which today constitute ethnic groups. The Tharu are one example; others are the Tamang, the Magar, and the Rai people of eastern Nepal (Höfer 1979: 142, 146–149). The state, through the instrument of the *Muluki Ain*, organized this multiethnic population on the model of the Hindu caste system; it divided the population into five strata, ranked hierarchically in relation to one another, and defined in terms of attributes of purity and pollution. This ranking in turn was modified by the political importance of the different groups to the state itself. Thus, while the high Hindu castes (whose elites dominated the state politically) and the untouchables occupied either end of this hierarchy, the state's solution to the problem of how to rank the various "tribal" groups reflects the exigencies of politics. These groups were divided into two categories, the nonenslaveable alcohol drinkers and the enslaveable alcohol drinkers (the consumption of alcohol was treated by the state as an attribute of impure, but not untouchable status). The higher ranked nonenslaveable category included the Gurung, the Magar, the Sunuwar,[6] the Rai, and Limbu and some Newar caste groups (Höfer 1979: 45). The enslaveable category includes, among others, the Tharu. The Tharu were thus included in the lowest category of the clean castes.

The Tharu are, relatively speaking, a large population; there are more Tharus in Nepal (nearly 1.2 million by ethnicity according to the 1991 census) than there are members of any of the higher ranked, nonenslaveable, alcohol-drinking groups. The key difference that relegated them to a lower social status in the eyes of the ruling elite in Kathmandu was probably their relative political marginality to the state. The Magars and the Gurungs—the "beau ideal" of the Gurkha soldier (Vansittart 1894: 223)—and later on the Rai and Limbu, formed and continue to form an important component of the Nepali military; they played a significant role in the expansion first of the principality of Gorkha and subsequently of the Nepali state. These ethnic groups were later characterized by the British as "martial races" and recruited into the British Indian army (Vansittart 1894; Des Chene 1993: 68–69). They were in effect population groups of some importance to the ruling elite. In contrast, the peaceable Tharus[7] posed no imaginable threat to the ruling order and were politically and geographically marginal. The other groups in the category of enslaveable matwāli were even more marginal: small, forest-dwelling groups whose population could be counted in the low thousands, or small groups of Tibetans living in the high reaches of the Himalaya.

The *Muluki Ain* set forth the view of the dominant Hindu castes on the proper form of social organization.[8] The impact of the *Muluki Ain* on social behavior appears to have been felt primarily in the sphere of inter-caste (interethnic) relations. According to Prayag Raj Sharma, the Rana regime permitted a great deal of leeway to individual caste/ethnic groups to follow their own customs; the final court of appeal, so to speak, being the Council of Nobles (Bharadāri) in Kathmandu (1997: 480–481). Sharma asserts that tribal groups "have lived under it for such a long time now that this model has extensively pervaded their own outlook" (Sharma 1978: 4). It is likely however, that the extent to which the *Muluki Ain* has had an impact on the thinking of "tribes" is a function of the effectiveness of the state administration. In more remote areas, the *Muluki Ain* probably had less influence than in more accessible places, where Kathmandu's writ was more strongly felt. Nepal's topography makes it an extremely difficult region to rule, and even earlier this century, communication between Kathmandu and the more remote regions in the high hills or the Himalayas could take several weeks if not months. James Fisher observes, "As official law governing such matters as caste hierarchy and inter-caste relations, it does not necessarily record what really happened, but it certainly indicates the Nepali government's strict Hindu hopes for its people" (Fisher 1985: 100). This is probably an accurate assessment of the situation in the more remote regions of the Himalayas, but the power of Kathmandu was more firmly felt in the

Middle Hills and the Tarai, particularly in those regions settled by Brahmans and Chhetris, whose own position was reinforced by the legal provisions of the state.

The *Muluki Ain* codified into law the existing interactions between different caste and ethnic groups, and attempted to organize their immense diversity[9] into a coherent hierarchy (see table 4). A central concept informing this act of organizing was ascribed status (Höfer 1979: 39). In this hierarchy, a key structuring principle, as in the caste system in general, was the opposition between the clean castes and the untouchables. Although both groups on each side of this divide were further subdivided into ranked groups, these subdivisions were not relevant for the interaction between the two. There was also another structuring principle which organized the hierarchy of the clean castes. This was the

---

Table 4. Caste hierarchy of the *Muluki Ain*

1. Caste group of the "Wearers of the holy cord" (tāgādhari)
   Upadhyaya Brahman
   Rajput (Thakuri) ("warrior")
   Jaisi Brahman
   Chhetri ("warrior")
   Newar Brahman
   Indian Brahman
   Ascetic sects
   Various Newar castes

2. Caste group of the "Non-enslaveable alcohol drinkers" (namasinyā matwāli)
   Magar
   Gurung
   Sunuwar
   Some other Newar castes

3. Caste group of the "Enslaveable alcohol drinkers" (masinyā matwāli)
   Bhote (people of Tibetan origin)
   Chepang
   Kumal (potters)
   Tharu
   Gharti (descendants of freed slaves)

4. Impure but "touchable" castes (pāni nachalnyā choi chito hālnu naparnyā)
   Kasai (Newar butchers)
   Kusle (Newar musicians)
   Hindu Dhobi (Newar washermen)
   Musulman
   Mlecch (Europeans)

5. Untouchable castes (pāni nachalnyā choi chito hālnu parnyā)
   Kami (blacksmiths) and Sarki (tanners)
   Kadara (stemming from unions between Kami and Sarki)
   Damai (tailors and musicians)
   Gaine (minstrels)
   Badi (musicians and prostitutes)
   Cyame (Newar scavengers)

Source: Modified after Höfer 1979: 45.

opposition between the matwāli or liquor-drinking castes and those castes whose members abstained, and were required to abstain, as a condition of their caste status, from the consumption of alcohol. This opposition was in effect the contrast between two cultural categories: on the one hand the high Hindu castes, which dominated political power, and on the other the so-called tribal groups, such as the Gurung, Magar, Rai, Limbu, Tamang, and, in the Tarai, the Tharu. As we saw earlier, the matwāli castes were further subdivided into two categories: the higher ranked nonenslaveable groups and lower ranked enslaveable ones.

The Tharu fell midway in the *Muluki Ain*'s hierarchy, within the category of enslaveable alcohol drinkers (*masinyā matwāli*). They were thus a pure caste, and Tharu women could be taken as wives or concubines by men of higher castes. Tharu men, however, could not take wives from the two categories that fell below them: the impure but "touchable" castes (among whom were reckoned Moslems and Europeans) and the untouchable castes—for example, the Kami (blacksmiths), Sarki (tanners), Damai (tailors and musicians) and the Badi (musicians) (Höfer 1979: 45). The provisions of the *Muluki Ain* as analyzed by Höfer seem to suggest that Tharu men could marry only with Tharu women or with women of other ethnic groups in the same category (of enslaveable alcohol drinker) in the hierarchy. But Tharu today assert that in the past, marriage between members of different Tharu communities was not permitted. It is possible that the *Muluki Ain* was intended to regulate relations among members of its fivefold hierarchy, while allowing local custom leeway within them. A Tharu man having sexual relations with a woman of higher status (that is, of the status of *tāgādhāri* or of nonenslaveable alcohol drinker) would be punished with enslavement plus a year's imprisonment if the woman were of a cord-wearing caste (see Höfer 1979: 71).

The *Muluki Ain* treats, in exhaustive detail, both of the attributes of different groups in the hierarchy it established, and of the appropriate forms of social intercourse among these groups. More than a third of it "deals with sexual relations, both inter-caste and intra-caste" (Höfer 1979: 69). It specifies which sorts of dangers are involved in what sort of contact between members of different caste groups. While the *Muluki Ain* ratified the traditional flexibility of intergroup relations in Nepal, it accorded high ritual status to Brahmans and upheld high-caste ideology in affording protection to the cow, banning the levirate, prohibiting sexual relations with members of untouchable castes, and punishing violations of the rules of commensality (Sharma 1978: 6). While high-caste men were permitted sexual relations with lower-caste women, provided they were not from the untouchable castes, rules of commensality had to be strictly observed in order to protect caste status. Thus, for example, a Brahman could take a Chhetri or a woman of matwāli caste as his wife or concubine, but he could not accept cooked food from her without losing his caste status. In practice therefore, high-caste men made their first marriage from within their caste group. The *Muluki Ain* established legally recognized forms of intermarriage between matwāli women and men of the high-status, cord-wearing castes—which provided an opportunity for change in caste status and social mobility for individuals.[10] The Chhetris, who are today the most numerous and widely settled group in Nepal, appear to have benefited most from this practice of hypergamy—the offspring of both Brahman-Chhetri and Brahman-Matwali unions being assigned to the category of Chhetri (Sharma 1978: 9–10).

An important concern of Nepal's ruling elite, ever since the unification of the country by Prithvi Narayan Shah in the eighteenth century, has been the question of India: more precisely, how Nepal should mark itself off from India as a separate political and cultural entity. In fact it was Nepal, in the popular dictum of Prithvi Narayan Shah, that was *asal hindusthān*, that is, the true Hindu homeland, India having been corrupted by Muslim influence (Höfer 1979: 153). Through the instrument of the *Muluki Ain*, the Nepali state organized its population in a coherent, systematic way along the lines of caste. By so structuring it, they tried to define it as something uniquely Nepali. The *Muluki Ain* thus served not only to legitimate the existence of Nepal as an autonomous political entity vis-à-vis British power but also, according to Höfer, "to motivate the solidarity of her citizens" (1979: 40), although whether it actually did so is open to question.

As the state shaped the caste system, so, in turn, the caste system helped to define the state in relation to other polities. In this context it is pertinent to note that the caste system throughout the subcontinent actually consists of innumerable local systems, which differ from each other in terms of caste categories, ranking, attributes, interactions, and so on. It is likely that this immense variety is related to the existence of innumerable states and principalities in India before the British period. Each region and polity had its own caste system, and as polities expanded, contracted, and fell, to be replaced by others, the local system of caste changed as well. The modern centralized Indian state that, ironically, upholds caste through constitutional provisions designed to redress the disadvantages of low castes, while simultaneously denying the system as a legitimate form of social organization, is merely the latest incarnation of this process.

The *Muluki Ain* of 1854 went through a number of editions in which certain provisions in the original were modified; the last of these editions to be prepared under the Ranas, in 1935, remained in force until the end of Rana rule in 1951. The *Muluki Ain* of 1854 was finally replaced by a new legal code introduced by King Mahendra in 1963, based on the country's first modern constitution (Höfer 1979: 39; Sharma 1977: 277). Höfer comments on these two pieces of legislation as follows:

> Undoubtedly, both Jaṅg Bahādur's [Muluki Ain] as well as King Mahendra's Muluki Ains each mark two turning points in the social history of Nepal. Jaṅg Bahādur's [Muluki Ain] is a codification of traditional social conditions; its central concept is that of ascribed status. King Mahendra's [Muluki Ain], while not explicitly abolishing the caste hierarchy, does not approve of it any longer. It thus clears the way to a competitive society to which the concept of achieved status is fundamental. King Mahendra's [Muluki Ain] was a reaction to a revolution which brought the Rānā rule and Nepal's isolation to an end. Jaṅg Bahādur's [Muluki Ain], by contrast, was the product of a dawning political consolidation after a period of wars and internal unrest between 1769 and 1846. (Höfer 1979: 39)

The modern state of Nepal no longer officially recognizes the institution of caste. Whereas the Nepali state today has formally enshrined in law the principle that there shall be no discrimination on the basis of caste or ethnicity, it promotes an ideology whose tenets are not compatible with caste principles as they were defined under the *Muluki Ain*. The state today promotes the twin ideas of "development" and "national integration." The instruments it uses to further these goals are the education system (an innovation in Nepal that is less than forty years old) and the universalizing of the language and culture of the dominant castes as the symbols of a common Nepali identity. Under the Ranas, the state attempted to organize the population on the basis of its diversity. Today, the state stresses that all Nepalese, whatever their cultural differences, share an essential unity in being citizens of the state with equal rights in law.

The State and Culture

Culture becomes politically relevant in Nepal in the context of a state predicated on the notion (even if unrealized) of popular sovereignty and oriented toward economic development and modernization. What is important here is that this reorganization of the state sets in motion other processes which affect its peoples. While Lord Macaulay's famous minute on education proposed to create a class of Indians who would be loyal to the British Empire, the processes it set in motion served to create a class of Indians that was instrumental in the dismantling of that same empire in India. In the same way, states seeking to modernize and create national societies may set in motion processes that serve to emphasize ethnic differences rather than undermine or homogenize them.

The requirements of a modern economy and of participation in an international system of states, particularly as a poor and dependent member, requires the institution of certain practices of rule: a modern bureaucracy, a rationalized system of revenue collection, the institution of the census as a form of social classification, some form of electoral politics, and a constitution that makes at least some ritual obeisance to the values of the European Enlightenment. The divine right of kings to rule is an ideology no longer respectable in the world, and even tyrants must claim to rule in the name of the people. Yet "the people" have a habit of taking such ideas to heart and of expressing them in different ways. The Rana state emphasized cultural difference even as it denied absolutely the right of people (who were, in any case, subjects and not citizens) to participate in the political process. When the principle of political equality is introduced into a society that was rigidly hierarchized, ethnic identities that had formed the basis of the now delegitimized hierarchy are likely to become politicized. When caste is abolished or delegitimized, it does not disappear; instead, in responding to new ideologies and practices of rule, it transforms into new social formations.

Of all of the processes of modernization, education is centrally significant; it is not only a means to modernization but also an attribute of it. Gellner (1983) has drawn our attention to the importance of education in engendering national identity and in homogenizing culture; his argument is perhaps overstated, but his point is well taken. The sort of state described in Gellner's analysis began to emerge globally in the nineteenth century; the successor states to the colonial regimes in Asia and Africa modeled themselves not on the agrarian polities which had preceded colonialism but on the Western model oriented toward economic growth. The important categories in the premodern agrarian polities were, if I might simplify here, that of lord and peasant; in the modern world, the politics of class has often been overwhelmed by the politics of ethnicity and nationalism. The Rana state exemplified very well Gellner's argument about the nature of agrarian polities:

In the characteristic agro-literate polity, the ruling class forms a small minority of the population, rigidly separate from the great majority of direct agricultural producers, or peasants. Generally speaking, its ideology exaggerates rather than underplays the inequality of classes and the degree of separation of the ruling stratum.... The most important point, however, is this: both for the ruling stratum as a whole, and for the various sub-strata within it, there is great stress on cultural differentiation rather than on homogeneity.... almost everything in [agro-literate society] militates against the definition of political units in terms of cultural boundaries. (Gellner 1983: 9–11)

In contrast, modern states must define themselves in terms of cultural boundaries; not culture in its "doxic" sense (Bourdieu 1977b: 164–171) but in the sense of an objectified system of key symbols, of which religion and language are usually the most important, and around which a national identity may be organized. In the modern world, unlike the old agrarian polities, nation and state are assumed to go together. While religion has been important as a symbol of identity for Nepal (it was Prithvi Narayan Shah, after all, who referred to his realm as asal hindusthān), it is language that serves to set it apart. The most successful achievement of the Nepali state's policy of cultural unification is the spread of Nepali as a national language. Frederick Gaige describes language as "a major component of Nepalese nationalism" (1975: 108). The development of a modern educational system has facilitated this process, but not without opposition from members of other language groups, particularly in the Tarai, where it was initially seen as an attempt to impose hill culture on plains people (108–111). Today Nepali is the lingua franca of the country, spoken as either a first or a second language by a majority of the population. It is also the official language of the state. While Nepali is the language of interethnic communication throughout the hills, it shares this position in the Tarai with Hindi and local languages such as Maithili and Bhojpuri. In the Tarai, while Nepali is the language of government and education, Hindi is used in commercial activity in urban centers, and Hindi movies are an important form of entertainment.

Among the Tharu of Chitwan, their own dialect tends to be restricted to domestic contexts, although it may also be used as a supplementary language in schools (for example, to explain a Nepali language textbook to students). Geeta Chand and her colleagues suggest that Bhojpuri-speaking Tharus adopted that language due to the influence of Bhojpuri speakers from India, and she suggests that in a similar fashion Tharu speakers in Chitwan will gradually relinquish their language in favor of

Nepali as their contacts with Nepali speakers deepen and increase (Chand et al. 1975: 13–17, 34). A Tharu woman in eastern Chitwan told me that her kinsmen in the western half of the district (the area most heavily settled by Nepali-speaking immigrants) spoke Nepali at home, an observation that, if generally true, would support Chand's hypothesis. While there is no sign of this happening in eastern Chitwan (and I have not been able to assess the degree to which it might have happened in the west), the young and educated Tharu men to whom I posed the question thought it possible. Indeed, one man remarked that he thought that half the Tharu population would "go in the direction of Nepal, and half in the direction of India," by which he meant that some Tharus would become assimilated to Nepali hill culture (which is happening to some extent in Chitwan) and some would be assimilated to the culture of the Indo-Gangetic plain (which is largely the case in the eastern Tarai).

ETHNICITY, CASTE, AND THE MODERN STATE

I see caste as a social formation dependent on the existence of a particular type of polity—one legitimized by the ideology of caste. Such polities no longer exist in South Asia, for these states regard their citizens as equal before the law, at least in principle. If social relations that were traditionally understood in ritual terms are no longer understood in that way, the concept of caste will be of little use in explaining them. Caste is then revealed in its elemental form: as ethnic groups ordered in relations of domination and subordination to one another, who compete with one another in a new political framework, that of the modern constitutional state.

Gloria Raheja (1988a, 1988b) and Declan Quigley (1993) understand caste systems as ritual systems whose purpose is to remove pollution (or inauspiciousness, in Raheja's terms) from the ruler or the dominant caste and thus maintain the harmony of the cosmos. Through the provision of various services essential for the successful completion of the ritual, client castes take on the pollution of the patron who sponsors it and who is its focus. I argue that systems of caste defined in these ritual terms are made possible only by a polity committed to maintaining and sanctioning such a state of affairs, and by the power of locally dominant castes to maintain a system that clearly works to their ritual, political, and economic advantage. Caste cannot endure for long in the absence of a caste-based polity—that is, a form of social and political organization that derives its legitimacy from the ideology of caste and where the ruler acts to uphold and maintain the caste order. Such polities are long gone from South Asia. In their absence, caste systems cease to be systems and decompose into their constituent ethnic components, whose mutual relations are organized along different bases of political competition and underpinned by different ideologies. The power wielded by locally dominant castes, which has been historically a conservative force upholding local caste orders, is vulnerable both to the exigencies of democratic politics and the forces of globalization and modernization. When caste systems are no longer guaranteed by the power of the state, as in modern India and Sri Lanka and in Nepal since the end of the Rana regime, they are transformed into systems of ethnic stratification where the ideology of caste as a legitimating value is absent or is openly questioned. This transformation has been occurring to varying degrees across South Asia depending on local social, political, and economic conditions.

For caste to exist as a formal system based on the principle of purity and pollution (as in the case of Nepal's old legal code, the *Muluki Ain*), it must be enforced. Caste cannot be separated from secular power. Power no doubt gathers its authority from a hegemonic ideology, but it is always backed up by the threat of force. In the recurrent caste atrocities in places like Bihar we see coercion—or more accurately terror—in its purest form, where neither cultural consensus nor authority validates the specific form that caste relationships take. Coercion is required because subaltern castes do not act in the manner that dominant cases have come to expect. Subaltern castes are able to reject certain traditional forms of behavior because the state does not recognize the "right" of dominant castes to expect subaltern groups to act in particular ways. The state therefore will not support (in principle at least) the traditional forms of social relationships.

The caste system in an agrarian polity was a hierarchically ordered institution of more or less endogamous groups[11] that was maintained and enforced by state power; the ruler of the polity settled disputes that arose over status between different endogamous groups and had the authority to modify the status of whole groups in the hierarchy (see Marriott and Inden 1974: 989). People of different languages and cultures could be absorbed into this system and given a defined place within it that determined their relationship to other such groups and to the state. The imposition of British rule, and the refusal of the British to assume the old caste responsibilities of the native rulers they had displaced, led to the transformation of this system.

South Asian states in the modern world have also been shaped by other globalizing forces originating outside their borders and bringing with them new ideologies and new forms of productive activities that are incompatible with the traditional ideology of caste; these include nationalism, the concept of citizenship, democratic politics, and the ideology and practices of modernity and development. South Asian states today have withdrawn from the business of regulating the caste order. R. Kothari argues that the involvement of caste groups in politics in India has decomposed the old order "and is gradually forging a reintegration on secular associational grounds" (1970: 23). The primacy of the old ideology of a hierarchy ranked on ritual principles of purity and pollution is being steadily replaced by groups defining themselves (and defined by the state) on attributes of modernity and of nonritual values.[12] The Nepali state, which once mandated in detail the forms that interethnic (caste) interaction should take, no longer involves itself in such matters and officially repudiates caste as the basis on which Nepali society should be organized. Status difference is now being explained in terms of various ideas about modernity, as the following account of contemporary interethnic relations in Chitwan attests.

Chitwan District until the 1950s was a malarial, sparsely populated, forested wilderness, inhabited mainly by the Tharu. In the 1950s malaria was brought under control in Chitwan and the valley was opened up for settlement. Hill people moved into the district in the thousands, soon reducing the native Tharu to a small minority of the population. In the village of my fieldwork, however, the Tharu continued to form a large proportion of the population, and the village's two largest landowners were Tharu, although many Tharu lost land as a result of the influx of new settlers.

I had not been in the village long when it became apparent that many Brahman men—wealthy and influential villagers and visiting government officials—paid little attention to maintaining the traditional attributes of their status. It was not unknown for them to eat cooked rice in Tharu homes (typically the homes of two large landowners), and indeed the visiting officials did so regularly. Under the *Muluki Ain* such social intercourse was clearly prohibited, a prohibition that certainly reflected and regularized customary practices of the time. What was even more striking was that Brahmans—of different social classes—would consume alcohol, in the village, in the tourist development in the neighboring village of Sauraha, and in the bazaar towns. Contemporary Brahmans do not seem to care much that alcohol consumption, in the "traditional" caste order, was an impure practice used to mark the inferior status of certain social groups.[13] In Rana times, the provisions of the *Muluki Ain* pertaining to proper caste behavior would have been enforced by the functionaries of the state, including at the village level jimidārs or revenue collectors (Guneratne 1996: 10–12). But the state no longer cares about traditional caste behavior, and no other institutions exist to enforce "traditional" caste norms.

The erosion of traditional forms of behavior and attributes of status does not mean that Brahmans and Tharus are unconscious of rank. Brahmans see themselves as superior to Tharus but attribute their superiority to their better education and general acumen. Invocations of ritual superiority and greater purity are seldom resorted to and in any case would be difficult to sustain, for the reasons alluded to above. Sharma mentions an emerging ethnic consciousness among the dominant Hindu castes (the Brahmans, Thakuris, and Chhetris), which he tells us, are each coming "to look upon themselves as distinct cultural groups with separate roots and origin" (1992: 8).

The favored way in Chitwan to explain status differences for both Tharus and Brahmans is couched in the rhetoric of forwardness and backwardness, concepts probably borrowed from India and referring to attributes decidedly unlinked to ritual: success in education, ability to engage successfully in business, and so on. These conceptual changes are linked to the transformation of Chitwan's society and economy, which have become increasingly closely integrated into both Nepal's national economy and the global economy. Brahmans are active participants in this economy, and this "modernization" has shaped both their behavior and their perception of it.

Tharus also share in this new idiom of understanding; that is, they see themselves as a backward social group.[14] Two reasons may be cited for why this is so. First, it serves to explain their lack of success in the new economy, a lack that they attribute to the general illiteracy of their community; illiteracy and a general lack of education are defining attributes of backwardness. Second, by defining themselves as backward, Tharus can demand of the state special provisions (such as reserved places in education and government service) to rectify this historical disadvantage. Unlike low-caste status, backwardness is not inscribed in the fundamental nature of the group but is a historically contingent condition that may be rectified by partaking in opportunities (such as schooling) that are open to all in a modern, more or less democratic state.

It is not just the economy that has been modernized. The ideology of the state has also been transformed. The nineteenth-century Nepali state shaped society in the image most familiar to its high-caste political elite: a caste society hierarchically ranked from the pure to the polluted. Since the fall of the Rana regime in 1951, however, Nepal has pursued a different tack. The international model of the nation-state, together with all its trappings (among which a constitution and an official ideology guaranteeing the equality of all citizens are the most significant), has been the path taken by the country's political elite. "National integration" was its buzzword until 1990, when the Democracy Movement opened the Pandora's box of ethnic self-assertion. The people of Nepal are now citizens rather than subjects: they are all equal in principle; caste cannot be invoked to defend privilege, and they participate in politics on the basis of one person, one vote. The state does not recognize caste and no longer plays any role in enforcing appropriate caste behavior. The power of the state is now deployed in an attempt to create a sense of Nepali nationhood, by promoting a common set of symbols, a process referred to as Nepalization (Bista 1982; Gaige 1975: 216).

The philosophy behind Nepalization has been succinctly put by the Nepali sociologist Kailash Pyakuryal: "It has become the aim of the government to integrate different ethnic groups towards a common goal of national development. Nepal aspires to achieve a common culture which could be the binding force, and attempts to create a socio-economic environment which could motivate everyone to achieve the national goals of development" (Pyakuryal 1982: 70). Of the two sorts of state policy (pluralistic and integrative) followed by multiethnic states (Brass 1974: 10), modern Nepal falls into the second.

Inasmuch as the symbols of Nepalization (for example, language and "national" dress) have been traditionally associated with the high castes, the Nepali state is now acting in contrast to its nineteenth-century predecessor: it is emphasizing not cultural distinctiveness but the possibility of a cultural commonality (albeit one based on the culture of the high castes). In such a context, a caste-based discourse cannot sustain Brahman self-conceptions about their superiority and is not particularly persuasive to others; modernity provides a plausible alternative discourse. While Tharus agree with Brahmans that they are a backward group, this is very different to being inferior due to some ritual or dharmic principle (see Cameron 1998: 141–153 for a discussion of caste and dharma in a Nepali context). If one is backward because one lacks education, that is a condition that in principle can be overcome, and it can be overcome by making use of facilities and resources provided by the state itself. The transformation in the nature and ideology of the state engenders this alternative framework of understanding.

The point is not that caste is changing; rather, the content of ethnic identities, the way that those identities are ideologically (or culturally) legitimized, and the ways in which the bearers of these identities interact with one another are changing in ways that can no longer be adequately described by the Western concept of caste.

THE PANCHĀYAT SYSTEM AND THE DEMOCRACY MOVEMENT

Despite the pervasive rhetoric of development, the Nepali state in the post-Rana period, first under King Mahendra and then under his sons Birendra and Gyanendra, has never been committed to fundamental social change as a way to resolve the country's deepening social inequities. In the Nepali context, as in much of Asia and Latin America, such change must have as its basis a systematic program of agrarian reform. Indeed, B. P. Koirala, the prime minister who was democratically elected in 1959, was committed to sweeping agrarian reform and promised to give the land to those who tilled it. But his policies threatened the landowning elite (Gaige 1975: 198) and were among the factors prompting King Mahendra to mount a coup barely a year later, thus bringing to an end Nepal's first brief fling with popular democracy. He introduced in its place a form of limited popular representation under strong monarchical direction known as the panchāyat system.

Despite its organs of repression that helped keep dissent in check for thirty years, the panchāyat state lacked broad support. While the British tacitly cooperated with the Rana regime in the maintenance of Rana rule, the government of Nehru and the Congress Party in India sympathized with Koirala and the Nepali Congress and were not prepared to follow the same policy. The king was supported by "a large majority of the landowning and commercial interests in Nepal" and by a variety of other, "tradition"-oriented groups opposed to the Koirala government's socialist tendencies (Joshi and Rose 1966: 388–389). Yet the monarchy had to assure not only the preservation of existing privilege but also, to legitimize itself, some measure of social and economic development. Foreign aid thus became a key component of this difficult balancing act. The Tarai, once freed of malaria, presented an appropriate locus of development activity that could be used to meet the aspirations of the hill peasantry while leaving the existing system of political and economic power untouched. As Gaige noted, "in the short run...foreign assistance has enhanced the monarchy's chances of survival and has inhibited the growth of pressures for fundamental change" (Gaige 1975: 200).

The demand for social change, articulated by the products of the newly developed educational system, could not be deflected indefinitely. The social, political, and economic contradictions within Nepali society generated by this process of limited development eventually burst out in the Democracy Movement of 1990, the last in a series of struggles mounted by opposition forces in Nepal against the panchāyat system of partyless government introduced by King Mahendra in 1960. The opposition, which consisted essentially of the Nepali Congress and the Communist Party, sought a restoration of the multiparty system and parliamentary government that Mahendra had abolished. The Democracy Movement itself lasted barely two months, a far shorter time than observers had predicted would take to make the regime capitulate; part of the explanation probably lies in the pressures brought to bear on the Nepali state by its aid donors in the West and in India to concede to popular demands for multiparty democracy. The period immediately following the Democracy Movement, when an interim government formed by representatives of the Nepali Congress and the Communist Party ruled Nepal, was characterized by a complete discrediting of state authorities throughout the country. The lack of a clear authority at the center, and the ideas of freedom and democracy that were very much in circulation at this time, would in any case have made it very difficult for the state to use the forces of repression at its command to halt the political organizing that was going on throughout the country.

Asserting Ethnic Identity

One of the consequences of the new freedoms has been the forceful articulation of ethnic consciousness on the part of the country's various ethnic groups. Ever since the success of the popular movement for democracy in 1990, long-suppressed ethnic aspirations have flourished in Nepal, and the country has seen the emergence of many ethnic organizations along the lines of the one described in this book (Fisher 1993). Nepal has also seen the birth of organizations that seek to unite all so-called janajāti to press for reforms in the political process and for the reorganization of the state to give a greater voice and role to the historically subordinate ethnic groups like the Gurung, Magar, Tamang, and Tharu. One such organization is the Nepal Janajāti Mahasangh (Nepal Federation of Nationalities), to which the Tharu Kalyankarini Sabha belongs. The federation, which maintains that the so-called tribal groups are the aboriginal people of Nepal, seeks to unite Nepal's various "nationalities" against Brahman-Chhetri dominance, and defines a janajāti as "fundamentally non-Hindu" (Fisher 1993:12). Although these organizations do not represent a significant political threat to the established order in Nepal and have made little headway in national electoral politics, they do suggest what the future contours of ethnic politics might look like.

The terms *sanskritization, Hinduization,* and *Nepalization,* when used in the Nepali context, are virtually interchangeable. They all describe much the same process, predicated on the adoption of the symbols of high Hinduism, although Nepalization includes as well the use of a common language as the basis of integration. The concepts of sanskritization and Hinduization describe the process by which low-caste or tribal groups raise their status within, or become absorbed into, the social system of a dominant Hindu polity. When used in the Nepali context, they all refer to the fact that the fostering of a common national identity based on Hindu symbols has been a preoccupation of the country's political elites since the political unification of Nepal in the eighteenth century. Dor Bahadur Bista, for example, presumably referring to the *Muluki Ain,* claims that the caste system in Nepal was introduced "as part of the political process of Nepalization aimed at an integration of different communities into an organized single structure" (Bista 1982: 4). Under the panchāyat regime, the rhetoric of "national integration" was an expression of the dominant political ideology; Harka Gurung remarks that "the Hindu kingdom of Nepal still considers discussion on ethnicity as anathema and therefore no official data are available on ethnicity and caste" (1992: 19). According to John Whelpton, while questions on caste/ethnic affiliation were included in previous censuses, the results were never released prior to the census of 1991 because of their potential sensitivity (1997: 51). The 1991 census is the first to make those numbers available.

The Nepali historian Prayag Raj Sharma has taken exception to the use of the concepts mentioned above, because he claims that the dichotomy imputed by the terms *Hindu* and *tribal* does not exist. In one sense he is correct. These are Western dichotomies imposed on South Asian societies. But there are two words widely used in India and Nepal, *ādivāsi* and *janajāti,* which approximates the Western notion of "tribal," although, as Tharus will tell you, one can be both ādivāsi and Hindu. The word *ādivāsi* means, literally, the "ancient inhabitants" or aborigines of a place, and is used by contemporary ethnic activists to assert the indigenousness of their group in a particular locality. According to Ajay Skaria (1999: 277–281), the term originated in the Chhotanagpur area of Bihar in 1930 and was used to refer in a nonderogatory way to so-called tribal groups. Groups that consider themselves to be ādivāsi (mainly those that have been called tribal) often mobilize and enter into political activity and into alliance with one another on that basis. While the provenance of the term appears to be rooted in the colonial distinction between caste and tribe (and in that sense Sharma is right), the concept, having established itself, has become a potent way in which subaltern groups contrast their identities with those of superordinate "caste" status. In Nepal, spokesmen for these groups often use the term *janajāti* to describe themselves, although the Tharu seldom do. They also refer to themselves using the English term *Mongolian*, claiming that the ādivāsi or janajāti of Nepal are a people of Mongolian or Mongoloid extraction, in contrast to the Aryan origins of the high Hindu castes. Thus they contrast themselves to high-caste Nepalese not only on a temporal scale (they were in Nepal first, Brahmans and Chhetris are descended from Indians who immigrated much later) but also in "racial" terms.

What is significant is that this ādivāsi identity is defined in opposition to the identity of the high Hindu castes—Brahman, Chhetri, and Thakuri—which dominate the Nepali state. The rejection of the Hindu-tribal dichotomy by scholars such as Sharma (see also Ghurye 1980 for a similar position) can be seen, then, not simply as part of an academic dispute but as a political argument arising from the public discourse on "national integration" that anchors any discussion of ethnic identity in Nepal. It is not so much the concept of tribe that political elites in Nepal take exception to as much as the idea that "tribe" must necessarily be counterposed to "Hindu." A core idea in the nationalist ideology promoted by the Nepali political elite is that all Nepalese share a common culture and identity focused on Hinduism. In a country where almost half the population falls into the "tribal" or ādivāsi category in their self-identification, such an identity challenges the state's ideological project.

One point of friction in the relationship between Tharus and the Janajati movement appears to be the janajāti definition of themselves as Buddhists. While this does not cause problems for some Tharus—mainly those who embrace the thesis put forward by Tharu intellectuals like Ramanand Prasad Singh that the Tharu are of Buddhist (Sakya) origin—it does annoy others, even those who accept the Buddhist origins theory but believe that Tharus today are Hindu, whatever they may have been in the past. Narendra Chaudhary, who is among the latter, puts it thus: "Janajātis are those who are the real inhabitants of this country, backward, socially, economically. Those who are not Hindus, *that* should be omitted from the definition." What he is asserting here is that the definition of janajāti should not be predicated on religion ("those who are not Hindus") but on autochthonous origins and the social and economic characteristics of backwardness. He also sees other janajātis—to whom he collectively refers as *Shetamaguraitha* (i.e., Sherpa-Tamang-Magar-Gurung-Rai-Tharu)—as being relatively more privileged and even advanced than the Tharu. They were able to take advantage of opportunities such as recruitment to the Indian and British armies, whereas the Tharu have remained farmers and are thus further behind the other backward groups. According to Narendra Chaudhary's logic, other janajātis should recognize this and allow extra opportunities for the Tharu to enable them to catch up; the Tharu should be first in line if and when the state accedes to their demands.

In Nepal, ādivāsi or janajāti groups are on the periphery of power. Where the Tharu are concerned, not only were they culturally peripheral to the state, they were geographically and politically peripheral as well. Sharma may be right when he questions the Hindu-tribal dichotomy as a cultural fact; but it indubitably exists as a political fact, in the differential distribution of power between high-caste Hindus and ādivāsis, and in the consciousness among ādivāsis generally (including Tharus) of that situation.

CHAPTER FOUR

Land, Labor, and Politics

A centrally important issue that has shaped Tharu experience in modern Nepal is that of land. We have seen that the Tarai has for centuries been under the suzerainty of various hill states, to whose economies it was vitally important. Even so, as Krauskopff (2000) has argued, Tharu chiefs enjoyed a great deal of autonomy. This autonomy was steadily eroded in the post-Gorkha conquest period as the revenue administration system became increasingly bureaucratized and rationalized, until, in modern times, the jimidāri system was abolished altogether. Many of the former jimidārs made the transition to become landlords, especially in the east and in some areas of the west, but they lost ground (both literally and figuratively) to immigration, first from India and then, in the post-1950s period, from the hills. The closing of the land frontier brought about by immigration, the pressures of an economy based increasingly on cash, fraudulent moneylending practices and debt foreclosures, all served to limit the expansion of Tharu landownership and reduce the amount of land controlled by the Tharu population overall. These processes affected Tharus of every social class, but its impact varied from district to district. In this chapter I shall examine Tharu experience of these processes in two districts, Dang and Chitwan. Although they resemble each other in many ways, the experience of Tharus in the two districts is very different.

I argue in this chapter that the class dimension of agrarian conflict in Nepal is often overshadowed by its ethnic aspect because of the close congruence between ethnicity and class in some areas of the country. Such low-intensity conflict, which often characterizes relations between high-caste and so-called tribal people in many areas of Nepal (Cox 1990a), contrasts with the large-scale and more intermittent violence of riot and pogrom that characterizes communal relations in other parts of South Asia.

In contrast to the rest of South Asia, Nepal often seems like an oasis of ethnic tranquility. Many Nepalese like to compare their apparent interethnic harmony to neighbors such as Sri Lanka, which have been consumed by violence. Even so, there have been incidents of violent interethnic conflict, a notable example being the 1948 Limbu uprising, in which many Brahmans were killed (Cox 1990a: 1318; see also Holmberg 2000: 13). While such incidents of large-scale violence have been quite rare, that should not imply that ethnic harmony always prevails. Low-intensity ethnic tension and conflicts exist in many parts of Nepal, and at their root are struggles over the control of land. I use the term "low-intensity" to refer to the quotidian violence that characterizes relations between social groups that are hierarchically situated in a very exploitative social system, in which, in Ranajit Guha's words, there is "domination without hegemony" (Guha 1989). A system of extreme inequality and exploitation can be sustained only by violence or the threat of it. However, the high-intensity violence of the Maoist insurgency in Nepal, in which well over 2,000 people have died since it began in 1996, is in part a reaction to the everyday violence of "normal" life and the grinding inequality of Nepal's agrarian sector. The Maoist movement, although based on class, has a strong ethnic dimension, for it recruits heavily among matwāli groups and untouchables (Hachhenthu 2000).

In terms of its identity politics, Nepal can be described as a land of minorities. It differs in that respect from the rest of South Asia, where majoritarian identities—typically defined in terms of language or religion—dominate interethnic relations within states. Nevertheless, in Nepal, one category of people, the tagadhāri or twice-born castes, consisting of the Brahmans, Chhetris, and Thakuris, occupies the dominant position in society. These castes collectively control the institutions of the state, and their culture and language provide the central symbolic elements of a common Nepali identity that seeks to encompass other ethnic groups. I shall refer to this social group, for the sake of convenient shorthand, as the Parbatiyā. The term literally means a hill person, but like the cognate term pahāṛiyā it is often used by Tharus to refer to the high castes. While most Parbatiyās, like other Nepalese, are peasants eking out a modest living from the land, as a group they have benefited more than others (with the exception of the Newar) from the creation and consolidation of the Nepali state. Although these three castes together constitute only about 30 percent of the population (Whelpton 1997: 53), they make up the overwhelming majority in the state bureaucracy, in the higher ranks of the military, and in parliament, and they are also the most literate and educated sector of the population. Throughout the nineteenth and twentieth centuries, an important aspect of the centralization of state power has been the settlement of Parbatiyās (a process encouraged by the state) in areas historically associated with other ethnic groups. The basis of power in Nepal has been control over land and the labor necessary to cultivate it, and the appropriation of land in this way has been a source of tension between Parbatiyās and other Nepalese communities. In this chapter I examine how this settlement policy has shaped relations between Parbatiyās and one such group, the Tharu.

In order to consolidate its hold over peripheral or "tribal" areas, the state encouraged high-caste Nepalese (who were the closest to the ruling elites in terms of caste affiliation, language, and culture) to settle on newly acquired territories (Gaige 1975: 73, 82; Caplan 1991: 310). Such consolidation became especially important following Indian independence, when Nepal had to define a national identity distinct from that of India. Most Tarai people, descended from immigrants from British India who had settled the Tarai at the behest of the Rana state, were viewed with suspicion (as "Indians") by the national elite in Kathmandu (Gaige 1975: 202).

Two such peripheral areas were the valleys of Chitwan and Dang, which lie between the main Mahabharat Range and an outlying range of hills known as the Churia or the Siwaliks. Such valleys are collectively known as the Inner Tarai. These valleys are similar in a number of respects. Historically, both valleys have been identified with the Tharu, who were their principal inhabitants. In both, the Tharu population, although obliged to pay taxes to the state, held independent control of the land before the land reform of the 1950s and early 1960s. The land reforms of the post-1961 period, which sought to vest title in the land with the cultivator and to impose a ceiling on ownership, occurred about the same time that immigrants from the hills were moving into these valleys. Malaria eradication, land reform, and immigration had different consequences for the Tharu in these two districts, however. Two factors are central to understanding interethnic relations as they have evolved: the degree to which Tharus retained control of their land and the degree to which they have been able to participate in the Parbatiyā-dominated process of local and national politics.

Despite Nepal's image of ethnic tranquility, as I observed, low-intensity ethnic conflict exists in certain areas between the high-caste population and other ethnic groups, including the Tharu. In an agrarian economy where land is largely controlled by one ethnic group and where ethnicity and class are congruent (in perception as much as in fact), ethnic tensions will develop. I shall elaborate this argument in this chapter by comparing the situation in Dang (where Tharus are subordinated to Parbatiyās in terms of both class and caste and where land is controlled by high-caste immigrants) to that prevailing in Chitwan, where Tharu-Brahman relations are not characterized by the same degree of interethnic hostility. I attribute this to the fact that Chitwan Tharus, unlike their counterparts in Dang, have been able to retain land and participate in the opportunities created by the development and settlement of the valley. As a group Chitwan Tharus are not landless, and their class structure is as complex as that of their Parbatiyā neighbors.

INTERETHNIC RELATIONS IN DANG

Dang is an Inner Tarai valley in western Nepal that was populated, until the 1960s, almost entirely by a Tharu subgroup known as the Dangaura. Hill people avoided the valley because of endemic malaria. For about three centuries until 1786, Dang had been under the control of a dynasty of Rajput chiefs. From 1790 to 1839 the ending of strong external control allowed the power of local Tharu chiefs to grow, although they were obliged to pay revenues to the Nepali state. After the Ranas seized state power in the mid-nineteenth century, Dang was included within the borders of the dependent principality of Salyan (Krauskopff 1990). Although Tharus were obliged to pay revenues to authorities outside the Dang Valley, and to provide corvée labor to the state and its functionaries, under the Rana regime and those that had preceded it they retained control over the land and the agrarian system in the valley (see Krauskopff 1999).

The fall of the Ranas in 1951 ushered in a period of economic development funded by foreign countries, principally the United States, India, and China. Among the more significant of these efforts, as I mentioned above, was the Malaria Eradication Project. Following the success of this program, the United States Agency for International Development (USAID) undertook various projects to develop the valley, including the building of roads and the provision of agricultural assistance.

Malaria was controlled in Dang in the 1950s and the valley opened up for settlement. With the fear of malaria removed, hill people, mainly Brahmans, Chhetris, and Thakuris, moved in increasing numbers into the valley, eventually reducing the Tharu to a minority of the population. This process was exacerbated by Tharu emigration from Dang in response to these pressures.[1] According to Thomas Cox, about 15,000 Tharus were rendered completely destitute, and at least 6,000 migrated out of Dang to districts further west (Cox 1990a: 1319). As in Chitwan, the Dang Tharu were mostly ignorant of government regulations concerning the registration of land. Some of the Parbatiyā settlers took advantage of this ignorance, as well as of their own ties to government officials, to register land controlled by Tharus in their own names. A Tharu farmer in Dang commented, "The *pahāṛi* [i.e., Parbatiyā] found it easy to destroy us; we weren't smart people [*nabujhne mānchhe*]." By a variety of fraudulent means, including the bribery of government functionaries, they dispossessed most Tharus of their lands, reducing them to tenant status or, even worse, to that of bonded labor. Intimidation was also used, as the following instance illustrates. A Tharu farmer in Chhakaura, the village in Dang where BASE initially began to organize, came under tremendous pressure from the Brahman landlord of a neighboring village to sell his land. The landlord threatened that if he did not sell his land voluntarily, he would take it without payment. The farmer, who told me the story, said that he was afraid the landlord would carry out his threat, so he sold him six or seven of the eighteen or nineteen bighās he owned at the time.[2]

Cox, citing a survey done by BASE, claims that "every bonded laborer in far-west Nepal is Tharu" and that "approximately 97% of the landlords are Brahmans, Chetris or Thakuris" (Cox 1995: 11). According to McDonaugh, "Whereas in the 1912 revenue settlement most of the landlords were Tharus, by the late 1960s...the great majority of landlords were Pahari [i.e., Parbatiyā]....In Dang by this date some 80% of the Tharu were tenants and the great majority of these tenants had little or no land of their own. Around 90% of the land cultivated by Tharu tenants belonged to Paharis" (1997: 281).

Violence between Tharus and high-caste immigrants from the hills, imminent in Dang for several decades, has been realized sporadically. This violence originates in class conflict—that between landlord and tenant, where hill people are the landlords and the Tharu are their tenants—but is thoroughly imbued by understandings of ethnic difference. Typically, Tharu have been at the receiving end; landlords have beaten them, and Tharu women have been raped while working in landlords' homes (Rankin 1999: 37; Robertson and Mishra 1997: 20). In the dynamic of interethnic violence, a crucial difference between Chitwan and Dang is the control that high castes in Dang have been able to exert over Tharu society through their monopoly over land. The situation could not contrast more starkly with that prevailing in Chitwan. The ethnic antagonisms that exist in Dang arise from the reduction of most of the Tharu population to tenant status following the appropriation of land by hill people, and from the distortion and abuse of the system of labor relations—the *kamaiyā* system—that existed in the valley, which has led to a situation of quasi-serfdom for many Tharu.

KAMAIYĀ LABOR IN THE FAR-WESTERN TARAI

The following description of the kamaiyā system as it operates in Kailali and Kanchanpur districts is drawn from Katharine Rankin's account (1999). In its broad outlines, it is relevant also to Dang. Such a labor system involves a peasant cultivator (kisān) and a laborer (the kamaiyā), whereby in exchange for the latter's labor, the cultivator undertakes to feed, clothe, and house him and his family. Relations between a kamaiyā and his patron are often mediated by debt. The kamaiyā is not necessarily landless; on occasion, a Tharu entered into a kamaiyā contract in order to obtain a loan. He was obliged to work for his master until the loan was repaid, but members of his family did not become kamaiyās also, and were free to work to raise the money to repay the loan. There were also opportunities for a kamaiyā to repay his debt and end his kamaiyā status. He could, for example, engage in seasonal wage labor or raise livestock on the side (Rankin 1999). But it is important to note that both the (Tharu) kamaiyā and his (Tharu) patron are members of one ritual and social world, and the line between them is finely drawn: a kisān in traditional Tharu society is only a few bad agricultural seasons away from being reduced to kamaiyā status. Kisāns and kamaiyās were traditionally linked by a shared ethnicity and often ties of kinship, and both participated in a common moral economy. The system of bonded labor that is widely prevalent today in the districts of the western Tarai developed out of this system of kamaiyā labor.[3] The incidence of debt-bondage or bonded labor is not uncommon in Nepal, and has been documented by Robertson and Mishra (1997) in a report to Anti-Slavery International.

This traditional system was distorted by certain actions taken by the Nepali state. Rankin (1999) argues that "state taxation and resettlement polices since unification" laid the basis for the extraordinarily oppressive and malignant system of bonded labor that developed in the Dang Valley in the aftermath of the Malaria Eradication Project of the 1950s. Revenue collection policies during the late nineteenth and the early twentieth century had created a new landlord class very unlike the peasant cultivators who had provided a livelihood and a degree of security to their kamaiyās—a class comprising absentee hill people of high caste who were appointed jimidārs (revenue collectors) or who had received *birtā* and *jagir* lands,[4] and including the Tharu headmen (*talukdār*s) they appointed to manage their lands in their absence. This new landlord class was socially and ritually removed from the Tharu society it came to dominate.

The second factor that helped to transform the kamaiyā system was the eradication of malaria, which enabled hill people to move into the Tarai. Rankin's argument is that originally the kamaiyā system, which bound a Tharu kamaiyā to a Tharu kisān, was ameliorated by strong kinship and ritual ties between the individuals involved. The new, ethnically different landlord class that took advantage of the labor system it found in Dang shares no such ties to its kamaiyā servants and was thus not bound by the constraints of customary practice or the moral economy in which the traditional kamaiyā system developed. The kamaiyā today is a bonded laborer, tied to his master through the debt he owes him, obliged to work for him until the debt is paid off but with no opportunity to work for wages to redeem the debt.

According to BASE, there were 3,807 kamaiyās in Dang in 1994 (BASE 1994). Corvée or *begari* was ubiquitous in the valley in 1991 and affected virtually every Tharu household in its western part. In the aftermath of the appropriation of their lands by immigrants from the hills, Tharu tenants were compelled to perform corvée labor for their new landlords. Under the most common form of tenure, *adhiyā* (fifty-fifty sharecropping), the tenant had to perform 30–35 days of corvée labor for the landlord in a given year. In 1991, in western Dang, the corvée included agricultural work of every kind: house construction, work on village roads and bridges at the behest of the landlord, and even work as porters to carry a palanquin when a member of the landlord's family wished to travel to a neighboring village or bazaar. Monuments to such a system of labor are evident wherever one travels in this area, in the form of the substantial brick houses of landlords with enclosed walled gardens, all constructed with unpaid Tharu labor. In addition, Tharu girls had to work all day as domestics for their landlords and were often subject to sexual abuse; BASE reports that the sexual exploitation of bonded Tharu women is widespread in far-western Nepal.[5] Not only did the landlord require corvée, but in many cases he did not even feed his workers and his domestic help, thus placing an additional burden on their shoulders. While interviewing people in half a dozen different villages in western Dang, I recorded three instances of suicide by Tharu servants following maltreatment at the hands of their landlords; according to statistics kept by BASE, there had been eighty-three such suicides in the area in 1989 and 1990.

Although it was legally abolished in 1951, corvée labor continued to flourish, particularly in the remote and poorly developed areas in the west of Nepal, due to the lack of political will to eradicate it. Landlords with kamaiyā labor were important local supporters of the panchāyat system, and also of the Nepali Congress and the Communist Party. It took the Communist Party of Nepal (United Marxist-Leninist) until June 8, 2000, to declare that it was unacceptable for their members to have kamaiyās and require their release, and even then, the Communists did so only because events had overtaken them (see below).[6] Refusal to perform corvée labor exposes Tharu tenants to violence at the hands of the landlord and his thugs, to harassment by the police, to harassment and noncooperation in government offices (many of whose functionaries come from or have ties to the landlord class in Dang), and to loss of access to land (see also McDonaugh 1997: 284–285). A report prepared by a member of the Land Reform Commission as early as 1954 observed of the situation in Dang that "the Government Offices meant for providing Justice take the side of the rich people and thus encourage further suppression of the poor."[7]

One response to the conditions sketched out above has been a mass migration of Tharus out of Dang in the last thirty years. Entire villages have moved out, to settle in the districts of Banke, Bardiya, Kailali, and Kanchanpur (Krauskopff 1990; Cox 1990a; McDonaugh 1997). According to McDonaugh, while the Tharu have been emigrating from Dang throughout this century, the rate of emigration increased sharply in the 1960s and early 1970s (McDonaugh 1997: 282). Even in these districts, however, they have been subject to similar forms of exploitation, as these formerly forested areas have been opened up for agricultural development by settlers from the hills.[8] The bitterness of Tharus over their circumstances was expressed in an article written by a Tharu intellectual in the western Tarai, in which he proposed the reintroduction of malaria into the Tarai to solve the problems of his community.[9]

The Emergence of BASE

The form of landlord-tenant exploitation sketched out above is seen by Tharus in unambiguously ethnic terms. That is, they see themselves as oppressed not simply by landlords but by Parbatiyās (a term that Tharus apply primarily to high-caste hill people). Young Tharus in western Dang began organizing against this situation in the late 1980s, primarily by conducting literacy classes in villages. These classes became the platform for building a broad-based movement against landlords: one that works to educate the Tharu, end corvée labor and debt bondage, and provide the Tharu with sources of income independent of land. The leader of this movement, now known as BASE, is a charismatic Tharu named Dilli Bahadur Chaudhari, who was recognized internationally for his efforts when he received the Reebok Human Rights Award in 1994. Dilli Bahadur had worked to organize Tharus since his early teens and had been in jail twice for his activities before he was eighteen. It was USAID, an organization not known for encouraging peasants to struggle against oppression, that gave an impetus to his activities.[10]

A Nepalese community development nongovernmental organization (NGO) named No Frills Consultancy, which was working under contract for USAID, hired Dilli Bahadur to help implement a rural development program designed to improve the economic circumstances of Tharu farmers around Tulsipur. The purpose of the project, known as the Vegetable, Fruit and Cash Crop Program, or VFC program, was to introduce new and improved varieties of crops and livestock. No Frills appears to have encouraged Dilli Bahadur in the community development work he was doing on his own initiative, and sent him to Thailand in August 1988 to attend a conference of indigenous peoples. This exposure, plus later travels in India, where he made contact with various tribal movements and observed the protests over the Narmada dam, created in him a consciousness of being ādivāsi (aboriginal) and the sense that ādivāsis everywhere share a common experience of dispossession and exploitation at the hands of more powerful groups. That experience strengthened his determination to organize Tharus to resist and overcome the situation they faced in Dang.

One of the activities begun by No Frills was a 4-H club intended to "provide a forum in which agricultural techniques could be taught" and "through which resources could be distributed" (Cox 1990b: 3). The 4-H club, however, turned out to be far more successful than No Frills had anticipated and in ways it did not perhaps intend. It became the forerunner to what is arguably the most successful peasant movement in modern Nepal and certainly one of the most significant examples of grassroots development work anywhere in South Asia.

The anthropologist Thomas Cox, who carried out a study of the VFC program for USAID, attributes the 4-H club's success to its promotion of "involvement in the VFC program as an essential, inseparable aspect of wider struggle [by the Tharu] to emancipate themselves from oppression by Brahman/Chhetri landlords" (Cox 1990b: 9). While the 4-H club was active in organizing literacy classes and doing agricultural extension work, much of its monthly meetings were taken up with discussing how to organize against exploitation. Cox describes an incident that took place at this time:

> Several Tharu farmers...told me that they hoped the 4-H club might eventually be able to get their land back for them. Indeed, the 4-H club's emphasis on land, and emancipation from landlords, has led to some tense and occasionally violent incidents. For example, three months ago [in early 1987] Tharus from the Tulsipur gaon (village) of Razura, at the urging of the 4-H club, cleared and laid legal claim to approximately 70 ropanis of unowned, previously uncultivated land. One day...they were approached by a group of landlords, who claimed that the Tharus had no right to the land. A huge fight ensued in which one Tharu was injured and three others thrown in jail. But the Razura people were able to hold onto their land. (Cox 1990b: 9)

This incident clearly violated established patterns of interethnic relations in Dang. In the first place, by laying claim to the land, the Tharu were attempting to establish an autonomy of tenure which, symbolically at least, threatened the dominance of Parbatiyā landlords. It was an initial move to unravel the hold these landlords had over Tharu society, an unraveling which would later be prosecuted with vigor and success in this part of Dang by BASE, the successor to the 4-H club. Secondly, the landlords probably did not expect the Tharu to resist; Tharus are characterized by other Nepalese as pacific and timid people, and in Dang were treated with contempt by landlords.

The USAID program clearly played a significant role in the emergence of Tharu resistance to their situation. This is not to claim that there would have been no organizing and no resistance without this development program, but such resistance would probably have been different. Relations between Tharu tenants and landlords in Dang were extremely tense at this time, and considerable potential existed for violence between the two groups. As Cox has noted, the response by both landlords as well as the local apparatus of the state to the activities of the 4-H club was violent and coercive. Tharu activists were beaten, and not only did local officials refuse to prosecute those responsible, they even accused the organization of planning terrorist activities against the government (Cox 1995: 13–14). A Tharu from the eastern Tarai, who had been working with No Frills in Dang, told me in early 1991 that the situation for the Tharu there was so extreme that he thought there was a possibility of large-scale violence in the valley within five years. While conditions for Tharus had actually eased somewhat by 1991 because of the People's Movement in Nepal and the activities of the organization led by Dilli Bahadur Chaudhari, he thought it possible that the landlords might initiate a "caste war" because their interests were being threatened by BASE. This is perhaps an exaggeration, but during this period violence was being directed against members of BASE, and I know of at least one attempt on the life of Dilli Bahadur Chaudhari. While such violence, if it had occurred, would have been generated by class antagonisms in the Dang Valley, it would have been seen as ethnic in nature because of the close congruence between ethnicity and class in the hinterland of Dang. Violent resistance by the Tharu to their situation would have met violent repression at the hands of the state. As the state apparatus in Dang is controlled by Parbatiyās, who have ties of kinship and sentiment to the local landlord class, there is little doubt which group would have suffered the most in those circumstances. The state would have found it easier to justify its response if it could have portrayed the violence as being communal—that is, the outcome of ethnic loyalties, which run counter to the state's official policy of "national integration."

That some at least among the Nepali elite are aware of these ethnic antagonisms and their relationship to the process of development is shown in the following comment by Pashupati Shamsher Rana, a prominent member of various Nepali governments in the panchāyat and post-panchāyat eras:

A small and limited class of traditionally powerful families, the capital's inhabitants and three castes have exploited and continue to exploit today the best that the country has to offer. With the process of development an increasing consciousness of this is growing among the rest of the country. Unless the government sets out to cure this natural and just resentment, we will turn the process of development itself into a time-bomb. (quoted in Ragsdale 1989: 7)

The establishment of BASE and the rapidity with which it expanded must be seen in the context of the vigorous political activity taking place in the country in the aftermath of the People's Movement. Shortly after the success of the movement in 1990, Brahman youths assaulted one of the leaders of the 4-H club, who had been urging his fellow villagers not to work for a landlord without pay. A couple of days after this incident occurred, activists from fifty-three Tharu villages met to decide how they should respond and concluded that they could not afford to let this act of violence pass unchallenged. It may be that the People's Movement itself had provided them with a salutary demonstration of the power of mass action. Deciding to confront the situation head on, they laid siege to the house of the instigator of the assault. The man's father emerged to pacify the crowd, apologizing for his son's actions and pledging that such violence would not recur. Having made their point, and having demonstrated the unity of their numbers, the Tharu dispersed. The landlords in this village were shaken by the incident, which was altogether novel; as in Cox's example of the land dispute in Razura, the contemptuous and disdainful view they had of Tharus had not prepared them for the possibility that the Tharu might respond so militantly.

This incident was a catalyst for the mobilization of the Tharu in Dang because it was a striking example to them of the effectiveness of unity. According to Dilli Bahadur Chaudhari, if this had not taken place, the movement might have had a much slower start. By the time I arrived in Dang for the first time in November 1990, more than eight months later, the movement had grown to include almost 16,000 villagers in over sixty-six villages in the valley. By January 1995, the organization's membership had grown to over 85,000 distributed in five districts in western Nepal (Cox 1995). The movement's dues-paying membership today is over 100,000.[11] The group is not only expanding into other areas of the western Tarai but also seeking to include low-caste groups and untouchables in its organizing.

The Tharu movement eventually outgrew the 4-H club and took on a new name: Shrāmik Mukti Sangathan (Free Labor Organization). In early 1991, the leadership of the organization, and principally Dilli Bahadur, decided it had to be renamed. After briefly considering the English name Community Organization for Development and Education (CODE), the acronym BASE (standing for Backward Society Education) was chosen. Dilli Bahadur believed the name Shrāmik Mukti Sangathan, with its reference to organized labor, would get the Tharu no cooperation from government offices and the all-important zonal commissioner, the most important government functionary in the region. On the other hand, he pointed out to me, who (apart from landlords) could object to educating a backward society? Tharus all over the Tarai consider themselves backward (*pichhaṛi*) in relation to Brahmans because of the low rate of literacy in the community as a whole; Brahmans, on the other hand, are associated with knowledge and education. The Tharu attribute their exploitation at the hands of Brahmans to their illiteracy and lack of knowledge of the wider world outside Dang. Knowledge,

A BASE night school, western Dang District, 1991. Classes in the elements of reading and writing take place after the evening meal. The room is lit by the single homemade kerosene lamp in the left foreground.

they see clearly, means power. The choice of this name is thus not merely a tactical move but also reflects one of the principal goals of the group, which is to raise the literacy rate among Tharus. BASE sees this as a fundamental act of emancipation. A report to the Royal Danish Embassy in Kathmandu (DANIDA, the Danish Agency for Development Assistance, is BASE's chief source of financial support) observed that "BASE is running the only literacy campaign in the country. While most District Education Offices are running 30 to 40 classes, BASE is running hundreds. There is little doubt that this effort will have and is already having an enormous impact on the Tharu communities of western Nepal" (PACT-Nepal 1993: 8).

Dilli Bahadur's second goal in renaming the organization was to facilitate communication with foreigners, who have been the principal source of financial and moral support to BASE. When I asked him why he didn't choose a Nepali name that would be readily understood in Nepal, he explained that he didn't think Tharus could expect much help from other Nepalese (by whom he meant principally Brahmans and Chhetris). Tharus of course understood perfectly well what the organization was about. If the membership of BASE consisted mostly of Tharus, that is because they were the ones who were suffering at the hands of (mostly high-caste) landlords.

In those early years, when BASE was still struggling to establish itself, Dilli Bahadur was keenly interested in having the organization written up in the foreign press, in order to give publicity to the organization and the condition of the Tharu in Dang. He felt there was no advantage to be gained in having BASE written up in the Nepali-language press because he believed that the press would not promote Tharu interests or cover the organization sympathetically but instead depict BASE as a communal organization. BASE's very visible contacts with and financial support from foreign agencies was an essential part of its strategy for survival, as it helped to deter repression and organized violence against the group from landlords (this is no longer a significant problem, although it was a serious one in 1991). The publicity that accrued to BASE after Dilli Bahadur went to Boston in 1994 to receive the Reebok Human Rights Award and after his reception by the king on his return (a photograph of the latter event hangs in every BASE office I visited in western Dang in 1997) greatly strengthened the organization's position. The substantial financial support given to BASE by DANIDA and other international aid organizations has enabled it to become so important locally that some high-caste landlords in Dang have come to it looking for employment for themselves or their kinsmen—undoubtedly a satisfying turn of events for the Tharu who founded the organization.

The situation in the western Tarai for kamaiyās has changed in dramatic fashion.[12] BASE, from its inception, has been focused on the task of ending bonded labor in Nepal, and throughout the 1990s it worked in cooperation with a number of other Nepali and international NGOs toward this end. In May 2000, nineteen bonded laborers filed a petition in the Geti Village Development Committee (VDC) office in Kailali against their landlord, a former cabinet minister named Shiva Raj Panta, demanding among other things that they be freed from debt-bondage, be compensated for their unpaid labor, and be paid the daily minimum wage of sixty rupees. Mr. Panta did not respond to a request from the VDC to a meeting to mediate the dispute. The kamaiyās then filed their case with the chief district officer (CDO) in Kailali, Tana Gautam, who refused to register it. A mass demonstration of seven or eight thousand people in the district capital of Dhangadhi and a sit-in at the CDO's office eventually compelled him to back down. The minister for land reform then visited the district to assess the situation for himself, only to assert that the problem of bonded labor was overblown, but that his government would solve it in four years. He also refused to state in writing that the kamaiyās were free from bondage, a strange reluctance, given that debt bondage is constitutionally prohibited in Nepal.[13] However, the initial modest attempt of these nineteen kamaiyās to improve their condition took on a life of its own and ballooned into a full-scale movement to finally end the system. Almost two months later, on July 18, following mass demonstrations, a spreading of kamaiyā demands for freedom to other districts, and the pressure of local and international NGOs as well as the parliamentary opposition, the minister for land reform announced in parliament that the cabinet had decided to prohibit bonded labor and also declared that no bonded laborer need repay debts owed to the landlord.

Landlord organizations, notably one in Kailali called the Kisan Hakhit Sanchalan Manch (Forum to Mobilize for Farmers' Rights), have responded to these events in a number of ways. They have rejected the term jamindār (landlord), for example, arguing that they are only kisāns (farmers) owning a few bighās each, and that their workers are not bonded but free to negotiate new contracts. They have also charged BASE with creating communal disaffection between (Tharu) kamaiyās and (upper-caste) landlords, thereby endangering communal harmony. For good measure, they accuse BASE of creating a situation in which liberated kamaiyās, with no other recourse, would take to crime, and they claim that BASE is facilitating religious conversions in Kailali (Onta 2000). These charges were apparently taken up by the CDO, Tana Gautam, who wrote to BASE accusing it of engaging in these activities; although the charges are manifestly absurd, Onta writes that "the power of jamindar discourses about Kamaiyas is so dominant that there is very little questioning of the above mentioned charges by the local press, intellectuals and state offices. In fact the local press is thoroughly pro-jamindar" (Onta 2000).

Although the emancipation of bonded labor has fulfilled one of BASE's major goals, the government's lack of enthusiasm in accomplishing this necessary step is reflected in its failure to provide for the thousands of people who were freed in this way. That inaction has led to a humanitarian crisis, with thousands of people living in makeshift camps (three thousand families in December 2000) and most of the burden of looking after them left to the NGOs, including BASE (Devkota 2000: 4). Freed bonded laborers were typically thrown off the farms they had been working on with no compensation from their erstwhile masters; they have been demanding land of the government (ten katthas per family, or about .34 hectares), but the government's response has been glacially slow. Some kamaiyās, tired of waiting, took matters into their own hands:

> From the early morning hours of Thursday, January 18, 2001, about 3,000 ex-Kamaiya families in Kailali and Kanchanpur districts started to move peacefully from 51 different makeshift camps into 19 undesignated chunks of government-owned but non-forest land, occupying a total of almost 1500 bighas of land. While doing so...the ex-Kamaiyas were careful not to encroach upon forest land, not to chop down trees, and not to build their sheds in privately-owned or otherwise contested properties. (Tiwari 2001)

The phenomenal success of BASE, the enthusiasm and engagement of its members, and the size of its membership can be directly attributed to the weight of oppression and exploitation of the Tharu in the western Tarai. The authors of an evaluation of BASE conducted for the Royal Danish Embassy in Nepal (BASE's principal aid donor) remarked that "its sudden emergence is an unprecedented phenomenon in the development [of] Nepal's NGO sector and shows the degree of motivation that can be engendered when people believe they are part of a movement that is going to lead to their genuine upliftment" (PACT-Nepal 1993: 4).

A Tharu organization in Chitwan provides us with a suitable contrast to BASE. Nepal Indigenous Development Society, or NIDS, founded by young men mostly from Pipariya (my field site in Chitwan), was expressly modeled on BASE (Dilli Bahadur sits on its advisory board) as a community development organization with the aim of "uplifting" the Tharu. There is nothing of a social movement about it, however; it lacks a broad-based membership with fee-paying members, the organizational structure is effectively restricted to the eight-member governing council, and it works closely with both Tharu and non-Tharu ethnic groups to achieve its goals of village development. NIDS is oriented entirely to fostering, with the assistance of foreign NGOs, income-generating projects (for example, pig raising), and village infrastructural projects (the construction of biogas plants and bridges). While income-generating projects are targeted mostly at Tharus, NIDS's most significant accomplishment to date, the construction of a ninety-meter concrete bridge across a river, was accomplished with the enthusiastic participation of all the ethnic groups locally present, including hill people of high caste.

While income-generating projects are an important aspect of what BASE does, at the core of its activities is education. BASE emphasized education from the beginning because it saw the lack of it in the Tharu community as the reason why the Tharu were so easily exploited, and because education was systematically denied to Tharus in Dang. In Sukhdewar village in western Dang, for example, when BASE attempted to start a night school during its initial phase of organizing, the landlord had the teacher beaten up while he was conducting a class. The social conditions in Dang that led to the emergence of BASE simply do not exist in Chitwan. While it is true that many Tharus in Chitwan lost land, most still continue to be landowners, there is no system of bonded labor, and there are no large landlords anywhere in the district. In the rural hinterland of Chitwan, class and ethnicity do not map neatly onto each other.

Tharu-Pahāṛiyā Relations in Chitwan

Until the 1950s, the sparsely populated Chitwan Valley's economic value to the state was much less than its importance as a hunting preserve for the Rana elite that had seized power in the mid-nineteenth century. The population (about 25,000 in the early 1950s) was mostly Tharu, with a scattering of other groups native to the area, such as the Bote, the Kumal, and the Darai. Here too hill people were reluctant to settle permanently in the valley because of their fear of malaria, and limited their contact with it to the winter months when the incidence of the disease was at its lowest. As elsewhere in the Tarai, the district was organized into the revenue-collecting units known as pragannās (five in Chitwan), each of which was further subdivided into maujās. A maujā consisted of one or more villages and hamlets. Each maujā was in charge of a jimidār, who was usually a Tharu. The jimidāri class in Chitwan, unlike their (mostly high-caste) counterparts in Dang, was very much a part of the local community; apart from his revenue-collecting and juridical functions, the jimidār played a central role in village rituals (Guneratne 1996).

The nineteenth-century Rana state had intended the jimidār to be an agricultural entrepreneur as well as a revenue collector; the two responsibilities were linked. The jimidār had to recruit settlers or tenants (known as *raiti*s) to cultivate the lands for whose revenue he was responsible, and if new land was being cleared, to provide settlers with credit until the first harvest had been gathered. Jimidārs in Chitwan were not, however, called upon to play the role of agricultural entrepreneurs for the most part, unlike their counterparts in other areas of the Tarai; the low population density and the lack of immigration into the valley generally precluded the formation of new maujās.

All this changed with the completion of a successful program to control the incidence of malaria, which, as in Dang, was carried out with American assistance. Chitwan was opened up for settlement, and by 1959, a graveled road was built that bisected the valley from east to west. Over the next two decades, large numbers of hill people, mostly Brahman and Chhetri, but including Tamangs, Newars, Gurungs, and Magars, began to move into the valley. While most of the initial settlements were in western Chitwan, where the Tharu population was relatively sparse, by the 1970s the Tharu villages of eastern Chitwan began to attract migrants. Today, in most of these villages, the population is mixed; the original Tharu village has become a neighborhood or *tol* in a greatly expanded village community. The forests that once separated one village from another were cleared for cultivation, and much of the pastureland on which Tharus grazed their large herds of cattle have also been brought under the plough.

The Bahāriyā of Chitwan

Prior to the successful implementation of the Malaria Eradication Project in the 1950s, Chitwan suffered from a shortage of labor, which enabled a segment of the society to avoid the status of raiti (i.e., peasants cultivating land as tenants of the state) and work instead as agricultural labor for raiti households (Guneratne 1996). These people were known locally as *bahāriyā*s. Land was not in short supply, and was consequently not much valued by those who chose to ensure their subsistence in this way.[14] A bahāriyā family would enter a yearlong contract with a tenant-cultivator (raiti) of the state; the contract could be renewed in the month of Phagun (February–March) by the verbal agreement of both parties. A bahāriyā would often move on after a few years of work in one place. In return for the labor of the bahāriyā family, the raiti undertook to feed, house, and clothe its members for a year, and provide them an annual payment in kind. In the context of labor scarcity, the presence of bahāriyās guaranteed the cultivator labor when he needed it. The labor problem was aggravated by the seminomadic tendencies of the population (Guneratne 1996); bahāriyās and even raitis would often work in a village or take land there for only a few years before moving on, leaving the cultivator the problem of recruiting new labor and the jimidār the problem of finding new tenants. Unlike in Dang in the post-Rana period, however, coercion and debt bondage were not characteristic of the relationship between the bahāriyā and his master.

The settlement of Chitwan that followed on the Malaria Eradication Project ended this system and left many Tharus landless. These were mostly bahāriyās who had failed to benefit from the land reforms of the 1960s that had vested title in land with the former tenants of the state. Not only was the land frontier closed off by the intensive settlement of the valley by immigrants, but the labor market became transformed to the cultivator's advantage, primarily because the construction of a metaled all-weather road connecting Chitwan to the districts of the eastern Tarai allowed for seasonal labor migration from those areas. The bahāriyā system had obliged the raitis to feed and clothe their workers and their families all year round, even when there was little demand for their labor; the expanded labor market made that no longer necessary. In 1989–91, during my initial research in Chitwan, vestiges of the bahāriyā system remained in my field site in the village of Pipariya; the two jimidāri[15] households maintained a couple of families of bahāriyā, and most middle-peasant households maintained at least one bahāriyā, usually a young boy or girl, to herd cattle or do domestic chores. By 1998 there were few bahāriyā of any kind in the village.

As part of the rationalization of land administration in the post-Rana period, an agrarian reform vested title in land with those who had been tenants of the state (raiti) and abolished the jimidāri system of revenue collection. Title to land was granted to both Tharus and immigrants. Many bahāriyā were initially reluctant to obtain title for fear of taxation (Guneratne 1996), and those who failed to do so were left landless. One factor accounting for landlessness among Chitwan Tharus today is the failure of some among them to grasp the significance of the administrative and social changes that were taking place, and their consequent failure to acquire land during the land reforms following the 1964 Land Act, which in principle they could have done (cf. Guneratne 1996). The more significant reason, however (as far as Tharu-Parbatiyā relations go), is the widespread perception among the Tharu that they were taken advantage of by Parbatiyās, who often colluded with government officials of their own caste to exploit Tharu illiteracy and take control of Tharu land through chicanery and fraud. While there is some truth to this perception, it is by no means the whole story; the rapid increase in population through immigration and the abolition of the old system of tenure has closed off the land frontier and ended the seminomadic existence of Tharus.

Tharus own or control less land now than they did during the land reform, and the explanation can be summed up in a word: debt. A common strategy of some of the hill people who immigrated into the valley was to make credit available on what seemed easy terms to the Tharu; many Tharus got deeply into debt as a result and were eventually forced to sell some (or in extreme cases all) of their land to pay it off. Tharus claim that the payment of interest on loans, as well as promissory notes, was introduced into economic transactions in Chitwan by hill immigrants. Before the development of Chitwan, there was little need for credit; living standards were low and little of what was required for life needed to be purchased. While the state had intended the jimidār to be a source of credit and entrepreneurial activity in the opening up of new lands, such agricultural development had stagnated in Chitwan. This was probably due to the relative scarcity of labor, the extremely malarial conditions, and the value of the area as a hunting preserve. Furthermore, Chitwan was not a destination for peasant immigrants from India; such immigration was the most important factor affecting population growth in the Tarai before the anti-malaria programs. Peasant cultivators in Chitwan, in the memory of Tharus living today, were therefore not faced with the startup costs of agriculture—incurred while clearing land and providing for subsistence until the first crop was ready—that the jimidāri system had been meant, in part, to address.

The Tharu economy prior to the 1950s was essentially nonmonetary; a man's property was calculated by the size of his crop, and a rich Tharu was one who could claim a large harvest from his fields. Cash was required to pay taxes and to buy a few essential items such as kerosene, cloth, and salt. Cash would be raised for this purpose by selling excess grain and oil seeds, and by hiring out one's oxcart to carry these items to sell in Bhikna Thori.[16] If a farmer suffered losses because of unfavorable weather, flooding, crop disease, or some other natural calamity, he would seek a loan to get by, but such loans were generally in kind, in the form of paddy or husked rice. More rarely, people would borrow money for weddings or death rituals. The loan was a verbal agreement and generally no interest was charged. One borrowed from one's relatives or one's mīt.[17] The jimidār was another source. The jimidār could turn to fellow jimidārs for help or borrow grain from well-to-do raiti, even compelling them, when necessary, to make such loans.

Caplan's account of how Limbus in the hills of eastern Nepal lost land to Brahman immigrants closely parallels accounts given by Tharus with reference to their own situation. For example, he describes a practice recounted to me by Tharus in both Chitwan and western Dang: "the creditor would provide a small loan and after obtaining the signature—or, more likely, the thumbprint—of the...owner, would then add 'a few zeros' to the amount, thus making it impossible for the...owner ever to raise the required amount to repay the loan and resume his lands" (Caplan 1970: 63–64).

Chand and her colleagues report in their 1975 study of bilingualism in Chitwan (this study would have been carried out not very long after hill immigration began into Pipariya) that "Tharus...claimed that they had been exploited by immigrants, whom they called Paharis. The Paharis, they said, came and took their land by subterfuge, getting them to sign over ownership in papers which they did not understand" (Chand et al. 1975: 6; see also Gaige 1975: 75). This method of land acquisition is illustrated by the account Tharus in Pipariya give of how a Brahman family in a neighboring village acquired its relative wealth. Tharus would go to a Brahman named Devkota (a pseudonym) for loans, which he would readily give, but they would find themselves unable to repay them in the time stipulated. He would grant them more time, but would obtain in return their consent to add another zero to the sum specified on the promissory note. Being illiterate and in any case unfamiliar with such things as promissory notes, the Tharu would readily agree to this. A loan of a hundred rupees would be transformed in this way into one of a thousand rupees, which was quite beyond the ability of a Tharu to repay. Eventually, the Tharu would lose all or part of his land to Devkota. A high-caste schoolteacher in Pipariya, who had read my dissertation,[18] told me that everything I had written about this matter was true and offered me, unsolicited, another example: the father of a well-known Brahman businessman would lend to Tharus at exorbitant rates of interest, as much as 200 percent per annum. Nevertheless, he insisted that such exploitation, while common in the past, no longer happened.

Almost all Tharu households in two villages in Chitwan which I surveyed in 1991 reported having had to sell some land during the last twenty years; many have had to sell land more than once, and almost invariably, the land was sold to a Parbatiyā. They have had to sell land to meet various obligations—debts to the cooperative, loans from moneylenders (usually Brahmans), unpaid medical expenses, purchases of consumption goods—and land has in the majority of cases been sold to hill immigrants, usually Brahmans. Parbatiyās are more likely to buy land than the Tharu because Tharus are unlikely to have the capital. In addition, many Tharu who reported that they sold their land may have had their debts foreclosed (Guneratne 1994: 188–193).

Land transactions deal in very small quantities, generally a fraction of a hectare. In the first place, every landowning household, even those whose members hold wage-paying or salaried jobs, depend on the land in very large measure (salaries and wages typically supplement what the land produces). Most families today sell land only when they have to, and then as little of it as possible. Second, land in Chitwan is expensive, selling in 1991 for Rs 150,000–200,000 per bighā (about $3,750–$5,000 in early 1991). Few people can afford to buy as much as a bighā, unless they are businessmen from one of the bazaar towns. Total indebtedness in Pipariya in 1991 seldom exceeded about 10,000 rupees for most families, and there is no need to sell a large amount of land in one transaction to meet such debts. Thus, land is usually sold in small parcels.

Nevertheless, despite the decline in Tharu landownership in absolute terms, the Tharu in Chitwan are by no means landless. Unlike other parts of the Tarai, Chitwan is a district of smallholders, almost 95 percent of landholdings being owned by the cultivators (His Majesty's Government 1990: 18). Most Tharu own some land. In Pipariya, 74 percent of households (about 81 percent of the Tharu population) owned land, the average landholding being 1.25 hectares.[19] Although the size of the average landholding per household has decreased sharply, the land is more intensively cultivated, producing three crops with irrigation where once it produced only one. While the Tharu, as a community, control less land than they used to, and seem unlikely to increase their holdings, some of the larger landowners (those owning ten or more hectares) in eastern Chitwan are the descendants of the former Tharu jimidāri families, many of whom acquired title to the lands for whose revenue they were responsible during the land reform. It is common in Chitwan for well-to-do Tharu to act as patrons to Brahman priests, summoning them to perform elaborate and expensive rituals like the Satya Narayan puja. In Pipariya, the most important Brahman political leader in the village depended on the local Tharu jimidāri family for access to land to cultivate as a part-time sharecropper. In this respect, there is a marked contrast between the situation in Chitwan and the Dang Valley. In Dang, very few Tharu are in a position to act as patrons to Brahmans, and the majority of Tharu there, in contrast to Chitwan, do not involve Brahmans at all in their rituals. Chitwan Tharu, in other words, are much more "Hinduized" than their counterparts in Dang. In Chitwan, most marriages and all funerals are conducted according to Hindu rites and are presided over by a Brahman priest; Brahman priests also preside over various religious rituals sponsored by well-to-do Tharu households, most importantly the Satya Narayan puja. Rajaure indicates that in Dang, while the small Tharu elite has sanskritized its customs, the life-cycle rites and religious rituals of the majority of Tharu are distinct from the Brahmanical tradition followed by high-caste Nepalis (Rajaure 1982a, 1982b).

The Tharu and Local Politics

The difference in the degree to which the Tharu have lost control of their land is an essential variable in the balance of political power between Tharus and Brahmans in both Chitwan and Dang. While the upper castes are dominant in both districts, the balance of power has not been tilted as sharply to Brahmans in rural areas of Chitwan. This is because, in Chitwan, the Tharu by and large continue to have an independent base in land. In Dang, for much of the period since the malaria eradication program, the Tharu lost ground extensively to hill people and became both subordinate to and dependent on them.

Political parties in Chitwan, as in Nepal generally, are overwhelmingly dominated by three groups, the Brahmans, Chhetris, and Newars. Fifty-two percent of political party leaders in Chitwan in the early 1990s were Brahmans, but Brahmans, Chhetris, and Thakuris together accounted for only about 40 percent of all voters in Chitwan. Seventy percent of the membership of party committees in the district was held by members of these three castes, together with Newars. The Tharu accounted for only 5 percent of party positions, although they constituted about 13 percent of the population of the district. In 1991 the Tharu were represented only in the committees of the Nepali Congress Party and the National Democratic Party (Chand); on the other hand, 85 percent of the leadership of the Nepal Communist Party (UML) were Brahman (the rest were Newar) (District Political Profile of Chitwan 1991: 5–6).

In Dang, although there was Tharu participation in formal politics as members and chairmen of village councils (panchāyat), the Tharu did not become an important force in the valley until after the emergence of BASE, when politicians began to try to cultivate Dilli Bahadur Chaudhari (without much success). Even at the local level, the leadership of both the Congress and the Communist Party in Dang consists of landlords, who have no interest in policies or programs that might benefit their Tharu tenants. The Tharu were nevertheless engaged in other forms of political activity, including struggles over tenancy rights. In the early 1970s, some radical Tharu set up an organization to promote literary activities; this association was also active, however, in encouraging Tharus "to stand together in the struggle for their rights against exploitative landlords" (McDonaugh 1997: 277). McDonaugh points out that "Tharu resistance had been going on some time before BASE" (personal communication) and notes "government pressure effectively prevented any further overt organization and expression of a more militant Tharu identity by this association" (1997: 277). None of these efforts, however, ever achieved the scope, level of activity, and success of BASE.

That BASE is, today, the most influential nongovernmental organization in Dang and very likely in the western Tarai is beyond question; Dilli Bahadur has served as the Chairman of Nepal's NGO federation, and in 1993, the home ministry invited him to become vice-chairman of the important Social Welfare Council, an honor he declined because of its political nature (Ødegaard 1997: 136–137). BASE has steered a resolutely neutral course where party politics are concerned, even though Sigrun Ødegaard quotes Dilli Bahadur as telling her that "BASE has now become so powerful that the politicians know we can change local government immediately" (136). In 1991, however, in western Dang, with the exception of a couple of important Tharu landlord families (as far as I could ascertain, the only two Tharu landlord families in the area), Tharus played very little part in formal political activity.

The situation in Chitwan has been very different. There, although high castes dominate political activity (as they do in most areas of Nepal), the Tharu are politically active, and in eastern Chitwan, where their population is concentrated, they are an important factor in local politics. Many Tharu activists played a locally prominent role in the People's Movement of 1990 that restored parliamentary democracy to Nepal, and several had to seek refuge in India from the Nepali police. Almost all Tharu jimidārs are active in party politics, and the Tharu vote is important. In Pipariya, the *pradhān panchas* (village council chairmen) in pre-Democracy days, and the chairmen of the Village Development Committee (VDC) in the post-1990 reorganization of local administration, have always been Tharus, as have many of the representatives of the nine wards of the VDC. Thus, while the real centers of power in Chitwan, especially at the district level, are in high-caste hands, and members of high castes tend to be the political power brokers, the importance of the Tharu vote is well understood. This is illustrated by the following two incidents.

The first took place a few years before I arrived in Chitwan. The pradhān panch of a certain panchāyat had always been a Tharu; his deputy at that time was a Brahman, who I shall call Adhikari. Adhikari was a locally important figure in the Nepali Congress, and a cleverer and politically more active man than Bikram Chaudhari, the Tharu pradhān panch, who also belonged to the party; it was Adhikari in fact who was running the affairs of the panchāyat. Not surprisingly, he decided that he would run for pradhān panch at the next election and he was accordingly nominated for that position by the local, Brahman-dominated branch of the Nepali Congress party. While thus rejecting Bikram, the party offered nothing to him in exchange. The Tharu activists in the Congress were very opposed to this turn of events, and one of them, a kinsman of Bikram's, challenged this decision. His position was that if the Congress did not want Bikram as pradhān panch, it ought to have nominated him to another position. He also held that a Tharu should have been nominated in any case, because the Tharu composed 70 percent of the population of this panchāyat (in reality, the figure was closer to 40 percent). When neither Adhikari nor the local (Brahman) party activists would consent to reconsider their decision, Bikram's kinsman vowed to work for his reelection—which he did, successfully. Bikram beat Adhikari by fourteen votes. The kinsman then proceeded to systematically (and successfully) oppose Adhikari's attempts to gain elected office at every turn, in order he said, "to teach him a lesson." As he observed, "It's not enough to be qualified; you must have the votes behind you." Since these events, this man has become a respected figure in local politics; most recently, he was invited to stand for president of the Village Development Committee (which replaced the panchāyat after the success of the People's Movement), but he declined; he explained to me that he was not wealthy and could not afford to take up what was essentially a full-time position which paid a salary of only 1,500 rupees per month.

The second incident concerned the Congress Party candidate for eastern Chitwan in the first general election following the People's Movement. The east is the one region of Chitwan where the Tharu constitute a substantial minority. Indeed, Tharus believe themselves to be in the majority there, but the available statistical data from the Malaria Eradication Project and the Family Planning Association of Nepal suggest their number is between 30 and 40 percent. Even the Pipariya Village Development Committee, which is in the heart of the Tharu populated area, does not have a majority Tharu population. Even so, during the run-up to the general election of 1991 there was a broad consensus among Tharu party activists in Pipariya in both the Nepali Congress and the Communist Party that a Tharu ought to represent eastern Chitwan in parliament. The Communist Party, however, already had its candidate, a veteran Brahman politician who had represented the district before in the national panchāyat and who was widely popular. Tharu political activists in the Nepali Congress wanted a Tharu to be nominated to oppose him, not only because they felt it was their due, given the preponderance of Tharus in the area, but also because they felt that tactically, it would pay off in Tharu votes that would otherwise go to the Communist Party. Many of the high-caste political activists were not opposed to this, and a consensus built up around a prominent and well-to-do Tharu jimidār who was said to be popular and capable of giving the Communist candidate a run for his money. I shall call this man Ramsaran. The district committee of the Congress Party sent up four names to party headquarters ranked in order of preference for the nomination to the east Chitwan electorate. A Brahman named Sharma headed the list, followed by Ramsaran; the individual who was eventually nominated was placed last (these are all pseudonyms). Sharma, who was well known and well liked by both Tharus and Brahmans, was a strong candidate, but I was told by Tharu political activists that he had preferred to support Ramsaran because, given the heavy concentration of Tharus there, he too felt a Tharu should represent eastern Chitwan.

According to Tharu Congress Party activists in the village, who gave me this account, at the time that the national party leadership was deciding on nominations, Sharma had been summoned to Kathmandu to meet the prime minister, K. P. Bhattarai. Sharma concluded that the summons meant he had been selected to contest. He felt it would not be proper of him to refuse when the prime minister offered him the nomination, particularly as he had told Ramsaran that he would support his candidacy. Instead of going to Kathmandu, therefore, he sent the prime minister a message to the effect that he supported Ramsaran as the best candidate.

Although Sharma did not go to Kathmandu, another party activist, a Tharu named Chandra Lal, went instead. This individual, like Ramsaran, was a notable figure in the Tharu Kalyankarini Sabha in Chitwan. Chandra Lal was said to be on bad terms with Ramsaran by people who knew them both, and it was alleged that he did not want that Ramsaran be given the nomination. Tharu workers for the Congress Party believed that Chandra Lal had urged the prime minister to nominate the man who in the event actually was given the ticket, and had assured the prime minister that he, Chandra Lal, could guarantee the Congress a majority of the Tharu vote. A Tharu supporter of the Communist Party opined that the prime minister believed him because he was a very important member of the local branch of the Tharu Kalyankarini Sabha. He added that

*A Tharu man votes in the first general election in May 1991 following the
restoration of democracy. On the right is a poster to show people how to vote:
by making a mark (depicted here by a swastika, an auspicious symbol) on the
ballot paper against the election symbol of the political party of their choice.*

although the Sabha has no political influence at the village level, in Kathmandu it claims (plausibly) to be the legitimate representatives of the
Tharu community. Village opinion considered the Brahman who was
given the nomination to be a loser from the very beginning, and so it
proved; he lost by a margin of over ten thousand votes.

Two days after the general election, I sat in a cattle shed with a number of young Tharu men, watching them play cards (a favorite pastime during the long lazy days between sowing and harvesting) and discussing Ramsaran's failure to get the nomination. There had been high hopes that he would get it, and many Tharus in Pipariya had been bitterly disappointed when that had not happened. The card players were universal in their condemnation of Chandra Lal; as one described him, he was "a Tharu cutting off another Tharu's legs." Another said angrily that Chandra Lal could not have obtained a thousand votes if he had stood for election. These young men believed that not giving the nomination to a Tharu in this instance was an attempt "to put Tharus down" (although in this case, by their own account, it was another Tharu who had done so, while Brahmans at the local level of the party had thrown their support behind the Tharu candidate). They also believed that if Ramsaran had been nominated, Tharus would have crossed party lines to vote for him. This was also the opinion of the young Tharu man who was the poll watcher in Pipariya for the Communist candidate at the election.

When the nomination was not given to Ramsaran, the Congress Party leadership in Chitwan clearly felt that damage control was necessary in the Tharu villages. In Pipariya, damage control took the form of an informal meeting at night in the courtyard of the jimidār, attended mostly by Tharus, but also by a number of hill people, generally the politically active among them. Several members of the party district leadership were present, and the meeting was addressed by Sharma, the man who had stepped aside in Ramsaran's favor. He spoke from a sitting position in a chair in the middle of the courtyard. A number of issues were raised, but the first, and from the point of view of the audience, the most important, was an explanation of why Ramsaran had not been given the nomination.[20] In reply, Sharma, speaking in both Tharu (in which he was fluent) and Nepali, emphasized the importance of voting for the party and not for the candidate, and he urged Tharus not to vote for someone simply because he was Tharu (in any case, the candidates of both major parties were Parbatiyās). Much later, at a Congress election rally in the village, Chandra Lal made an impassioned speech in Tharu (the only speaker on the platform to speak in that language) in which he called on Tharus to vote not for the man but for the party.

As the two instances described above demonstrate, Chitwan Tharus can and do shape important political events to suit themselves. They do not vote blindly for a candidate (as Sharma seemed to fear) simply because he is Tharu. Tharu political behavior seems dependent on a number of complex, intertwining factors, including political affiliation or political sympathy of the voter and candidate, ethnic affiliation, and personal kinship ties. Which of these factors becomes important in the mind of any voter presumably depends on a number of circumstances. For example, the Tharu candidate of the National Democratic Party (which represented the interests of the now-discredited former panchāyat regime) lost badly in the Chitwan-3 electorate in southern Chitwan, which has a substantial population of Tharus. Nor do Tharus vote for a non-Tharu candidate simply because he is endorsed by the Tharu elite, which may campaign on his behalf. The Congress candidate in eastern Chitwan lost heavily in villages with substantial Tharu populations, where the local Tharu leadership was firmly in the Congress camp. Even though the Communist candidate, a Brahman well known for taking up cudgels on behalf of the landless and small peasants, would have been a formidable candidate to defeat, the local Tharu elite was also weak in providing political leadership of its own community. They had a misleading idea of the impact of their own activities in swaying Tharu political opinion because the village poor tend to dissemble before them.

Those members of the Tharu elite in eastern Chitwan who were supporters of the Congress tended to believe that villagers would take their cue from their jimidār; where the jimidār supported the Congress, the village, they believed, was also likely to. Ironically, some of the Congress's most committed supporters in this class believed that only the influence of Brahmans could wean Tharus away from the "correct" political path. The wife of a Tharu activist in the Nepali Congress told me that the village into which her husband's sister had married was solidly behind the Congress; it is almost entirely Tharu, with the pahāris (Parbatiyās) living on its periphery. The Tharu supporters of the Congress in this village had stayed up the night before the election, she said, to prevent any pahāris from coming into the village to persuade Tharus to vote for another party. She remarked a little sadly that contact with pahāris in Pipariya had "corrupted" Tharus to support the Communists. On the other hand, some ordinary Tharus decried what they perceived as the inordinate influence of Brahmans on the Tharu elite.

The political dependence of the Tharu elite on the Brahman political leadership is a subject of much criticism among some sections of Pipariya's Tharu population, notably those families that tacitly support the Communists. In conversation with me, the head of one such household angrily denounced the way the jimidār "followed the lead" of a Brahman political activist unpopular among Tharus in the village. By following this man, he said, the jimidār was not showing "the right way" for Tharus. The Tharu, he said, were here first, and they understood the *wātāvaraṇ* (environment) of this place. The Brahman activist ought to be coming to the Tharu, it should not be the other way around. His brother, who was listening to our conversation, interrupted to remark that this was how the Tharu had come to grief (*bigriyo*). He was critical of the jimidār for what he saw as his weakness and pliability in the hands of Brahman activists. Why, he asked rhetorically, should the jimidār follow this Brahman, who was not nearly as well educated as either the jimidār or many members of his family?

Both the Pipariya and the Padampur Village Development Committees, with large Tharu populations, and a Tharu leadership firmly in the Congress camp, had been considered to be Congress strongholds; the Congress is very visible, all the important Tharu landowners are Congress Party activists, and the Congress had set up a small building for its activities in Pipariya, in which village youths like to gather to play carrom and generally to pass the time. In contrast, the Communist Party is virtually invisible; its supporters are the village poor, who sensibly keep their political opinions to themselves.

The relative isolation of the Communists is illustrated by an incident that happened before the election. There was a quarrel between two Brahman political activists, one a Communist and the other a well known and active worker for the Congress. The Communist, said Congress supporters, had assaulted the other; the Communists (at a political rally in the village for the Communist Party candidate a few days later) denied the charge, and claimed it was their man who had been assaulted. Whatever the facts of the case, a meeting was called the evening of the quarrel, attended by many villagers and the village political elite, all members of the Congress. The men involved in the quarrel were also present. The pros and cons of the matter were publicly discussed, but there was never any doubt as to where the assembly's sympathies lay. The Communist was forced to publicly apologize to his antagonist and beg his forgiveness, which was magnanimously given. As one villager remarked to me, the Communist sympathizers had pretended to be Congress out of fear of the Congress leadership in the village (*Kāngresko ḍarle ḍarāerā*). The Congress candidate in the general election to parliament won the Pipariya VDC by a couple of hundred votes (less than two thousand were cast altogether) and lost Padampur by a wide margin.

It is clear that the forms of political activity in which Chitwan Tharus and Dangaura Tharus engage are shaped by their circumstances. Chitwan Tharus are able to participate fully in formal political activity, as members of political parties, and to occupy positions of leadership at least at the village level and sometimes at higher levels of organization. They are able to do this because many of them have land, education, and employment in the formal sector and because the Parbatiyās do not have a significant structural advantage over them. Concomitantly, there is no "underground" activity of any consequence; despite widely held distrust of Parbatiyās and resentment at the way their fathers were cheated of land, there is no target for Tharus to organize against as an ethnic group. In Dang, by contrast, most of the Tharu have been landless tenants, with Tharu landowners of consequence rare. The formal political sector, whether of the Congress or the Communist Party, is firmly controlled by landlords (one significant exception is a Tharu who was elected to the national legislature as a member of the Communist Party; even so, he is the son of one of the few remaining Tharu landlords in western Dang). With that avenue of activity closed to them, Tharu efforts to transform their situation had to be channeled into other areas.

DANG AND CHITWAN COMPARED

I have discussed in this chapter the central importance of land and labor as factors shaping relations between high-caste immigrants into the Tarai and the Tharu. I have done so by comparing two situations of interethnic contact that have had different outcomes. That the interethnic dynamic described here is not peculiar to Chitwan and Dang but is generally true of many areas of Nepal is evident from other accounts (Ødegaard 1997; Cox 1990a; Caplan 1970; Gaige 1975). Both Chitwan and Dang are Inner Tarai valleys, formerly malarial, that were populated almost entirely by Tharus less than fifty years ago. Both became initial loci for the most significant national development program carried out in the decade after the demise of the Rana state—the Malaria Eradication Project—and both became the destination of tens of thousands of hill immigrants who came into these valleys in search of land. In both cases Tharu society was subjected to a fundamental and far-reaching social and economic transformation.

While both valleys were originally relatively peripheral to the Nepali state, Chitwan became increasingly more important after the Malaria Eradication Project, while Dang, like the other western districts of Nepal, remained on the periphery. Part of the reason for Chitwan's importance is that it straddles the most vital road junction in Nepal: in Narayanghat, where the east-west highway meets the road to Pokhara and Kathmandu. While the east-west highway facilitated immigration into Chit-

wan, it also made it easy for large Tharu landowners to send their sons
to the new schools in Birganj set up after the fall of the Rana dictatorship,
and even to India. Tharus in Chitwan were able to make use of newly
created opportunities for education; Tharus in Dang were denied them.
This is probably one factor that minimized the impact of immigration
into Chitwan and allowed a jimidāri-derived Tharu elite to survive (and
even prosper) in most Tharu villages.

Chitwan today is not only an important agricultural area; it is also a
center for industrial development. In addition, the presence of the Royal
Chitwan National Park, conveniently close to Kathmandu, has made it a
locus of tourist development. The indigenous Tharu population of the
valley was relatively small in comparison to that of Dang and was not an
adequate source of labor for the greatly increased acreage brought under
cultivation.[21] Several factors eased the labor shortage: as a district of
smallholders, many holdings were small enough to cultivate with family
labor; the east-west highway facilitated the movement of itinerant agricultural laborers from the eastern Tarai and led to the development of a
labor market; and the closer integration of Chitwan into the market and
the much more favorable terrain has resulted in a greater use of tractors,
which were introduced early into the district. Most importantly, however, Chitwan lacked the form of labor relations—the kamaiyā system—
that enabled the new landlord class in Dang to control its labor through
a system of quasi-serfdom. Debt-bondage, although ameliorated by
being embedded in a moral economy, existed prior to the immigration
into the Dang valley; immigrants were able to co-opt this system while
stripping it of the shared moral economy that bound master and servant.
The bahāriyā system, while superficially similar, contains no element of
debt bondage, and in any case, given the proximity of Chitwan to Kathmandu, the rapid development of Chitwan's labor market, and the relatively high degree of economic development achieved in the district, a
system of bonded labor would have been very difficult to sustain, even
had it emerged.

Dang is still a relatively peripheral region. Communications are
poorly developed and there are no paved roads. The air service that
links Dang to Kathmandu has little relevance to the vast majority of the
inhabitants of the valley. By contrast with Chitwan, it is poorly developed in economic terms: there was no labor market of any significance in
western Dang in 1991, although this may be changing, and there are few
industries of any consequence in the district. The agricultural labor force
continues to be primarily Tharu, and because communications are so
difficult, it is unlikely that the sort of large-scale labor migration com-

mon in the Outer Tarai and Chitwan will develop here in the near future. In western Dang, the villages in the interior are mostly inhabited by Tharus, with a high-caste elite controlling most of the land. This situation has actually worked today to the advantage of the Tharu: after BASE had organized them and this NGO had become highly visible and well funded, Tharus in these villages were able to end or substantially reduce the practice of forced labor and negotiate more equitable relations with their landlords.

Apart from the emancipation of the kamaiyās, there has been another political development affecting the Tharu of the western districts. This is the developing Maoist insurgency in the country, which undoubtedly includes Tharus within its ranks. The Maoists are active in most of the Tarai districts, from Jhapa to Kanchanpur, with the western districts being the worst affected by incidents of violence. I have been told by Dilli Chaudhari that many NGOs have withdrawn from Dang as a result of the insurgency, and that although an uneasy peace exists between BASE and the Maoists, BASE workers have nevertheless been harassed. While a great deal of material is now available that discusses the Maoist movement, mostly on the Internet and in the popular press, there is to the best of my knowledge nothing published in a Western language that specifically addresses these issues from the perspective of their impact on the Tharu.[22]

Ethnic tensions are very pronounced in Dang and much less so in Chitwan because in the latter district a substantial portion of the Tharu population retained control of some land and were able to benefit from the opportunities provided by development and modernization, including, most significantly, the opportunity to receive some schooling and find employment in nonagricultural occupations such as tourism, industry, and trade. Ethnic tensions have not been significant in Chitwan despite some antagonism and distrust between the two principal communities because, apart from the reasons alluded to, the local Tharu elite is well integrated into national party politics. It is relevant that the politically active Brahmans in villages in Chitwan are not landlords (a largely unknown breed in any case in this district), and in most cases not even large landowners, unlike in Dang. They are thus able to articulate policies and fight for political causes that cut across ethnic lines and can appeal to an enfranchised Tharu electorate; hence the popularity of the Communist Party's candidate in eastern Chitwan. In short, the difference between Chitwan and Dang where politics is concerned is that in Dang the Tharu used to be marginal to politics before BASE emerged in the district, while in Chitwan they participate fully, albeit as junior partners. BASE is, in effect, an example of ethnicized politics, even though it is not oriented to formal party politics; its aim is to alter the balance of power in Dang between Parbatiyās and Tharus, a profoundly political goal but one couched in the rhetoric of development. On the other hand, the organization it inspired in Chitwan, NIDS, is oriented purely toward development work and has neither political purpose nor political effect. It lacks, and is unlikely ever to acquire, the broad-based support BASE enjoys because the circumstances that gave rise to BASE do not exist in Chitwan. It would be a considerable exaggeration to say that Brahmans oppress Tharus in Chitwan; concerning western Dang, however, it is a statement of historical fact. The Dang Tharu need BASE to engage Parbatiyā society as they seek to redress the injustices of the last forty years; in contrast, Chitwan Tharu engage their Brahman neighbors from an independent base of their own in land, and that has made the difference.

CHAPTER FIVE

Organizing the Elite

In the preceding chapters I have discussed the social, political, and economic forces that make possible the emergence of a shared sense of peoplehood among ethnic groups as culturally dissimilar as the Tharu. But a sense of peoplehood does not just emerge; it must be shaped through acts both concrete and symbolic. Not every social stratum participates in such processes of group fashioning; the very poor typically do not because they have neither the time, the resources, nor the standing in society to be persuasive. Considering that ethnicity, like nationalism, is a form of identity that seeks to subsume or collapse all of the manifold divisions within a society into an overarching unity, the question of who is most likely not only to carry out such a reshaping of identity but also to benefit from it, is pivotal. The answer is that it is those sectors of society that have the time, resources and interest to do so—the social, political and economic elite. In this chapter I examine the origins and structure of the most important organization of the Tharu elite in Nepal—the Tharu Kalyankarini Sabha or Tharu Welfare Society. I shall refer to it in the following pages simply as the Sabha. I will also discuss other ethnic organizations of the Tharu that are more local in their scope and their activity. I shall leave a discussion of the work of the Sabha—its cultural refashioning of Tharu identity—to the next chapter.

THE THARU ELITE

The traditional elite in Tharu society comprised the large landlords and large landowners, the people whose historical relationship to the state I discussed in chapter 2. By reason of their relative wealth, they were able to obtain an education, either in India or, after the fall of the Rana autocracy, in the new schools opened in Nepal. This traditional elite had risen to positions of power and influence in Tharu society by serving either the state itself as revenue collectors (jimidārs) or those to whom the state had alienated land in recompense for services rendered. As agents of the state at village level, however, these jimidārs were also vested with the authority to resolve local disputes and adjudicate on matters of customary law (cf. Guneratne 1996: 10–12; Krauskopff 1989: 67). In Chitwan, not only did the jimidārs exercise juridical and revenue authority, but they were also important ritual specialists in their own right, being responsible for the conduct of regular rituals to the village deities to assure the prosperity and well-being of the village and its lands.

The power that the jimidār exercised was often arbitrary and cruel, and they had a great deal of leeway in terms of the punishments they could impose on people. Although the state might intervene from time to time, the only real restraint on such capriciousness was the threat that tenant farmers would abandon too tyrannical a jimidār. Older Tharus in Chitwan told me how they exercised their power. For example, if a man and woman eloped who were closely related to each other, thus violating customary law, and if the jimidār was personally hostile to one or both of them, he would have them tied hand and foot to two posts with their legs spread apart, and light a fire under them as punishment. The victims would be questioned while this was being done to them, and if the jimidār found their answers unsatisfactory, they would be beaten. "This was the jimidār's job," a Tharu man commented. Another described how a jimidār would administer corporal punishment. The victim was forced to stand on two bricks, legs spread, and was then beaten on the thighs and calves. If he moved his legs he would be beaten even more.

Prabhunarayan Chaudhary recounts in *Thāru Saṁskār*, a magazine published in Sunsari, how in 1958 jimidārs imposed a similar punishment on an ordinary peasant for some offense (Chaudhary 2045: 50–54). The man was made to stand in the sun on one leg with an areca nut on his head and, on top of the nut, a full pot of water. He was finally rescued by a jimidār named Manik Lal Chaudhary. Manik Lal was both wealthy and despotic, and people in the district had a healthy fear of him, but he apparently did not approve of this sort of punishment. The author of this article writes that the jimidār rode out on his elephant to where the punishment was taking place and told the man to drop the pot and get up behind him. He took the man back to his own village, and when the other jimidārs followed him to protest, he beat them and chased them away. That was the last time such punishment was inflicted. The author is writing to explain some aspects of the history of the Tharu Kalyankarini Sabha and how such unacceptable practices were ended. People began to back the Sabha because it sought to end arbitrary punishments of this type. Its critique of the traditional Tharu leadership of that time (out of which it had itself emerged) was that it did nothing to promote the interests of Tharus as a community but instead simply abused its power.

Thus the elite in the formative years of the Sabha was often divided, with some wishing to preserve the old ways and others wanting change and reform. In Saptari the first group was called the *buṛojugiyā*, from *buṛo* (old) and *yug* (epoch or era), while the faction that wanted to introduce reforms was called the *nawajugiyā* (new era). The nawajugiyā may have been originally a group advocating the sanskritization of traditional Tharu customs defended by their opponents, the buṛojugiyā. For example, the nawajugiyā advocated a mourning period of thirteen days whereas tradition called for thirty (Hindus observe thirteen days of mourning for a woman and twelve days for a man). I was told this by Tribhuwan Choudhary, a Tharu from Saptari who now lives in New Mexico. His family was buṛojugiyā. He attributes an economic motive to this reform, for a thirty-day mourning period interferes with the conduct of one's economic activities. Nor did the nawajugiyā initially take a stance against child marriage; instead, they wanted the child bride to visit her husband's home for a few days after the ceremony, whereas the buṛojugiyā were opposed to this; they favored retaining the custom whereby the bride went to her husband's home only after attaining puberty. But the nawajugiyā were more open to social reform than their opponents and came to be identified with those agitating for change.

While the elite are in the forefront of Tharu ethnic refashioning, in the sense that the founders of the Tharu Kalyankarini Sabha were drawn from this stratum, the social composition of the elite has been transformed and expanded since the agrarian reforms of the 1960s. The agrarian reform both rationalized the revenue collection system by vesting it in a government bureaucracy and abolished birtā and jagir tenure, vesting land instead in the cultivator. The ranks of the elite have grown by the entry of an educated younger generation that hails from more modest social backgrounds: the sons of "middle peasants" who have succeeded in Nepal's education system and become technicians, clerks, engineers, schoolteachers, and the like and who have moved into administrative, technical, and professional positions. Such people are not necessarily landholders of any significance; they may have come from modest backgrounds but done well in the new economic conditions of post-Rana Nepal, or, conversely, they may be from old landholding families that lost much of their land as immigrants from the hills settled in the Tarai. Nevertheless, loopholes in the law limiting landownership have allowed many of the powerful jimidāri families of the past to retain large holdings (running sometimes into the hundreds of hectares). These families continue to be a visible and powerful presence in the Tharu Kalyankarini Sabha. In sum then, the Tharu elite consists of wealthy landowners who have secured for themselves a niche among the national, Kathmandu-based elite; of locally important landowners in every district, typically the descendants of the revenue collectors of former times; and of the well educated (schoolteachers, college students, government officials, and those with professional degrees) from the large landowning class and the middle peasantry.

It is impossible to estimate the proportion of the elite in the Tharu population. But professional and clerical occupations are suggestive of elite status, and the 1991 census of Nepal indicates that about 2.5 percent of the working Tharu population (which is 37.2 percent of the total population of Tharus as enumerated by ethnicity) are employed in "white-collar" jobs—professions, administration, clerical work, and sales (His Majesty's Government 1993b: table 28). Of course, this does not take into account landownership, but usually, where a household owns a significant amount of land, it is able to translate that into education and clerical or professional occupations. In Chitwan, where landownership is much less concentrated within Tharu society (as indicated in the very low incidence of tenancy), a few households in every village could be regarded as belonging to the elite. In all of western Dang, on the other hand, where the rural population is predominantly Tharu, there were less than half a dozen landowning Tharu households of any significance in 1991; the overwhelming majority of the Tharu there were tenants of Brahman and Chhetri landlords. To put this another way, every Tharu village in Chitwan had some Tharu households that could be accorded the status of elite; in western Dang, most Tharu villages were dominated by a Brahman-Chhetri elite that had taken control of the land, and a native Tharu elite was lacking. The eastern Tarai presents a more complex picture, but unfortunately one that has not been adequately researched. A relatively larger proportion of Tharu men there, sometimes from fairly modest backgrounds, have been to college and acquired professional qualifications, and are active in the Tharu Kalyankarini Sabha; but the eastern Tarai is also home to extensive estates and pervasive poverty, extremes one does not find in Chitwan. The eastern Tarai is the heartland of the Tharu Kalyankarini Sabha, the area in which it is most active and where it is probably the most broadly based. The most important Tharu intellectuals—Ramanand Prasad Singh and Tej Narayan Panjiar, who together have articulated an interpretation of Tharu identity that seeks clearly and forcefully to delineate the Tharu as Buddhist and non-Hindu—come from the eastern Tarai. Singh is from Saptari and Panjiar hails from neighboring Udaypur.[1]

Tharu elites, as I explain in this chapter, have attempted to organize and project the ethnic category *Tharu* into a cohesive, natural, enduring social entity, and they see themselves as spokesmen for it. While the Tharu Kalyankarini Sabha appears to have originated, according to R. P. Singh, partly as a reaction of young, educated Tharus from the eastern Tarai to the political and social conservatism of their elders, young Tharus today are reacting to it in a similar way. I discuss some instances later in this chapter.

The Origins of the Tharu Kalyankarini Sabha

The Tharu Kalyankarini Sabha is a Nepali variation of a phenomenon that originated in India about the mid-nineteenth century: the caste association. These associations have been described by Robert Hardgrave (1969), R. S. Khare (1970), and Lloyd Rudolph and Susanne Rudolph (1960), and by William Fisher (1987) in the case of Nepal. One of the early catalysts for the caste association was the British preoccupation with attempting to list, and rank in a hierarchy, every caste group in India. The principal vehicle for that endeavor was the decennial census. That exercise, as far as its professed aim was concerned, was futile, but, as Bernard Cohn (1987) has shown, it did succeed in giving "caste" a political importance and resonance that it may not have had before. The groups that may be categorized as a caste are to all intents and purposes potentially limitless, and organized in an immense variety of local systems. Nor is the caste system, in general, as rigid as it is sometimes made out to be; there is potential for mobility of entire caste groups, through sanskritization or the intervention of royal authority. In the nineteenth century, elites in many different caste groups saw this British preoccupation as a way to advance their own claims for higher status, and began to form caste associations in order to petition the census authorities to certify their claims as valid. Initially, these caste associations operated within the paradigm of sanskritization. Their claims to higher status were based on caste histories tracing the origin of a particular community to some ancestral high-status condition; they encouraged the adoption of high-caste ritual practices and behavior among their caste fellows, and eschewed customary practices associated with low status. But as a modern economy developed, as communications improved, and as the framework emerged for popular participation in politics, the nature of caste associations changed. They took on an increasingly political aspect; as Rudolph and Rudolph have pointed out (1960), caste became one of the chief ways in which the Indian electorate's participation in democratic politics was organized. Status, once interpreted through the idiom of ritual ranking, became based on the acquisition of the fruits of economic development and modernization.

The Tharu Kalyankarini Sabha is similar to these caste associations in its origin, evolution, and activities. The term *caste* itself has been assimilated to the Nepali lexicon; when a Tharu talks about the category Tharu, he may refer to it as jāt (the commonest term used), *samāj* (society), or more rarely, as caste. When the English word *caste* is used, it is generally by elites. Caste or ethnic associations in Nepal appear not to have been as well studied or documented as those in India. In part, this is because their origins are more recent; they essentially date from the end of Rana rule. Political conditions under the Ranas were not conducive for the emergence of ethnic associations of this sort, and the *Muluki Ain* lent a degree of structural rigidity to the Nepali caste system that was absent in the Indian context.

The Tharu Kalyankarini Sabha may be the oldest ethnic association in Nepal; certainly it is the oldest to be formally recognized by the state. It came into existence at a time when the (Rana) state had little tolerance for ethnic associations. That it was allowed to exist suggests, first, that the Ranas did not see the Tharu elite as a possible threat to their rule. This is the view of Parshu Narayan Chaudhari, one of the most politically prominent Tharus in Nepal, who discussed with me the founding of the Tharu Kalyankarini Sabha. Speaking in English, he said, "Since Ranas knew that these Tharus...are very—not political persons, they are very backward people, illiterate people, so they allowed this institution... they get permission to open Tharu Kalyankarini Sabha." It also suggests the degree of that elite's ties to the Ranas. As we saw earlier, many members of the Tharu elite occupied locally important positions as jimidārs. The *baḍa hakim* (governor) of Palpa, one of the most important posts in the state administrative system of the time, was Mahikar Dev Narayan Singh of Saptari, who was assassinated during the uprising against the Ranas in 1951. One of his three sons is Ramanand Prasad Singh.

The story of the Tharu Welfare Society begins with a man named Amar Bahadur Singh from a village named Gadahal in what was then called Bara (which is today divided into the districts of Bara, Parsa, and Rautahat). Amar Bahadur, according to Narendra Chaudhary of Rautahat, who was president of the Sabha in 1999 when it celebrated its fiftieth anniversary, was the uncle of Kewal Chaudhary, the organization's founder. Narendra Chaudhary, who is from Sunsari, is Kewal Chaudhary's son-in-law. Amar Bahadur, like other sons of the Tharu elite (he was the son of a jimidār), was sent to India to study, probably toward the end of the nineteenth century; Parshu Narayan Chaudhari told me Amar Bahadur was an old man when he founded the Sabha's precursor. He came back with a very different perspective on the society he had left behind; he now saw it as backward and full of social evils like liquor, extravagant rituals, illiteracy, and bridewealth ("taking money to marry your daughter").

Amar Bahadur—who was probably a village level magistrate and tax collector, as he is referred to as a *phaujdār* (Chaudhary 2055: 2; Tharu 2054: 5)—set out to reform these practices. He summoned a meeting at Kakadi village in Bara in B.S. 1980 (1923/24) to propose that a number of customary practices—such as polygamy, extravagant feasts and the consumption of alcohol, which he saw as either degrading or economically ruinous—be prohibited. He seems to have succeeded in persuading other important people (*demān*) like himself in the local society to go along with his ideas,[2] at least for a time; but these others had little commitment to the social and economic reforms Amar Bahadur was proposing, and after his death in B.S. 1988 (1931/32) little if any effort was made to promote his ideas (Chaudhary 2055; Tharu 2054).

The social work that had ended with the death of Amar Bahadur Singh was taken up by Kewal Chaudhary, who returned to his home in Rautahat from his studies in India that same year. We have a brief biography of the man by Govinda Chaudhari, a former parliamentarian and member of the Tharu Kalyankarini Sabha's central committee (Chaudhari 2052: 46–47). Kewal Chaudhari was born in 1908 to a wealthy family in Rautahat district; he was educated at home and, when he entered his late teens, at a secondary school in Kalaiya, Bara. He was sent to Banaras to continue his education in B.S. 1986 (1929/30), but various family crises compelled him to return to Rautahat. His experiences in India may have sensitized him to what he came to see as social evils in his village, and he became known as a social worker. After his return he set up a primary school in his village and also established a health post. His importance as an influential member of his community was recognized by the Rana prime minister Mohan Shamsher, who appointed him to his "mock" parliament[3] in B.S. 2005; he remained a member until B.S. 2007 (Chaudhari 2052: 46). Kewal Chaudhari subsequently served in a number of posts during the panchāyat era, including a stint as the official in charge of elections in Janakpur in B.S. 2036 (1979/80) and a term in the Land Reform Commission in the 1950s.

The revival of Amar Bahadur's work began at a meeting in Kakadi in B.S. 2005 (1949). A group of influential Tharu men, including Kewal Chaudhary and Chiranjivi Prasad Chaudhary, on whose account (2055) the following is based, met to attend a Satya Narayan puja. At this gathering, apparently, the conversation turned to the work on social reform carried out earlier by Amar Bahadur Singh, and those present decided to revive his organization. They set a date for the first convention (Baisākh 1, B.S. 2007, which corresponds to mid-April 1950), and then set out to organize it. However, it is not clear from his account whether Chiranjivi Prasad is describing the B.S. 2005 meeting in Kakadi or whether this is a different gathering.

The first convention turned out a success. It was well attended, and those present elected Kewal Chaudhary the first secretary of the newly renamed organization, the Tharu Kalyankarini Sabha. Things did not go smoothly however. There was opposition from the older Tharu elite, who saw their privileges threatened by the young social reformers. The reformers were concerned that the Sabha would not be recognized by the Rana government, which was then in its waning days, and Chiranjivi Chaudhary was dispatched to Kathmandu to intercede directly with the Rana prime minister, Mohan Shamsher (Chaudhary 2055). The prime minister referred his petition for recognition of the Tharu Kalyankarini Sabha to the constitutional committee (*vaidhānik samiti*), which reported to him that in their opinion it was likely to promote communal feeling. Chiranjivi then submitted another petition and met with Bijaya Shamsher, Mohan Shamsher's son, who told him that the Sabha would be recognized, as there was nothing inappropriate in the constitution. Unfortunately, Chiranjivi does not tell us what arguments he brought to bear to obtain that more favorable outcome. Official approval of the Sabha dates from Magh 12, B.S. 2007 (January 1951).

The founding members of the Tharu Kalyankarini Sabha came from the eastern Tarai. Even today, it is in this part of the Tarai that the Sabha is strongest and has the most influence. The eastern districts have historically been the most prosperous part of the Tarai region because of their agricultural productivity, including cash crops such as jute, and more recently their industrial development. While Chitwan was a backwater under the Ranas, who treated it mostly as a hunting preserve, the eastern Tarai provided a substantial portion of the regime's revenue. The Chitwan Tharu consider the Tharu of the eastern districts to be much better educated than they are (since more of them have completed school and gone on to college), a view that is shared by many Tharu in the eastern districts as well. But Tharus I interviewed in Chitwan also believe that the Tharu communities in the east are characterized by much greater economic inequality.

Large Tharu landowners in the eastern Tarai made use of their resources and the ease of travel into India to have their sons educated across the border (schools were few and far between in Rana Nepal). Mahikar Singh, the governor of Palpa, was educated at Ripon College in Calcutta and received a law degree from Patna in 1918. His sons, who are among the most prominent members of the Sabha, were all educated in India. Ramanand Prasad Singh, for example, went to school in Darbhanga, North Bihar (Dharbanga District and Saptari share a common border) and went on to study history at Banaras Hindu University. He later studied law and became the attorney general of Nepal under King Mahendra in 1971. His brother Durganand Prasad Singh received a B.A. from the University of Bihar and a law degree from Patna University and then went into politics. He was elected to parliament in 1959 from Saptari, and after King Mahendra's coup he was appointed to the National Planning Commission, where he helped to draft the Third Five Year Plan. After serving on that commission for twenty months, he was appointed to the Public Service Commission. Another example is Parshu Narayan Chaudhari, a large landowner from Deukhuri who was also educated in India. He joined the Nepali Congress and was minister of education in B. P. Koirala's 1959 cabinet, also serving a term as general secretary of the Party. In 1981 however he left the Congress and joined the panchayāt system, holding cabinet posts in a number of governments. He was minister of education again in 1988–89, and after the success of the people's movement joined the pro-monarchical Rashtriya Prajatantra Party (National Democratic Party) in which he became a vice-president.

Tej Narayan Panjiar, who served the Sabha for a time as its treasurer and is today one of the two most prominent Tharu intellectuals in Nepal (R. P. Singh is the other), was born the son of a government official who rose to the rank of Subba (district head). His father served his entire life in the inner Tarai valley of Udaypur and never traveled far from it. He had Tej Narayan educated in Lahan Bazaar, the principal town in Siraha, which is an eight-hour walk from his home village in Udaypur. When Tej was nine years old, his father took him on horseback to Lahan and left him there to attend a newly established school. His father was not a well-educated man but he could read English; he had brought someone from India to Udaypur to teach him the language. (In Pipariya the father of the jimidār had also brought a schoolteacher from India to the village to teach the village boys.) Tej Narayan graduated from the Lahan school in 1957 after completing a high-school education and eventually, after a brief stay in Kathmandu, went to India to study at Ram Krishna College in Madubhani. When he returned to Nepal, he obtained a position as a headmaster and served in that capacity for a number of years, interrupted only by a two-year political appointment in government service, which ended with the dissolution of the government of the day. Tej Narayan eventually obtained a B.A. from Tri Chandra College in Kathmandu (the money came from his father, who was always willing, Tej Narayan remarks, to educate him). He joined the government service in 1970 and in 1977 was sponsored by the government to study for a master's degree program in bio-statistics from the University of North Carolina at Chapel Hill. That was his second trip to the United States and the highest educational qualification he has received; a few years earlier he had gone to the United States for training in population statistics and demographic analysis as part of his work for the census bureau.

The impetus to found an organization that would define and promote the interests of Tharus came from men like these. The interests of the organization are in effect the interests of this elite and their allies at the local level.

I interviewed Kewal Chaudhary in his home in Bhawanipur in 1997 when he was about eighty-nine or ninety. I met him again in 1999 at the Sabha's Jubilee celebration in Hadiya; he passed away a year or so later. He recalled the date of the founding of the Sabha as B.S. 2007 (c. 1951), but he was clearly thinking of the first official convention, which the *Thāru Saṁskṛti* gives as B.S. 2007 (Tharu Kalyankarini Sabha 2055: 50; see table 5). A commemorative pamphlet issued by the Morang district committee of the Sabha to mark the thirteenth convention of the organization gives the date for the founding of the organization as B.S. 2005 (c. 1949), which is also the date cited by Tej Narayan Panjiar (personal communication) and Chandra Tharu (2054). The officially accepted date is B.S. 2005, and the Tharu Welfare Society celebrated its golden jubilee in B.S. 2055 (1999).

Kewal Chaudhary, founder of the Tharu Kalyankarini Sabha (1997)

Kewal Chaudhary recalled another meeting, this one in B.S. 2009 (c. 1952), being organized in Gadahal village in Bara, to which were invited Parshu Narayan Chaudhary of Dang and another man from Bardiya whose name he had forgotten. He described this meeting as the first interdistrict meeting the organization had held, probably a reference to the presence of these men from the western Tarai. Most of the men present were from the local area, which Kewal Chaudhary defined as 2–4 *kos* distant from Gadahal (roughly, 4–8 kilometers). The Gadahal meeting was followed by another in B.S. 2010 (c. 1954) in Gobardiha, Parshu Narayan Chaudhary's home village, and after that in Rajbiraj in Saptari District in B.S. 2011. (Rajbiraj was presumably the venue for the opening; as in Morang in 1991, the actual conference took place in a village, Padariya. See table 5).

The initial phase of expansion appears to have proceeded through the development of personal contacts, much in the way that Kewal Chaudhary had recruited Parshu Narayan to the cause. In 1952, Parsu Narayan Chaudhary, then newly returned home from his studies at Banaras Hindu University, was invited to attend the meeting at Rangapur. Kewal Chaudhary had learned about Parsu Narayan when he casually mentioned to a (non-Tharu) district commissioner that he intended to organize a meeting for the Tharu of Bara (which then included the districts of Rautahat and Parsa as well). The district commissioner told him that he knew of a young educated Tharu man who had recently returned from India and suggested that he be invited. In an account evocative of the difficulties of travel at that time, Parsu Narayan recalls,

> So he [the district commissioner] gave him my address and then at the time he sent a telegram via India and then we got that telegram, and then…my younger brother—cousin brother—he also came with me, so we traveled all the way from Dang, then we came to India. At the time there was no road, communication, transport was very difficult. We had to walk whole day on horseback and came to the Indian railway station and we got the train, went to Gorakhpur…came to Birganj and Rautahat.… From Rautahat, we got a cart, and from that cart we traveled all night and all day and then reached that place [Rangapur village].

As a consequence of his participation, the annual meeting was organized in Parsu Narayan's home village of Gobardiha in Deukhuri in 1954. The Sabha would not meet in the far west of Nepal again until B.S. 2040 (1984/85), when it met in Kailali.

Tharus such as Tej Narayan Panjiar and Parshu Narayan Chaudhari, who have been members of the Sabha almost from its inception, remember Kewal Chaudhari as an indefatigable organizer willing to travel the length and breadth of the Tarai to proselytize his cause. On one occasion, there was in B.S. 2013 (c. 1956) a royal visit (*sawāri*) to Chitwan. Kewal Chaudhary went to Chitwan on that occasion, stayed a month in the district, and publicized the Sabha among the people there. Whenever the organizers of the Sabha got to know of an important or prominent Tharu

Table 5. National meetings of the Tharu Kalyankarini Sabha

B.S. (C.E.)	Place	Chief guest
2007 (1950)	Kakadi, Bara	
2008 (1951/52)	Rangapur, Rautahat	
2009 (1952/53)	Gadhal, Bara	Matrika Prasad Koirala
2010 (1953/54)	Gobardiha, Dang	
2011 (1954/55)	Padariya, Saptari	Bishweshwar Prasad Koirala
2012 (1955/56)	Kanchanbari, Morang	Niranjan Shamser
2013 (1956/57)	Keutaliya, Rupandehi	
2021 (1964/65)	Soknaha, Sarlahi	Rishikesh Shaha
2036 (1979)	Haripur, Sarlahi	
2038 (1981/82)	Amuwa, Rupandehi	
2040 (1983/84)	Pavera, Kailali	
2043 (1986/87)	Murgiya, Rupandehi	
2047 (1991)	Biratnagar, Morang	Krishna Prasad Bhattarai
2049 (1993)	Duhavi, Sunsari	Girija Prasad Koirala
2051 (1995)	Baganaha, Bardiya	Man Mohan Adhkari
2053 (1997)	Joshipur, Kailali	Lokendra Bahadur Chand
2055 (1999)	Hadiya, Udayapur	Girija Prasad Koirala

Source: Tharu Kalyankarini Sabha 2055: 50.

in some district or other, they would write to him and ask him to organize a meeting and invite the local notables. Parshu Narayan described (in English) what happened on such occasions:

> we used to lecture in the morning, we used to discuss our social problems, how to read, and then in the afternoon, after taking food, the lecture went on—[Lecture on what kinds of topic? I asked.] On social reforms. How should we go ahead, how the people are changing themselves according to the time, we should change it, so they have to open the schools, they have to send our children to these schools, they should abolish child marriage because due to this children can't get an education.

The initial response by Tharus to the message of ethnic unity that Kewal Chaudhary and other ethnic activists were spreading in these early years appears sometimes to have been one of skepticism, a skepticism overcome by force of argument. I asked Narendra Chaudhary how Kewal Chaudhary was received when he went into an unfamiliar district to propagate his message of Tharu unity. He replied, "Definitely the people reacted [saying] you are not Tharu. But when he talked to [them] they were convinced. Then they come and join." One such argument might have been the one articulated (in English) by Ramanand Prasad Singh:

> When you realize that you are treated differently than others, then you want to unite...And for unity you want the common indices and you appeal to them...we are one race, you are looked down upon by others, people have come and now begun exploiting us, so what we can do is to come together and educate our children, unless we get educated there's no way out...so educating and giving up all these superstitious ideas, that is how it...it was social reformist.

Following the founding of the Tharu Kalyankarini Sabha in 1950, the organization appears to have gone through a period of great activity, during which it met regularly every year. At two of these annual meetings, the prime minister of the day was present as chief guest; at a third meeting, the chief guest was the state's most important local official. That meeting was inaugurated by Niranjan Shamsher, the chief district officer (presumably of Morang District, where the meeting was held). Thirty-five years later, at the thirteenth convention, the prime minister of Nepal was once again present as chief guest, an index of the Sabha's success in establishing itself as an ethnic organization of some importance. The prime minister of the time was present at the four conventions that followed the one in 1991; Girija Prasad Koirala in 1993, Man Mohan Adhikari in 1995, Lokendra Bahadur Chand in 1997, and Girija Prasad Koirala again in 1999, when the Sabha celebrated its jubilee in a remote village in Udaypur District. The list spans the political spectrum in Nepal. By this time the nature of politics itself had changed; political parties in a parliamentary system cannot afford to ignore organizations that claim to speak for a significant constituency.

Table 5 indicates the growth across national space of the Tharu Kalyankarini Sabha. Until 1980, almost all its meetings were in the eastern Tarai, in the home district of its founder Kewal Chaudhary (Bara) or, after the subdivision of Bara, in Rautahat. The relative scarcity until recently of venues in the far west suggests that active local organizations of the Sabha did not exist there.

After 1957 the regular annual meetings came to an end, probably due in part to the unfavorable political conditions following King Mahendra's palace coup. A cardinal feature of the years of panchāyat rule was the suppression of ethnic affirmation; the political emphasis was on nation building and "national integration," and the assertion of ethnic distinctiveness was frowned upon. The only meeting that took place at this time was in Sarlahi, and the chief guest was Rishikesh Shaha, who had served as finance and foreign minister after King Mahendra's seizure of power in 1960. He had, however, been dismissed from the cabinet in 1963 and had become a critic of the regime (Hoftun, Raeper, and Whelpton 1999: 79–80). A Tharu writer refers to this period (post-1965) as the "dark age" of the Tharu Kalyankarini Sabha, when political conditions in the country prevented it from being active (Chaudhary "Tharu" 2055: 46).

The reemergence of the Sabha as an active organization dates from 1979, following the referendum called by King Mahendra's successor King Birendra, which reaffirmed the panchāyat system. The commemorative souvenir published for the Sabha's thirteenth convention in 1991 hails the ninth convention—which took place in Sarlahi in the month of Aswin, B.S. 2036 (September–October 1979)—as an important one in the social history of the Tharu because it was the first meeting attended by all the Tharu groups, including representatives from Naini Tal and Champaran.[4] Another Tharu writer notes that two Tharus from Champaran came to the third convention in 1953, and in 1957 "eminent Tharus" from Gorakhpur in India attended the seventh convention in Rupandehi. The 1979 meeting is notable for another reason: it was the first meeting of the Sabha since it entered its "dark age."

THE AIMS OF THE THARU KALYANKARINI SABHA

Although in its earliest phase, a large proportion of the Sabha's goals were oriented toward sanskritizing activities, its focus today is on economic or material welfare. This focus arises from the principal experience that the Tharu share throughout the Tarai, an experience that underlies their consciousness of unity; that of losing land to immigrants from the hills. To quote R. P. Singh, "We were the landowners everywhere, and we could see that our lands are being taken away, even by deceptions." Closely connected to this is another, that of being treated with contempt or disdain by high-caste immigrants; this, too, is a universal experience of Tharu throughout the Tarai. In all these areas, the Tharu blame their lack of education for the ease with which they were exploited, and, not surprisingly, the promotion of education among Tharus is one of the publicly stated goals of the Sabha. Members of the Tharu Kalyankarini Sabha, like Tharus in general, believe that it is through education that the welfare of the Tharu may be assured.

The catalyst for the founding of the Sabha was the perception that the Tharu were backward, and the necessity to make their status equal to that of other castes (jāt). The causes of this backwardness was identified as the general illiteracy of the Tharu, which made them vulnerable to exploitation by other groups, and the consequent inability of the Tharu to produce the doctors and engineers who, by virtue of their professional status, might raise the status of the group as whole. Education has been seen as the means by which a "backward" society may be transformed to a "forward" status (see Guneratne 1999). As a consequence, a large proportion of the Tharu Kalyankarini Sabha's activities have been devoted to the promotion of education. Among other things, Kewal Chaudhary established in B.S. 2007 (1951) a student hostel in the Tarai border town of Birganj, to benefit Tharu students in local schools and colleges. In B.S. 2032 (c. 1975) another building was erected next to it to provide hostel facilities for women, with funds provided by the king. Although these facilities were primarily intended for Tharus, Govinda Chaudhari writes that students from other "backward" communities were also allowed to stay there (2052: 47).

The Sabha has also been asking the government to reserve a certain number of places in the university for Tharu students, but without success. According to Narendra Chaudhary, during the panchāyat era King Birendra had agreed to award scholarships to Tharus in a number of different faculties including medicine and engineering, but these grants had been terminated after the restoration of democracy. Narendra Chaudhary then persuaded Koirala to reinstate the scholarships. The scholarships serve no purpose, however, unless Tharus are admitted to colleges and universities; hence the pressure on the government to reserve places for them, which it has so far resisted. (The model that inspires this is the system of reservations for backward classes guaranteed in the Indian constitution.)

The shift in the aims of the Sabha is illustrated by the resolutions adopted at the conventions of 1956 and 1980. The first convention took place at a time when the ideology of bikās (development) had not yet taken firm root in Nepali soil; by 1980 the business of bikās was well established. The 1956 convention, like the ones I attended in the 1990s, was conducted in Hindi, Tharu, and Nepali; Hindi and Nepali were, and continue to be, the link languages that enable Tharus from one region of the Tarai to communicate with those in another. The resolutions adopted in 1956 were as follows (Chaudhari 2047):

a. to limit dowries or gifts to the bride to one dhoti, one plate, one lohota (a small metal waterpot), and one rupee
b. to end the tax for honey

c. to encourage education
d. to pay attention to health
e. to reduce expenditure on feasts *(bhoj-bhater)*
f. to reduce the number of people who participate in a wedding party
g. to give up liquor
h. as Marwaris do, to live simply in order to make economic progress
i. to give up raising pigs and chickens
j. in place of *uchara-khadki,* to wear sarees and blouses

As I noted above, there have been changes of emphasis in the sorts of activities on which the Tharu Kalyankarini Sabha has focused. Much of this early list from 1956 is concerned with matters pertaining to sanskritization *(g, i,* and possibly *j),* social reform *(a),* controlling social expenditures *(e, f,* and *h),* and modernization *(c* and *d). Uchara-khadki* presumably refers to the white cloth worn by Tharu women in the eastern Tarai. However, Tribhuwan Choudhary, a Tharu from Saptari now living in New Mexico, tells me that it refers (in Saptari) to the white skirt worn by prepubescent girls and cannot refer to the clothes of adult women. The reference to a honey tax is unclear; this again might have been a traditional levy on Tharu peasants in the Eastern Tarai. The Marwaris are a wealthy Indian trading community in Nepal, considered by Nepalese to be frugal in their daily life.[5]

In 1979 (B.S. 2036), which the UN declared the International Year of the Child, the Tharu Kalyankarini Sabha met in the village of Haripur, in the district of Sarlahi, and declared it the year in which they would put an end to child marriage *(bāl vivāha nised varsā).*[6] According to Amar Lal Chaudhary of Saptari, a leading role in putting an end to child marriage was played by Ramanand Prasad Singh during his tenure as attorney general in the 1970s; he prosecuted violators of the law prohibiting child marriage, including his own maternal uncle. According to Tribhuwan Choudhary, however, although he often threatened prosecution, he never actually did so. Singh played an important role in getting legislation passed to prohibit child marriage; in this, as in other issues of interest to the Sabha, he says, "the times were in our favor."

Tribhuwan Choudhary, although not a member of the Sabha at the time, is one of those who worked to end child marriage in Saptari. In 1968 he worked for six months as the headmaster in Ramanand Prasad Singh's home village of Prasbani. He was not acquainted with Singh at the time but knew of him and was influenced by his ideas. Tribhuwan was opposed to child marriage because it interfered with education; he would point out that while Tharu students were well represented in every high school in Saptari, they never went on to college because they were burdened with responsibilities for the families they had started at a young age. He would go to where child marriages were taking place to lobby against it; people would listen politely to him because he was an educated man and the headmaster, but his arguments never prevented a marriage that was already taking place. Nevertheless, he says, child marriage came to an end in Saptari over the space of a decade between the late 1960s, when activism against it began, and 1979, because younger people were motivated to give it up.

The 1979 convention also resolved that it would

a. take special measures for women's education
b. establish a hostel for Tharu women (presumably students)
c. pay more attention to adult education
d. give special encouragement to creating an interest in diverse occupations
e. make an effort to set up cottage industries
f. encourage young men to go to the towns and acquire modern skills and means of livelihood

This list suggests the extent to which the Sabha's priorities have shifted. There is no mention here of anything that we could connect to sanskritization in the sense defined by Srinivas; these are the concerns of a modernizing elite. Tharus are to be encouraged to participate in the modern economy and acquire the skills with which to do so. This is plainly put in a document circulated for discussion at the jubilee convention in Udayapur in 1999, which proposed various strategies to develop the organization. It states: "Through the district committee, the village committees will be mobilized for the promotion of education and eradication of deeply rooted, anti-development, traditional prejudices and outdated institutions."

The Organization of the Tharu Kalyankarini Sabha

One of the strengths of the Tharu Kalyankarini Sabha is the ubiquity of its organization in every district of the Tarai, an organization which reaches, probably in most districts and certainly in the east, to the village level. But while the Sabha has a decentralized structure based on district committees with separate constitutions, actual power is in the hands of a central committee located in Kathmandu, made up of a small number of

Tharu men (and in 1991, one woman) who have achieved some degree of national prominence or who have become part of the urbanized elite. For all of its existence, the Tharu Kalyankarini Sabha's principal executive positions, that of president and secretary, have been monopolized by two individuals from the eastern Tarai who were affines: Kewal Chaudhary and Danalal Chaudhary. Narendra Chaudhary is Danalal's son and Kewal's son-in-law. All those who have served the Sabha as president, secretary, and treasurer, with the exception of Parshu Narayan Chaudhari, have been from the eastern Tarai and from Chitwan (see table 6). As we shall see in the next chapter, the lack of turnover at the upper levels of the Sabha has been a point of stress between the leadership and younger activists.

Women are virtually invisible in the leadership of the Sabha at every level. The B.S. 2055 issue of *Thāru Saṁskṛti* lists all the members of sixteen district committees, including the Kathmandu valley. Of 140 individuals

Table 6. Principal office bearers of the Tharu Kalyankarini Sabha

	Period in office (B.S.)	Years in office
President		
Balibanta Chaudhari (Bara)	2007–13	6
Danalal Chaudhari (Sunsari)	2013–43	30
Ramdin Chaudhari (Chitwan)	2043–49	6
Parshu Narayan Chaudhari (Dang)	2049–53	4
Narendra Kumar Chaudhari (Sunsari)	2053–present[a]	
General secretary		
Keval Chaudhari (Rautahat)	2007–47	40
Parshu Narayan Chaudhari (Dang)	2043–49	6
Ramanand Prasad Singh Tharu (Saptari)	2049–51	2
Satya Narayan Chaudhari (Siraha)	2051–53	2
Amrit Prasad Khañ Tharu (Rautahat)	2053–present	
Treasurer		
Ramanand Prasad Singh Tharu (Saptari)	No data	
Tej Narayan Panjiar (Udayapur)	No data	
Narendra Kumar Chaudhari (Sunsari)	No data	
Shiva Narayan Chaudhari (Saptari)	No data	

Source: Tharu Kalyankarini Sabha 2055:50; the dates are taken from Chaudhary "Tharu" (2055: 44–45), who provides no data for the tenure of office of the treasurers of the Sabha.
[a] B.S. 2055 or C.E. 1999.

listed only fifteen are women. Only in Udaypur, where women occupy the posts of treasurer and assistant secretary, and in Siraha, where a woman is treasurer, do women hold any key positions. Although many women attend the national conventions, they are there as spectators. The only woman in the central committee of the Sabha in 1991 was Shanti Choudhary.

Shanti Choudhary's life has been very different from the lives of the men described earlier, and her goals within the Sabha have been correspondingly different. She has written about herself in a brief autobiography, translated and mimeographed into English (Choudhary 1990). This autobiography, written from the perspective of a Nepali feminist, is a critique of the patriarchal domination of Tharu society and also its domination by elite, privileged males. She was born in Bara, the daughter of an influential and well-educated landowner and politician named Radha Krishna Choudhary, and was married quite young. By her account, she was an activist for women's rights from early on. In 1979, when she was sixteen, she was deeply affected by the attempted rape of an untouchable woman by one of her kinsman. Although the woman escaped, Shanti Choudhary writes that the woman's husband was later shot dead by the man who had attempted to rape her. Although the culprit was her kinsman, Shanti Choudhary, motivated by this incident, began to organize ordinary villagers to resist the oppression of their social elites. This sort of abuse was also what the Tharu Kalyankarini Sabha was organizing against, and may have been what drew her to it.

When I met her in Kathmandu, she was running a center for women, the Creative Development Center (Shreejana Vikash Kendra), which was intended to help underprivileged women of both rural and urban areas to set up income-generating activities. She began to help underprivileged women in her youth, when she would take baskets woven by poor women in her village and sell them in Kathmandu. In 1984 her mother tried to have land that had belonged to Shanti Choudhary's father (who had died some years earlier) transferred to her name, but that attempt was stopped by an affinal kinsman (a senior official in the police), who claimed a share in the property. This may have been in retaliation for Shanti Choudhary's early activism. When her mother was unable to assert her rights in the local courts, Shanti Choudhary moved to Kathmandu to seek legal redress there. There she met a lawyer and appears to have found an opportunity to study the law through him, something she says she had wanted to do for a long time because she saw the law as an avenue through which to fight for justice, both for herself and for the less privileged sectors in society.

Senior members of the central committee of the Tharu Kalyankarini Sabha have access to the highest levels of power in Kathmandu; Parshu Narayan Chaudhari, for example, was one of the most powerful figures in the central committee and had held cabinet positions in various panchāyat governments. Kewal Chaudhary had been a member of the National Council and the Land Reform Commission, Ramanand Singh had been attorney general, and Narendra Kumar Chaudhary had been commissioner for the Bagmati Zone, the administrative area in which the capital city of Kathmandu is located.

The Tharu Kalyankarini Sabha has district branches in every Tarai district, including those like Makwanpur and Dhanusha that, according to the 1991 census, have negligible Tharu populations. In the following pages I shall discuss the district committee structure as it is organized in Chitwan. The Chitwan District branch had its own constitution; presumably other district committees also do.[7] These constitutions are subordinate to the constitution of the national organization, which prevails in matters of dispute. A district committee on average has nine members, who are elected at an annual general meeting of the organization. The district committee is required to meet four times a year but may call other meetings as the need arises. In 1991 the headquarters of the district committee in Chitwan was in Sultana, one of the wealthiest Tharu villages in Chitwan and the home village of the national president at the time, Ramdin Chaudhary. The local elite in Sultana is strongly represented in the local Sabha at every level (district committee, advisory committee, and area committee); the national president of the Tharu Kalyankarini Sabha in 1991 was the biggest landowner of this village.

The district committee in turn acts as an apex for area committees. Chitwan, for example, is divided into six areas (*kṣetra*), each with a committee of local notables (ideally every Tharu village in any given area has a representative on this committee), which is responsible in theory for implementing the programs and goals decided upon at a higher level. The constitution of the Chitwan district committee requires each area committee to appoint an advisory committee of at most five people, who should be among the most distinguished individuals in its area of jurisdiction. The area committee must meet at least three times a year, and the presence of the president, secretary, or assistant secretary of the district committee is mandatory at such meeting. The meetings are supposed to be a forum in which the members of the area committee can evaluate the progress they have made toward realizing the goals set out in the district organization's constitution.

In addition to these various executive committees, the constitution of the Tharu Kalyankarini Sabha in Chitwan requires the district committee to appoint an advisory committee (in 1985, this committee consisted of eleven men, whose names, like the names of all the other members of these various committees, are listed in an appendix to the constitution). The constitution specifies that these men should be from among those who have distinguished themselves nationally and locally. In the event, the membership of the district committee and the advisory committee include some of the most important Tharu landowners in the district. The number of people appointed to this committee is at the discretion of the district committee, and members serve for the same length of time as the district committee itself.

In 1985, according to the lists of names and villages appended to the constitution, 157 individuals from about 119 villages were formally members of different committees of the Chitwan District branch of the Tharu Kalyankarini Sabha. Some villages were better represented than others. Altogether, six men from the important and prosperous village of Sultana were members of the various committees (district, advisory, and area). Three other villages had three people each involved in the councils of the Sabha, twenty-one had two, and ninety-one had just one (their representative on the area committee). Some villages (probably those in areas with a small Tharu population) had more than one representative on the area committee. Kumhiya village in western Chitwan, for example, had contributed three members to an area committee of seven. While this was the smallest area committee, the four largest (all in eastern Chitwan, where the Tharu population is concentrated) each had nineteen members. The representative of the village at the level of the area committee is typically the jimidār or, in the absence of a jimidār, one of the larger landowners.

This elaborate organizational structure is entrusted with the implementation of a program of social reform, economic advancement, and cultural preservation. Whether it actually does so is another matter; with the exception of one important event (discussed below) that took place toward the end of my stay in Pipariya, the home village of a member of the district committee, I saw little evidence of any activity on its part. Most Tharus (including the committee member referred to above) felt it had done little if anything to promote its various goals. But that it may have achieved little in terms of social reform and economic advancement is less significant than that it has provided a common forum for the Tharu elite in virtually every Tharu village in the district.

The constitution lays out the aims and purposes of the organization under four headings. The first, which deals with social issues, is by far the largest, listing sixteen separate aims and purposes. The other three are concerned with economic (four aims), educational (three aims), and cultural issues (three aims). The sixteen social aims may be broadly grouped into four categories. The first is the prohibition or reform of certain marriage practices that are considered, in the modern context, to be backward or degrading. The constitution proclaims the Tharu Kalyankarini Sabha's intent to end the practices of child marriage, "discordant" marriage (i.e., of an old man with a young girl), and polygyny. Bridewealth is marked out as an undesirable practice to be rooted out from Tharu society, but dowry, characterized here as a custom penetrating into Tharu society from elsewhere, is also to be discouraged and resisted. I believe there are two matters of concern here to the Tharu elite. On the one hand, bridewealth has come to be thought of as the buying and selling of one's daughters, and hence demeaning. Dowry is also considered demeaning because, although one should endow one's daughter with the goods she needs to start off in her new life, one should not be compelled to offer gifts in order to make the marriage possible (the resistance here is to the idea that the groom has a right to demand gifts from the bride's household as a condition of marriage).

On the other (and this brings me to the second set of concerns under the rubric of social issues), the constitution is at pains to discourage lavish expenditure on social ceremony. Dowry, of course, adds significantly to the cost of a wedding. In addition, the constitution proposes limiting how many people participate in the *janti* (the procession in which a Nepali groom goes to his bride's home for the marriage ceremony), how many escort the bride to her new home after the marriage ceremony, how many attend the *bhoj* (feast) that marks the betrothal, and so on. Expensive customs (for example, the customary slaughter of a castrated goat by the members of the janti at the bride's house) are prohibited. The constitution limits the length of the *khersār* (the fine white cotton cloth traditionally presented to the bride's mother) to sixteen hands (a hand equals the length of a man's forearm). Previously, the bride's household would specify the length or the customary length might vary from village to village.

The constitution also specifies the fine to be paid for elopements after marriage to be one thousand rupees. Were a woman to elope after the feast of betrothal has been eaten but before the marriage has taken place, the constitution sets the fine at five hundred rupees. It is this aspect of the Chitwan Tharu Kalyankarini Sabha's activities that is best known to the ordinary villager in Pipariya. Finally (and significantly), the Chitwan district committee proposes to vigorously encourage marriages with Tharus from other districts.

The section on economic aims deals with fundraising (members of district and area committees are asked to contribute according to their status and circumstance). There are three provisions for promoting education: make it mandatory for children to attend primary school, provide scholarships for poor Tharus to attend secondary school, and reserve one place for Tharus in each college campus in the district. In the area of cultural affairs, the district committee proposes that magazines and papers be published to protect the Tharu language and develop its literature, that Tharu cultural practices in danger of disappearing be preserved and fostered, and that the priceless cultural heritage of the Tharu, such as folk songs and folk stories, be protected and developed through continual activity.

Apart from the role it plays in adjudicating infringements of traditional rules and customs, especially those pertaining to marriage, the local district organization of the Tharu Kalyankarini Sabha has another significant impact on the lives of villagers. Apparently in response to a petition submitted by important Tharus in the district, who were alarmed at the rapidity with which men in their community were losing control of land, King Mahendra ruled that future land transactions between Tharus and non-Tharus should receive the approval of the Tharu community (in effect, of its leading men). All land transactions must be registered before the chief district officer, who must give his consent to the sale; if a Tharu wishes to sell land, the CDO will usually refer the matter to the local district committee of the Sabha for its approval. The Sabha must take a decision on the matter in his presence. My research assistant told me he had been present on one such occasion as an observer, presumably when his own family had sold land a few years earlier to a Brahman. He claimed that the policy of referring land transactions to the Sabha had been commonly resorted to during the panchāyat era; he knew of several cases. The CDO is not obliged to consult the Tharu Kalyankarini Sabha, although he usually does so.

OTHER THARU ORGANIZATIONS

The Tharu Kalyankarini Sabha is not the only organization of Tharus, although it is the only one with a real claim to a national presence. BASE has had a much greater impact on the lives of ordinary Tharus, but its scope is confined to Dang-Deokhuri and the districts of the far-western Tarai. Another organization of national scope is mentioned by Ødegaard: the Tharu Samskrti Samaj, or Tharu Culture Society, which also has local committees in various districts. Its aim, Ødegaard writes, is "to preserve and promote Tharu culture" while at the same time facilitating interdistrict contact among Tharus (1997: 140). At the time of her writing, it was led by a wealthy landowner from Deukhuri named Dinesh Kumar Chaudhary. This organization was responsible for the First International Tharu Culture Conference in Saptari and was funded in part by BASE. The conference lasted three days and featured among other things dance, poetry, and song competitions for representatives from various districts. BASE is as committed to the pan-Tharu ideology as the Tharu Kalyankarini Sabha, but being an organization firmly rooted among the poor, the focus of its activities is different. That it is prepared to financially support an event far from its stamping grounds in the western Tarai, and an organization whose purpose has nothing to do with the improvement of the material conditions under which Tharus live, indicates its commitment to the idea of pan-Tharu unity. This is also despite the fact that there is much less recognition or involvement in the cause of pan-Tharu unity in the west than in the east (McDonaugh 1989; Ødegaard 1997: 52, 91–96).

Most districts in the Tarai have their own organizations dedicated to much the same aims as the Sabha and BASE, aims that fall under the general rubric of Tharu upliftment. I have already described one in the previous chapter, the community development NGO in Chitwan named NIDS. They are often organizations of the youth, although Ødegaard describes another elite-driven organization, the Rana Sudhar Samaj, or Rana Reform Society, which brings together members of the rich, educated, Rana Tharu elite in Kailali and Kanchanpur (1997: 145–150). In contrast to the modernist ideology of both BASE and the Tharu Kalyankarini Sabha, this organization appears to be motivated by more traditional ideas of sanskritization or "caste mobility" (1997: 150).

Youth organizations speak to the same sort of motivations and frustrations that draw people to the Sabha. Unlike the Sabha, they have roots in particular villages, districts, or other local areas. While some have come into existence without any reference or relationship to the Tharu Kalyankarini Sabha, others have emerged out of a sense of dissatisfaction with what the Sabha has accomplished.

The professed aims of these organizations are all very similar. The Tharu Vikash Samanvya Parishad (Tharu Development Coordination Council—TVSP), for example, which was founded by college students from Morang, Sunsari, and Saptari studying in Biratnagar, wanted to work to improve the economic condition of Tharus, to preserve their culture, and to improve Tharu education. They would like all Tharu women to be literate. But as one TVSP member told me, when I met him at the Tharu Kalyankarini Sabha's convention in Tetariya, all this was at the talking stage, they had not actually done anything as yet (they had been in existence then about two years). Lack of funding prevented their expansion, he said, but he hoped that the TVSP could eventually organize Tharu students throughout Nepal. He claimed that its members, about three or four hundred students, had formed the group to counter the discrimination and isolation they felt on campuses at the hands of Brahman students and the (Brahman-dominated) administration. They had met in secret (or informally) before the Democracy Movement, but were now organizing openly.

I came across another youth club in Madi, in southern Chitwan, called the Tharu Yuva Club (Tharu Youth Club). The founder, a young man in his early twenties named Kishore Chaudhari,[8] told me he had appended the word Tharu to it deliberately, even though it meant that the government might not recognize it on the grounds that it was meant for only one community and hence was communal. He wanted the club to devote itself to the welfare of Tharus and to the development of the (Chitwan) Tharu language. He meant by this the removal of obscenities from the language, its purification, and the development of a literature. The club would devote itself to the development of "Tharutva," a neologism coined to describe everything that pertains to being a Tharu, including, as he put it, culture, language, and society. The goal of the Tharu Yuva Club was to halt the decline in the social and economic conditions of the Tharu community which was "getting weaker as a society day by day." Kishore believed that as long as Tharus remained uneducated, they would not be able to develop. The club had about 40–45 members, mostly male, all drawn from Kishore's and the surrounding villages. Kishore knew of the Tharu Kalyankarini Sabha and its work, and his club had been founded partly in reaction to it. He had originally thought well of the Tharu Kalyankarini Sabha because its goal had been to work for the development of Tharus, who were, as he put it, a fallen jāt (*gireko jāt*). But it could not succeed in this effort because of the intrusion of politics. The local area committee of the Tharu Kalyankarini Sabha in Madi, he observed, had split because its members, who had different political affiliations, tried to bring party politics into the organization. He believed, perhaps as a result of this experience, that Tharus should have their own political party.

Another group, founded in 1989, which was also critical of the Tharu Kalyankarini Sabha was the Tharu Kalyankarinikari Yuva Sabha (Tharu Welfare Youth Association), established by an individual with close ties to the former panchāyat regime. The Tharu Kalyankarini Sabha in Chitwan is dominated by supporters of the Nepali Congress. This man, once a member of the Congress, had switched his political loyalty to the panchāyat government and had set up the Yuva Sabha. He explained to me that he had done so because the youth were dissatisfied with the "slowness" of the Tharu Kalyankarini Sabha's approach; they wanted "quick results." However, a few years later he became district president of the local committee of the Tharu Kalyankarini Sabha, so presumably a reconciliation had been effected. It was the Yuva Sabha that had brought out the inaugural issue of a magazine *Hamār Saṁskṛti* (Our culture) to promote Chitwan Tharu language and culture. His description of his organization's aims is not a list of activities accomplished or even in process, but rather a wish list of items. It illustrates what the elite feels to be important to Tharu society, to wit, a preoccupation not with concerns about ritual rank or sanskritization but with economic betterment. "It's like this," he said. "We would like to teach how to do agriculture in a developed, modern way.... Now, how, from a limited amount of land, how to get a large crop: should there be a vegetable farm, or a poultry farm there, or what should there be?...Why are [we Tharus] going back step by step [referring to their socio-economic status]? We have paid most attention to this question."

My research assistant, himself a member of the Congress who sympathized with the Tharu Kalyankarini Sabha, alleged that the Yuva Sabha had been set up to erode the Congress's support base among the Tharu. The secretary to the Chitwan District branch of the Tharu Kalyankarini Sabha, a schoolmaster, was the editor of *Hamār Saṁskṛti*, and thus closely associated with the Yuva Sabha in its production, but he was a strong supporter of the Communist Party candidate at the general election. As I noted in the last chapter, the alleged support base for the Congress was probably illusory; communist candidates swept the election in Chitwan, and in eastern Chitwan, where Pipariya is located, the communist candidate won by an overwhelming margin.

My research assistant's reasoning, in making a claim for a strong Tharu support base for the Congress, was as follows. He believed that Tharus were 60 to 70 percent of the population of Chitwan (although, in fact, they are less than half the population in eastern Chitwan alone, where Tharus are concentrated, and less than 14 per cent of the district's population overall). If all the Tharu were united (presumably through the good offices of the Tharu Kalyankarini Sabha) and supported the Congress, this would seriously affect the prospects of panchāyat candidates. The Yuva Sabha, he reasoned, was thus set up to provide a panchāyat-backed alternative to the Tharu Kalyankarini Sabha. His analysis may have been correct, but in the event, neither the Congress nor the Panchas carried the day at the election.

❖

CHAPTER SIX

The Making of Tharu Identity

I shall discuss in this chapter the practical and symbolic work engaged in by Tharu social elites as they strive to shape a common ethnic identity for the various social groups subsumed by the ethnonym *Tharu*. The focus of this chapter is the work of the Tharu Kalyankarini Sabha, which, I have argued, is the only ethnic organization available to the Tharu with a truly national reach and organizational infrastructure. Despite the absence of shared cultural symbols like language or religion, the sustained symbolic activity of this organization over a period of fifty years has instilled in Tharus throughout the Tarai a sense of ethnic unity. One aspect of this activity—the institutional structure of the organization itself, with its central committee in Kathmandu and subcommittees all the way down to the village level—has been described in the previous chapter. This organizational structure is a necessary prerequisite to the work of cultural production described below.

The first meeting of the Sabha that I attended was of the central committee. It met at Gaushala in Kathmandu on October 8, 1990, and was attended by delegates from various districts. I believe this was the first meeting following the success of the People's Movement the previous April, which had restored party-based parliamentary democracy to Nepal. Gaushala is a large rest house providing accommodation to the pilgrims who come to the Pasupatinath temple. More than fifty men were present, seated on mats in a large room, facing the leaders of the organization, who were similarly seated. The men in positions of national leadership were then in their fifties and sixties. Many of the district representatives present, however, were younger, in their thirties and forties. The younger men, particularly from the eastern Tarai, represented a more radical faction of the organization. Many were supporters of the Communist Party; the older men were either supporters of the Nepali Congress or of the old regime. All those present, however, were drawn from the elite: wealthy landlords, jimidārs, salaried workers, professionals, and college students.

The meeting had been called to discuss what Nepal's new circumstances in the wake of the People's Movement meant for Tharus, and how Tharus could take advantage of them. Six resolutions had been put forward for consideration, including one that the next convention be held in Biratnagar and another calling upon Tharus to give their language as "Tharu" at the forthcoming census (see below). Unfortunately, I was unable to ascertain what the rest of the resolutions were about.[1] The debates and speeches at the meeting seemed to have less to do with these resolutions themselves (in the event, they were all adopted) and more to do with factional disputes and disagreements within the Sabha. In particular, a good portion of the meeting was taken up with a sustained criticism of the national leadership, made by younger representatives from the eastern Tarai districts, one of whom described the national leadership to me, in English, as "blame persons."

The chair of this meeting was Narendra Chaudhary, the former commissioner for Bagmati Zone (in which administrative unit Kathmandu is located). He would call on speakers from a list he held; people who wanted to speak would make a gesture indicating they wanted their names added to it. As I entered the hall, a young man from Sunsari was making a pointed criticism of the central committee, alleging that it did not reply to letters sent it from district committees. Another criticism of the central committee (articulated primarily by representatives from the Eastern Tarai and apparently an important theme in the debates) was that it was not democratic; it did not consult the district committees, and it was self-appointed rather than elected. This criticism would be reiterated at the Biratnagar convention a few months later and lead to a serious and acrimonious dispute.

Halfway through the meeting, there was a disturbance at the other end of the room, and Ramanand Prasad Singh entered. He is one of the most influential men in the organization, and among its principal power brokers. Because of the high position he has held in the ranks of government and his reputation as a scholar, he is accorded enormous respect and deference by other Tharus. Singh, whose late entrance interrupted a mild-mannered man from Dang who had the floor and now waited in embarrassed silence for an opportunity to continue, insisted that the gathering observe one minute of silence in memory of the martyrs of the People's Movement. The meeting agreed, and afterward the man from Dang was allowed to continue.

Later in the afternoon, Singh rose to speak. He is a good orator, and clearly enjoyed the opportunity to speak to this audience. He spoke in Hindi, Nepali, and what I assumed was his native Saptari dialect, switching back and forth between the various languages as he made his points. His speech dealt with what he considered to be the core of Tharu identity: he asserted that Tharus are descended from the Buddha, or more precisely, from the Sakya clan. His point was to assert the high status of the Tharu; the emperor Ashoka himself was of their jāt, and what other jāt could claim a greater pedigree? Singh grew eloquent as he switched from the origins of the Tharu to a critique of Babu Ram Acharya (a Nepali historian who had failed to discuss the Tharu in his work)[2] and to an attack on the central committee (of which he was a member) for its lack of activity.

SINGH'S THESIS ON THARU ORIGINS

Ramanand Prasad Singh has set out his ideas on the origins of the Tharu in a pamphlet entitled "The Real Story of the Tharus" published by the *Thāru Saṁskṛti* (a magazine published by the Tharu Kalyankarini Sabha and edited by himself) in 1988. Briefly, his thesis is as follows. The Tharu, he says, are a "pre-Aryan race of Mongoloid origin"; he cites the Indian anthropologist D. N. Majumdar to support this view (Majumdar 1944: 71). Other authorities he has used in developing his ideas on the antecedents of the Tharu include the French Orientalist Sylvain Lèvi, Brian Hodgson, T. W. Rhys Davids, Vincent Smith, and Buchanan Hamilton. The Tharu, he argues, are the original Sakyas, whose most distinguished scion is the Buddha Gautama: "The book 'The Historical tradition of India' written by learned Pargitar has suggested that if there be any remnants of the Buddha's tribe, it is the Tharus.... Prof. Rhys Davids is positive that Buddha belonged to a Mongoloid tribe, Vincent Smith is of the same View" (Singh 1988: 5).

Singh argues that the Tharu originated not in the Thar Desert or Rajasthan, as some have said, but in Nepal and are descended from the kings of Banaras (see also Panjiar 1993: 20). These descendants, divided into two clans known as the Sakyas and the Kolyas, settled in the woods around Kapilavastu; the Buddha's father Suddhodana was an elected leader of his people, the Sakyas. He was not a king but a large *bhūmipati*, or landlord. That Suddhodana was an elected leader is important, because Singh envisages the Tharu as having lived in self-governing village republics with elected leaders. To quote him again on his view of the etymology of the term *Tharu*,

It was the Sakya and the Kolian people who became initiated later on in Buddhism, after the Buddha having gained enlightenment and having many deciples [*sic*] came to Kapilavastu to meet his family. The people of those two clans who conducted themselves according to Buddha's original doctrines as reported by their elders came to be known as Therabadins. These followers of Therabad Buddhism came to be called "Sthavir." It is from this word that the name "Tharu" derives. From sthavir to thavir and from thavir to Tharu is an easy and logical verbal transition. This interpretation of the word "Tharu" is logical and in keeping with their traditional values and behaviour. The Tharus live a simple life and are renowned for their honesty. (Singh 1988)[3]

Ramanand Prasad Singh is the best known and most articulate of the small number of Tharu intellectuals. The idea that Tharus are descended from the clan of the Buddha Gautama is not necessarily shared by all Tharus, at least not those of Chitwan. Singh's thesis is a flattering one, and many Tharus who consider themselves to be Hindu are willing to entertain it; there is no contradiction being Hindu in the present but being descended from the clan of the Buddha. In Chitwan, the Tharu subscribe to the theory of Rajput origins, which has also been recorded for Tharu groups elsewhere in the Tarai (Roy Choudhuri 1952: 247; Kochar 1963; Majumdar 1937: 119; Risley 1892: 312–313). Ramanand Singh is dismissive of this claim, which, he points out, is a theory advanced by people of low status in order to improve their self-image (within a society dominated by upper-caste Hindus and their values). As far as he is concerned, the Tharu are an ancient people who existed before Rajputs were even thought of. As he told the assembled delegates at the Tharu Kalyankarini Sabha's convention in Biratnagar, "Hāmi buddhako santān ho" [We are the descendants of the Buddha]. In Singh's view, Tharus have been the victims of both Hindu and Moslem civilizations.

Singh is rejecting the ideological incorporation of Tharus into Hinduism as a subordinate caste by positing for them an origin that places them completely outside the Hindu community. He also positions the Tharu as an ancient people, whose identity has endured over three thousand years and who are kinsmen to the Buddha and to the Emperor Ashoka, one of the chief royal patrons of early Buddhism. The claim to kinship with Ashoka is based on Ashoka's having been born in Champaran, the region identified by Taranatha (according to some translations of his work) as the land of the Tharu.[4] In the Nepali context, his position may be understood as a response to domination by a high-caste national elite that has defined the polity as essentially Hindu. Singh is not simply claiming that Tharus were, and should be, Buddhists, thereby attempting to separate their identity from Hindu society. Rather, he is claiming that Tharus are descended from the clan of the Buddha, and that they are of the same blood as the emperor Ashoka. Tharus are ignorant of their history and their distinguished lineage because Buddhism, the religion founded by one of their own, was destroyed and replaced by Hinduism. Their lineage is thus more ancient and more distinguished than that of the high Hindu castes that today dominate the Nepali state. As he put it to me, switching into English in order to make his point in a conversation carried on mainly in Nepali, "Buddha was humanity personified and he was a Tharu." In Singh's view, to posit a Rajput origin for Tharus is to accept the Hindu paradigm; the point (for him) is to liberate oneself from it.

Tej Narayan Panjiar puts the critique of Hinduism even more strongly. He sees Buddhism as superior to Hinduism because it is a religion of peace (further proof of the link between Tharus and Buddhism, because Tharus are an inherently peaceful people). Hindu gods are depicted carrying weapons, whereas the Buddha's power does not derive from his ability to mobilize violence. And Tharus, asserts Panjiar, are not Hindus; rather, they are compelled by a Hindu state to observe Hindu practices. I doubt that any Tharu I know in Chitwan would agree with this view.

I mentioned above that most Tharus refer to themselves as a jāt, which is also the term used in the *Muluki Ain*. Ramanand Singh is a rare exception; he makes a point of insisting that Tharus comprise a samāj (society) and not a jāt. Commenting on scholars who claim that Tharus belong to a number of different jāts, he observed, "Everyone has misinterpreted us. . . . The Tharus aren't a jāt; the Tharus are a society. . . . We are a community without caste. Newars also were casteless, but Jayasthiti [Malla] brought in castes."[5] Singh is here treating the word *jāt* as being synonymous with the English *caste*, and he opposes jāt/caste to samāj/tribe. The Tharu are a tribe, and not a caste: he points out that Manu treats the Sakyas (the putative ancestors of today's Tharus) as a tribe, not as a caste. The Tharu in fact, stand outside the whole system of varna.

To define the Tharu as Singh does, as a society rather than as a single jāt, is one way to accommodate the differences among them. It enables Tharu intellectuals to posit that the differences among Tharus arose from the simple fact of their isolation from each other. It ignores, however, the existence until recently of strict rules of endogamy, one of the chief defining features of a jāt/caste group.

MARRIAGE, CLASS, AND THE BOUNDARIES OF JĀT

Rules about who one may or may not marry are among the most fundamental ways of maintaining group boundaries. Mary Cameron's observation about Nepali hill society, that the honor (*ijjat*) of both the patriline and the household "become manifest and reinforced when marriage prescriptions are followed" (1998: 245; see also 135ff.) applies to the Tharu as well. To redefine the boundary of the jāt is therefore not simply a matter of cultural refashioning, it is a profoundly political act and, as in the case described below, one that is consciously taken. To make alliances through marriage in this way is to make kinsmen out of people with whom one had little or no connection formerly.

The Sabha determined early on that all those recognized as Tharu were within the acceptable conditions of marriageability; whatever restrictions might have applied to their intercourse with other Tharu communities in the past no longer obtained. While this is a significant symbolic statement of Tharu unity, it has had little practical consequences for the Tharu population at large, at least as far as intermarriage between Tharus living in different districts is concerned. The expense involved in seeking a marriage partner from a village more distant than a bullock cart can travel in a day is prohibitive by village standards. Almost all the marriages I know of that have taken place between Tharus of geographically separate groups were those of the elite, who have the resources and motivation to seek marriage partners outside the district. But it does serve to legitimize unions between members of hierarchically ranked Tharu groups living in the same district; this is the principal way in which ordinary Tharus experience this particular decision of the Tharu Welfare Society. In other words, they can no longer turn to the village elite for help in imposing sanctions on members of their family who might have married a Tharu of "inferior" status. This is not an issue for younger Tharu, at least as far as my field site in Chitwan was concerned, but it is an issue on which some members of the older generation are not in agreement with the position taken by their elites. I discuss one such instance later in this chapter.

The Tharu population in Chitwan belongs overwhelmingly to one Tharu subgroup. Consequently, the opportunity for intermarriage with other groups does not frequently occur. But in some parts of the Tarai, particularly in the west, Tharu populations are more intermingled, and marriage across group boundaries becomes possible, even for the poor. I am referring here to the formally arranged, socially approved marital union, the *bihe*. Krauskopff notes of Kailali, a Tarai district in the west populated both by Katharya Tharus and Dangaura Tharus, that both groups affirm a common identity and have begun to intermarry (1989: 33). It is not clear whether, by marriage, she refers to arranged marriage or elopement. The former is significant, the latter is not, because marriages are typically arranged only within the confines of the jāt. Inter-jāt marriages are usually by elopement. Nor do we know whether this has anything to do with the Tharu Kalyankarini Sabha's activities or whether it is the result of an independent dynamic in Kailali.

The salience of the symbolism of marriage for Tharu ethnic unity is captured in a description by Ødegaard of a marriage between a Tharu man from Deukhuri in the west and a Tharu woman from Sunsari in the east. The marriage had apparently been negotiated by Dilli Bahadur Chaudhary, the leader of BASE, and BASE had agreed to meet the cost of the groom's party's travel to Sunsari for the wedding. Ødegaard writes,

> The marriage...took place in May...and it received a lot of attention in the pan-Tharu environment. When the bus left...Deukheri for the long journey eastwards, it was only half-full. All along the Tarai belt, however, the bus picked up new people: Tharus from Kathmandu as well as from the other Tarai districts.... The wedding had become a collective Tharu affair and a symbolic statement of their unity. (Ødegaard 1997: 142)

Ødegaard also writes that the wedding was a cultural encounter between women from different parts of the Tarai, who, unlike their more mobile male counterparts, seldom got the opportunity to travel outside their own districts. Such weddings become an arena in which cultural differences are negotiated—in customs, in food, and in language.

The Tharu elite constitutes a very small fraction of the Tharu population. Where Chitwan is concerned, considerations of class and economic status appear to have been much less important before the area's economic development (starting in the early sixties) than they are today. Among the older generation of Tharus in Chitwan, the children of revenue collectors and other influential villagers appear to have married from time to time with humbler families, including those of their servants. In terms of the material conditions of life in Chitwan, there was no significant gap between the standard of living of the dominant stratum in village society and the poor. What distinguished them was quantity of material goods rather than their kind or quality; this reflected the existence of a largely unmonetized economy. The economic development of Chitwan has led to increased monetary wealth and consumption among the economically dominant Tharu and to a marked symbolic differentiation of class. One consequence has been the decline in marriages between members of the elite and the ordinary peasantry. Because the pool of suitable marriage partners within a particular endogamous group is thus reduced (especially for the national elite, who dominate the Tharu Welfare Society), the abrogation of rules of group endogamy is a strategy with definite benefits for the elite. In essence it expands the pool of possible marriage partners and permits people who are locally powerful or influential to establish alliances with others of their class throughout the Tarai.

Kewal Chaudhary himself appears to have led by example at a very early date. Sometime around 1968 Kewal Chaudhary (who is a Kochila Tharu) married one of his granddaughters to a Katharya Tharu from Nawalparasi. He then married his daughter to Narendra Chaudhary of Sunsari, thereby cementing an alliance with Narendra Chaudhary's father, Danalal Chaudhary, who was president of the Sabha for much of the time that Kewal Chaudhary served as secretary (see table 6). Although both are Kochila Tharu, people from Rautahat (who speak Bhojpuri) had not traditionally intermarried with the Maithili-speaking districts to the east. Kewal Chaudhary told me that the Tharu of Bara, Rautahat, and Sarlahi traditionally considered themselves to belong to one jāt. Those three districts would have comprised the traditional limits of marriage alliances. Finally and perhaps most significantly, Kewal Chaudhary married another granddaughter to a Rajghariya Tharu from Sunsari. The Kochila Tharu of that district regard the Rajghariya as inferior and have not traditionally intermarried with that subgroup. Narendra Chaudhary told me that although such intermarriages are now accepted, in the past a Kochila man who married (i.e., eloped with) a Rajghariya woman would have been forced to leave the Kochila community, and his children would not have been permitted to marry with other Kochila. Kewal Chaudhary therefore was addressing the divisions in Tharu society head on. Intermarriage among Tharus from different districts and different subgroups is now common among the elite. If it is much less so among poorer peasants, this is usually due to economic reasons rather than cultural ones about the honor (ijjat) of the jāt that must be preserved through the regulating of marriage relations. Cultural factors are important in other ways, however, as a conversation I had with a fairly well-to-do farmer in Chitwan indicates. When I asked him how he would react to a proposal of marriage for his son or daughter from Dang or Morang (or some other district), he answered,

> I would like it very much. The child's mother will say, "Let's not give our daughter away to a far-off place. If we do that we won't get to see them that well. If they fall sick, we won't know about it." But that's not what the father thinks. If the son-in-law is accomplished, if he is a good person, it doesn't matter how far away he lives, we can marry our daughter to him.
>
> But when you take into account the environment (*watāvaran*), it's better to marry within your district. Chaudharys of other districts speak somewhat differently. So one would need to make some changes in the way one speaks [i.e., learn their dialect]. This will be a little difficult for one's daughter. But if you marry her off within your own district, there is no language problem ["language" is also a metonym for culture in general]. So we prefer to marry within our own district.

Even so, old beliefs do not disappear easily, especially among the older generation. To quote the daughter-in-law of a jimidār in Chitwan, who would have been in her late thirties when I interviewed her in 1991, "We are a superior Tharu jāt, we are the Bahuns of all Tharu. [She is referring here to the Rajput Tharu, who are the dominant subgroup in Chitwan; she means the Rajput Tharu are at the top of the local hierarchy.] The others are of lower status. Because the *pad* [rank, title, degree] of Bantars and Botes is of a *sāno thar* [i.e., of lower status], I wouldn't like it if they married with us."

Why should ordinary Tharus accept the resolutions of the Tharu Welfare Society on such personal matters as matrimonial decisions? Traditionally, of course, they have not been personal matters but social ones, and the jimidār was entrusted with the task of ensuring that the interests of society were properly taken into account. Under the Ranas, the jimidārs not only were responsible for the collection of revenue and the exercise of juridical authority within the village, but were also the arbiters of that compendium of traditions and customs that we may term "caste law." It was the jimidār who decided when caste law, particularly in the case of marriage relations, had been infringed, and he had the authority to punish violators and annul inappropriate marriages. Today, however, the jimidār has no power to enforce caste law, and as many Tharus in Chitwan admit, there is little if anything anyone can do to sanction such infringement.

Although the *institution* of jimidār was abolished almost thirty years ago and the former jimidārs no longer carry institutional authority or exercise formal coercive power, the strength of this institution in the imagination of ordinary Tharus (or at least older ones who grew up under its authority), and the political and economic influence former jimidārs still wield in their villages, continue to be important factors in social life in Chitwan. If this elite, traditionally vested with the authority to rule on such matters, decides to redefine the boundaries of the jāt, there is no other group or institution with either the prestige, authority, or interest to oppose or deny this. As far as most Tharu are concerned, there is no reason why others sharing their ethnonym should not also be Tharus, the same *kind* of people as themselves, different and distinct from non-Tharus. They all occupy adjacent districts of the Tarai, experience similar forms of discrimination and exploitation, and define themselves in common opposition to the category of *pahāriyā* (hill person). Furthermore, other Tharu groups may be symbolically linked to their own society through marriages between their respective elites. These observations apply clearly to the eastern and central Tarai; it is in the far west that the idea of Tharu unity is at its weakest, although I suspect that here too, especially with the rise of BASE, the movement is toward ethnic unification. BASE is an important organization for poor Tharus in the west and is firmly committed to pan-Tharu unity.

While the state and its works are the conduit through which Tharu elites are able to establish relationships with each other, those same elite are the conduit through which different Tharu societies begin to forge relationships with others like themselves. As the jimidār has been the traditional source of authority on these matters, the perception Tharus have of others sharing their ethnonym is influenced by the thinking of elites in their own local society; in this matter, the elite has acted to liberalize the social norms that formerly it was responsible for upholding. In any case, ordinary Tharus (which is to say the vast majority) are in no position to ostracize or outcaste the elite; ultimately whether the poor agree or disagree is irrelevant.

The Tharu Kalyankarini Sabha has positioned itself to be the inheritor of this traditional authority, which now, however, lacks any legal base. That is to say, if any Tharu chooses to reject the authority of the Sabha to promulgate rules regulating how or whom he marries, there is nothing the Sabha can do legally to compel him. Whether a Tharu man or woman obeys the dictates of the Sabha will depend on the particular nature of power relationships in any given instance, on whether the Sabha can mobilize popular opinion to pressure a recalcitrant individual to conform. Better-off individuals are less susceptible to these pressures than their poorer neighbors, who may depend on the elite for help in times of hardship and crisis. We shall see later how this dynamic operated in a particular instance in Chitwan.

The poor, of course do not blindly follow the lead of their elites. The proposition that all Tharus are one jāt does not contradict their own experience; rather, it is either neutral or it reinforces that experience, by reaching out to others who have been similarly disabled by the transformation of the Tarai (thus, the opposition between Tharu and pahāṛiyā maps onto that between Tarai and Hill [pahāṛ]). Class and ethnic identity exist in tension with each other. Class consciousness (of being poor, "backward," and exploited, a belief that is widespread among Tharus throughout the Tarai), dovetails easily with the belief that those in the Tarai who are poor, backward, and exploited are *Tharus*. Class and ethnicity converge. The existence of the common ethnonym facilitates this process.

LANGUAGE, IDENTITY, AND THE CENSUS

The permitting of marriage between people formerly defined as belonging to different jāt may be understood as a symbolic statement of ethnic (jāt) unity. But Tharus also believe that a defining aspect of a jāt is that its members must share a language in common. Ramanand Singh put it in dire terms to the Tharu convention in Tetariya: "Bhāsa gayo bhane thāru jāti chainā" [If the language is lost, there won't be a Tharu jāt].[6] This presents a problem (which must be resolved intellectually), for Tharus, on the face of it, do not share such a language. The Tharu elite holds that Tharus shared a common language at some time in the distant past, and that this language has become differentiated over time. Ramanand Prasad Singh, for example, argues that all Tharus speak a single language which has regional variations and dialects, even difference of intonation. But Tharu intellectuals cannot agree on which existing language most closely resembles the original; all assert that their own particular tongue is primal and the others are deviant. Because (according to Singh) Tharus now lack a system of writing, they have no books and magazines, and are thus unable to standardize their language (even though all of the different Tharu languages are readily written in the Devanagari script). Singh claims that Tharus once had such a system of writing, but the policy of the Ranas was to destroy all publications in Tharu and other tribal languages.

Tharus speak Indo-European languages that are variants of, or influenced by, the languages spoken generally in the regions in which they live. From west to east, these are Awadhi, Bhojpuri, and Maithili. This diversity is clearly incompatible with the single-language thesis put forward by Ramanand Prasad Singh and other Tharu intellectuals. Most Tharus acknowledge that they speak different languages. Thus Parshu Narayan Chaudhari, in a speech to the meeting in Kathmandu described earlier, observed that it was difficult to establish one language because Tharus had lived separately in different districts, and their languages had consequently been influenced by other tongues. As a result, he said, Tharus now spoke different languages. Narendra Chaudhary acknowledges the problem posed to Tharu unity by language and offers his own solution (he speaks here in English):

> We have the different languages, this is the problem.... We have not decided which language should be the real Tharu language, this is a very difficult task. In my view, when we all said we are one Tharu, I said: let us allow the Dang people's language to be the real Tharu language. It has a different dialect no other community speaks, so that language would be the best for the Tharus if all Tharu agrees. But this is very difficult!

What is important for Narendra Chaudhary is that no one else speaks the Dangaura language; as a symbol of Tharu identity, it would serve as a definitive boundary marker if only all Tharus would agree to adopt it and learn it.

Ramanand Prasad Singh's home district of Saptari lies within the boundaries of ancient Mithila. One of his goals is to establish the Tharu dialect he speaks as a distinct language from Maithili (other Tharus from that area, however, will simply say that they speak Maithili, and presumably return this answer at the census, for the census returns up to 1981 show negligible numbers of Tharus in districts such as Sunsari and Saptari, which have large Tharu populations; see table 7). Until the 1991 census, returns were made by language only, and not by ethnicity.[7] Unlike in Chitwan, where language is an unambiguous aspect of Tharu identity (only Tharus, and some peripheral groups such as the Darai and Musaher, speak Chitwan Tharu), in the Maithili-speaking east it is a significant area of contestation. Here, almost everyone speaks Maithili, and language has been defined in the census as a key symbol of identity. One

Tharu writer suggests that the discrepancy in the numbers of Tharus enumerated in the 1991 census by language (989,541) and by ethnicity (1,194,224) may be attributed to Tharus in Mahottari, Sarlahi, and Dhanusha giving their language as Maithili and Tharus in Bara, Parsa, and Rautahat reporting it as Bhojpuri (Chaudhary "Tharu" 2055: 1).

If one is Tharu, then one, by definition, must speak Tharu. Prior to the 1991 census, it was only by demarcating themselves linguistically from other Maithili speakers that Tharus in these districts could make themselves visible in the Nepali polity. If, in Chitwan and the western Tarai, Tharu identity defines itself in contrast to that of hill immigrants, it is very likely (and this is a subject for further research) that in the east, Tharus contrast themselves with the Maithili- and Bhojpuri-speaking descendants of Indian immigrants who were encouraged by the Ranas to settle in the Tarai.

It is not surprising then that Ramanand Prasad Singh, the most articulate and forceful Tharu intellectual in Nepal, has committed a good deal of his energy to demonstrate that Tharu (the dialect spoken in the eastern Tarai) is a different language from Maithili. Maithili, he says, has its roots in Tharu; he attempts to demonstrate this by investigating the etymology of various Maithili words. More generally, he places great emphasis on developing and standardizing the various Tharu languages. When I met him in 1991 he was in the process of compiling a comparative dictionary (or vocabulary list) of different dialects. Similar linguistic research is also being carried out by Amar Lal Chaudhary of Saptari, who is Tej Narayan Panjiar's son-in-law.

The census figures over the years have given a misleading idea of the actual numbers of people in Nepal who consider themselves to be of the Tharu jāt. The under-enumeration was virtually total in the Bhojpuri- and Maithili-speaking eastern Tarai districts prior to the 1981 census. In Saptari, the home district of Ramanand Prasad Singh, the 1971 census recorded only five Tharus (table 7). The 1981 census shows a dramatic change in the numbers; the Tharu population has increased from 5 to 35,511 individuals. This increase can probably be attributed to the consciousness-raising work of Tharu ethnic activists. In 1991 the Tharu Kalyankarini Sabha made a determined effort to address the situation posed by the under-enumeration of Tharus in the census. One of the resolutions adopted at the Biratnagar convention was that Tharus should be urged to give their native language as Tharu, rather than as Maithili, at the 1991 census. For good measure, Parshu Narayan Chaudhari, in his closing speech at the convention, urged Tharus to append the term *Tharu* after their name in the census returns

Table 7. Tharus in the censuses of Nepal, 1971–1991

	1991 (ethnicity)		1991 (language)		1981 (language)		1971 (language)	
	N	%	N	%	N	%	N	%
Jhapa	9,600	1.62	4,801	0.81	1,461	0.30	2,518	1.02
Morang	60,391	8.95	52,460	7.77	33,772	6.32	35,640	11.82
Sunsari	75,079	16.20	73,274	15.80	44,704	12.97	56,731	24.30
Udaypur	18,369	8.30	19,512	8.82	11,341	7.10	3	0.00
Saptari	61,640	13.24	80,526	17.30	35,511	9.37	5	0.00
Siraha	20,617	4.47	11,523	2.50	3,541	0.94	17	0.01
Dhanusha	1,697	0.31	145	0.02	33	0.01	9	0.00
Mahottari	7,522	1.71	4,598	1.04	1,144	0.32	190	0.06
Sarlahi	15,359	3.12	11,371	2.31	7,941	1.99	406	0.23
Makwanpur	526	0.17	134	0.04	24	0.01	13	0.01
Rautahat	21,821	5.27	14,759	3.56	6,337	1.91	258	0.08
Bara	49,389	11.88	19,779	4.76	16,356	5.13	718	0.30
Parsa	32,701	8.78	1,203	0.32	246	0.09	110	0.05
Chitwan	45,392	12.80	44,640	12.60	31,179	12.01	24,718	13.00
Nawalparasi	73,494	16.85	31,598	7.24	15,710	5.09	36,928	25.20
Rupandehi	55,803	10.69	20,056	3.84	482	0.13	7,510	3.08
Kapilavastu	43,709	11.76	37,571	10.10	13,431	4.97	21,969	10.70
Dang-Deukhuri	111,574	31.48	105,018	29.60	84,061	31.56	72,475	43.19
Banke	45,564	15.95	44,197	15.50	17,519	8.53	22,121	17.60
Bardiya	153,322	52.81	149,865	51.60	73,876	37.12	77,469	76.10
Surkhet	4,941	2.19	4,498	1.99	1,610	0.97	2,171	2.07
Kailali	206,933	49.52	198,497	47.50	120,534	46.74	103,939	80.85
Kanchanpur	70,544	27.35	59,795	23.20	22,369	13.24	29,452	43.00
Total Tharu	1,194,224	6.45	993,388	5.37	545,685	3.63	495,881	4.29

Sources: His Majesty's Government 1984; Aryal, Regmi, and Rimal 1982; His Majesty's Government 1999.

Note: The sum of Tharus in the districts listed in the table does not equal the figure for Total Tharu, which includes those Tharu who have settled outside the Tarai in Kathmandu and elsewhere.

[a] Until the 1991 census, returns were made by language only, and not by ethnicity.

(also one of the decisions taken at the meeting). A leaflet issued by the Progressive Tharu Youth Organization, a group based in Lalitpur, Kathmandu, was printed up to be distributed in the villages. An edited translation of it, with interpolations to clarify possible ambiguities, is given below. The document is entitled "An Appeal to the Tharu Society." It clearly demonstrates Ramanand Singh's views on the Maithili question.

> This is an appeal, to protect, foster and to firmly establish our...honored traditions.... Therefore, in the national census of the coming year 2048 [c.e. 1991], let all the individuals in Tharu society not forget to write down, and cause to be written down, that their mother tongue is Tharu bhāsā.
>
> It has already been proved that the Maithili language, which, up to now, has obtained for itself the position of Nepal's second language, is the Tharu language in disguise. In reality, the progenitor of Maithili is the Tharu language. In a majority of the Tarai districts Tharu bhāsā is spoken. There is only a small percentage, not even worth counting, of Maithili speakers. In terms of districts, in only two or three [is Maithili spoken] and even in those, one finds it spoken by only one or two jāt in a few pockets.
>
> Those individuals deputed [to carry out the census] in past censuses (...of whom a majority supported Maithili) took advantage of the simplicity and uprightness of the illiterate rural members of Tharu society to mislead them, and because, in place of Tharu bhāsā, they wrote down Maithili [i.e., in the census return], Maithili has come to occupy the position of Nepal's second language.... This organization makes a heartfelt appeal to Tharu society, to all intellectuals, teachers, government officials, students, businessmen and farmers, let us enter our mother tongue in the forthcoming national census as "Tharu bhāsā" and cause [the census enumerators] to do the same [i.e., ensure that census enumerators enter the language in the return as Tharu, not Maithili].

The most significant aspect of this document is the last paragraph. It accuses the census enumerators of deliberately entering the language of Tharus as Maithili in the census returns. The point was explicitly made to me by Narendra Chaudhary: "They [census enumerators] have totally cut down our population numbers.... the Tharus are still even more than 30 lakhs [3 million] living in this country but the census was hardly 15 to 18 lakhs. So what we thought when the new census comes, we all write Tharu so the real number of Tharus will come." It is because

Tharus speak different languages in different regions that "they have got the opportunity to cut down our population."

The effect of such an action is to swell the apparent support base for various political organizations which claim to represent the interests of "Tarai" people. This category is thought of as those people in the Tarai who are of recent Indian descent, and who may be identified in the census by the languages they speak—Maithili, Bhojpuri, and Awadhi. The Tharu, on the other hand, have been part of the Nepali polity since its creation, and their elites functioned as revenue collectors for the state in the Tarai. In other words, the Tharu consider themselves to be of "Nepali extraction" rather than Indian. The census enumerators are also those people—such as schoolteachers and minor government officials—who are likely to be active in ethnic or caste associations of their own, and to have an interest in swelling the number of one linguistic category rather than another. Implicit in this document is the accusation that the census enumerators were working to further the interests of those who stood to gain some political benefit from expanding statistically the number of Maithili speakers in the population. Thus, the last sentence in the "Appeal" emphasizes that not only must the Tharu affirm that his mother tongue is Tharu, but he must also ensure that that is what the enumerator writes down. Whether the language spoken by Tharus in Siraha and Saptari is distinct from the Maithili spoken by others in those districts is a moot point; what is important is that the state recognizes the linguistic category *Tharu*, which is implicitly identified with a particular ethnic community. What is at issue in the census is not language per se, but *identity*, for which language, in this instance, is simply the vehicle.

A comparison of the 1991 census data by language and ethnicity seems to bear out the argument that the numbers of people who identify themselves *ethnically* as Tharu have not been accurately represented by calculations based on language (table 7). There is, however, a significant anomaly in the data that I cannot explain, and it pertains to one of the most politically significant districts of all, Saptari. In almost every case, the numbers of Tharus in each district show an increase when enumerated by ethnicity as opposed to language. This is what one might expect. Significant increases are posted in Siraha, Rautahat, Bara, and Nawalparasi, but in Saptari, the numbers drop from 80,526 to 61,640. I can offer no reason why people who are not ethnically Tharu would claim to speak the "Tharu" language, especially as only five people had claimed to speak it in Saptari in 1971.

The Tharu elite's insistence that there is (and has to be) a common Tharu language, and its inability to determine what that language might be, has had an unexpected consequence. Following the success of the 1990 popular movement for democracy in Nepal, the Nepali state abandoned its attempts to discourage the use of the many local languages spoken in the country and introduced a more liberal policy regarding the use of the various ethnic languages (Sonntag 1995). One consequence of this policy was that beginning in August 1994 Radio Nepal began to broadcast the news and other programs in the languages spoken by the country's major ethnic groups.[8] This posed an immediate problem for the Sabha, to which Radio Nepal turned for help to identify the appropriate Tharu language, for it forced the Tharu elite to confront practically an issue which they had hitherto been able to deal with purely on the theoretical level. Sonntag writes that the Sabha never responded because it could not agree on the answer. Narendra Chaudhary told me, however, that the Tharu Kalyankarini Sabha eventually decided to recommend that in the eastern Tarai the news be read in the Morangiya Tharu language because it was distinct from Maithili, which most Kochila Tharus speak, and that in the west the Dangaura Tharu language should be substituted. The news was already being read in Maithili, in recognition of the large Maithili-speaking population in the eastern Tarai. This appears to be a tacit recognition on the part of the Tharu leadership that, given the politics of language in the eastern Tarai, it would serve no purpose to insist on a (Maithili) Tharu broadcast that would be effectively indistinguishable from the Maithili broadcasts that were already taking place.[9]

Radio Nepal's attempt to democratize the airwaves was condemned by Ramanand Prasad Singh on the grounds that the government was trying to sow dissension among Tharus by forcing them to make an invidious choice among their various languages. What Singh wanted the government to do instead was to "help unify the Tharus by employing linguists, using scientific methods, to determine what is the Tharu language," for he was convinced that such an exercise would confirm his own arguments (Sonntag 1995: 117).

SHAPING IDENTITY THROUGH LITERARY ACTIVITIES

Literary activities, in particular the collection and publication of folk songs, is another important activity for the Tharu Kalyankarini Sabha and other locally based Tharu ethnic organizations throughout the Tarai.

Local elites in different areas of the Tarai publish magazines and pamphlets in their regional languages. Typically, the contents consist of poetry, folk songs, essays, and short stories and carry such titles as *Hamār Saṁskṛti* (Our culture) or *Thāru Saṁskār* (Tharu ritual).

Hamār Saṁskṛti was published by a Tharu youth organization in Chitwan known as the Tharu Kalyankarini Yuva Sabha. The publishers raised money for it by screening videos of Hindi movies in the villages, but the scarcity of funds meant that only one issue was ever published. It is typical of such publications, of which I collected many from Chitwan and districts of the Eastern Tarai. It carried original poetry, folk songs, and essays on "Our Chitwan," "Tharu History" *(itihās)*, "Tharu Society," and so on. These were all in the Chitwan Tharu dialect.

One poem published in this magazine is an exhortation to the young to avoid the temptation of the bazaar and its cinema halls and to become educated; another, in the same vein, proclaims,

> We Tharus are a backward jāt!
> Our only work is to till the fields!
> (Let's) make knowledge reading and writing!
> Let's abandon our bad speech!

In this context speech may be interpreted two ways, either as custom (and in fact culture and language are often taken as synonyms for each other) or in its literal sense. In the latter case, what the writer may be referring to are the obscenities to which Chitwan Tharu village speech is sometimes casually given, and which is considered by the elite to be another sign of backwardness.

Literary production of this sort appears to have been more highly developed in Dang than in Chitwan, and at least initially, more overtly political in content (McDonaugh 1989; 1997: 277). McDonaugh describes a journal in the Dangaura Tharu language, *Gotcāli*, of which only one issue appears to have been published (in the early 1970s) before it was banned. Several members of the editorial committee were jailed. Copies of the journal are no longer available, and McDonaugh says people are not willing to talk about it. As far as he has been able to ascertain, however, apart from calls for social reform and the championing of language and literature, which all such publications have in common, the more overtly political content called for "the Tharu to unite in the face of adversity to fight for their rights" against the oppression they faced at the hands of Brahman-Chhetri landlords. McDonaugh adds that "At times the language may have been frankly left-wing with the implication that the Tharu farmers' predicament should be seen in the more global context of the peasant class struggle" (1989: 200).

At the national level, these literary endeavors are encouraged by the central committee of the Tharu Kalyankarini Sabha. It publishes annually *Thāru Saṁskṛti* (Tharu Culture). What is interesting about this magazine is that it is a self-conscious example of the attempt to create a unifying symbol for Tharus built around language. Its articles, covering the same subject matter as described above, are reproduced in the original languages of the authors, who represent virtually every Tharu language group in the Tarai. It is, as it were, a symbol of unity in diversity.

The story of the founding of *Thāru Saṁskṛti*, as told by Tribhuwan Choudhary, illustrates the preeminent position that Ramanand Singh gives to language as an essential attribute of Tharu identity. In the early 1970s there were few Tharus in Kathmandu, and most of them were from Saptari and lived in rented apartments. Because Singh owned a house, it became a gathering place for Tharus living in the valley. Every Saturday they would meet to discuss how to bring about progress for their community, but, according to Tribhuwan, who was newly returned from the Soviet Union where he had gone to pursue his education (he is an economist), their activism never advanced very far beyond talk. Feeling that something needed to be done, he approached another Tharu, Shanker Chaudhary, with the suggestion that they raise funds for scholarships for Tharus. He and Shanker put up twenty-five rupees each as seed money and took it to the next Saturday meeting with their proposal. But Ramanand Singh was adamant that the highest priority was the preservation of the Tharu language and culture and that the publication of a magazine was a key instrument to achieve this. He persuaded the meeting that any funds raised should be used to publish a magazine and not be used for scholarships. The first issue of *Thāru Saṁskṛti* came out in 1977/78 and the magazine was published continuously until 1985, when it became dormant, to be revived in the 1990s.

From the meetings held in Singh's house was born the Kathmandu chapter of the Tharu Kalyankarini Sabha. It needed permission from the zonal commissioner to raise funds for its activities, including the publication of *Thāru Saṁskṛti*. The zonal commissioner refused permission, alleging that the Tharu Kalyankarini Sabha was an illegal organization; all such organizations, he claimed, were illegal since the institution of King Mahendra's system of panchāyat government. But the Sabha had invited King Mahendra to attend their B.S. 2021 convention in Sarlahi. He had sent them a polite refusal thanking them for the invitation. The Sabha had kept the letter, which Tribhuwan showed to the zonal commissioner as proof that the king did not disapprove of their existence. The zonal commissioner's opposition, says Tribhuwan, then ceased, and the Sabha was allowed to collect funds.

The way Tharus think about themselves and their place in Nepalese society is illustrated in this translation of an unpublished poem in Tharu made available to me by the author, who is the founder of the Tharu Yuva Club in southern Chitwan, described in the last chapter. The sentiments expressed in the poem represent the way many Tharus in Chitwan, whatever their social position, think about themselves and their relationship to the rest of Nepali society:

> We became Tharu
> Having no knowledge of our title [thar]
> Where our origin was
> We knew not our home.
>
> We came from Chitragarh
> To be squatters in the Tarai
> Calling it Chitwan
> The Rapti became its fence.
>
> Depending on the *ghar guruwā*[10]
> The Tharus have begotten many descendants
> Giving goats,[11] pigeons, and doves to the gods
> And if this is to no avail, giving to other spirits.
>
> The time of the Chitrasari *melā* came
> The Tharus all gathered there
> Saying they have to give a bottle to the *kul devatā*[12]
> They drink it themselves.
>
> These Tharus are like oxen, honest and generous
> One is an animal, the other a poor peasant
> Jogis, beggars, exploiters, and businessmen
> The Tharus, being farmers, support them all.

The poem touches on a number of themes that recur in different contexts of Tharu discourse in Chitwan. The first is ignorance, the ignorance Tharus have of their history, specifically their origin. This ignorance is taken to be a sign of backwardness both by Tharus and by Brahman-Chhetris (see Guneratne 1999). But in the next verse the poet seeks to explain Tharu origins by positing that they were refugees from Chitragarh, a Rajput city which fell to a Muslim army. It recalls their claim to Rajput status. It is an uncertain claim, though; not everyone subscribes to it, and it is vigorously disputed by others.

Another theme the author touches on is what he sees as the moral weakness of Tharu society, the inability of Tharus to do things properly and carry out a project to its successful fulfillment. Their weakness for liquor and their alleged inability to focus on the essential issues leads them to deny the offering to the god for whom it is intended. (The Chitrasari melā is an important fair that takes place in November on the day when Tharus go to do puja at the temple of the god Chitrasen Baba in eastern Chitwan.) The final theme is the exploitation of Tharus; they carry the weight of a wider society on their shoulders, which they must sustain through their labor. Satya Narayan Chaudhary of Chitwan, who helped me translate this poem, suggested that the comparison with oxen in the last verse had a dual meaning. On the one hand, the Tharu, like the ox, was the one who did the work, slow, patient and uncomplaining.[13] The ox obeys the ploughman or his driver, going wherever he is directed. On the other hand, he pointed out, the ox is the relative of the cow and shares in her sacredness; the ox is like a god.

THE REPRESENTATION OF ETHNIC UNITY

The Tharu Kalyankarini Sabha has had seventeen nationwide conventions since its founding up to 1999, when the organization celebrated its jubilee (see table 5). Important men from many different villages within the district, and others from elsewhere in the Tarai attend these meetings. Few Tharus (from that particular district), especially those with social and economic power, can be unaware that it is taking place. Many individuals from my field site in Chitwan, both well-to-do and poor, remembered a meeting (probably a meeting of the national committee or a district-level meeting) that had been held in a village located about a ninety-minute walk from Pipariya. That meeting provided an opportunity for many of them to learn about the Sabha and its professed goals.

These national conventions of the Sabha, held biannually since 1991, are the most important ritual events in the organization's calendar. They are not only public affirmations of the unity of Tharus throughout the Tarai, they are also an arena in which that unity can be shaped and ordered. But they are also the circumstances in which tensions within Tharu society are oftentimes revealed. I was able to attend two of these conventions, in 1991 (Morang District) and 1999 (Udaypur District). The late Norwegian anthropologist Sigrun Ødegaard attended a third, the 1995 meeting in Bardiya District; I draw on her description (Ødegaard 1997) in what follows.

The Thirteenth Convention of the Tharu Kalyankarini Sabha was held in the Morang District on January 6–8, 1991. The opening ceremony was held in the Biratnagar town hall; Biratnagar is the largest town in Morang, and one of the most important towns in the Tarai. It was attended by Krishna Prasad Bhattarai, the prime minister, as chief guest. But the actual business of the convention, which took up two full days of meetings, was held in the village of Tetariya, several kilometers distant. The large hall was filled to capacity, there being approximately equal numbers of men and women, sitting in separate sections. The audience consisted of members of the Sabha from various districts, local Tharus from Morang District, journalists, policemen, and others. The prime minister was late in arriving, and Ramanand Prasad Singh occupied the time by making a speech to the assembly. He touched on all the points elaborated above; the three-thousand-year history of the Tharu, their settlement in the Tarai from the Mechi to the Mahakali rivers, their Buddhist antecedents, and the theme of Tharu unity in diversity. The prime minister finally arrived two hours late, to be garlanded, and filmed by camera crews. The presence of the prime minister thus assured some television coverage of the event. The remainder of the proceedings consisted mainly of speeches, three of which are of note here.

The first was by Parshuram Bhagat Chaudhari, a reader at the local college and an important personage among the Tharu of the district. The core of his speech centered on how Tharus had become indebted to exploitative moneylenders and had lost their land; they had fallen on hard times and had been forced to emigrate to places as distant, he claimed, as Punjab or Kashmir. His speech was in Nepali, but he interpolated in English the comment, "This is the survival of the fittest *yug* [epoch; age]; either be able or be perished." He ended by appealing to the prime minister to institute reservations for Tharus (on the Indian model for Scheduled Castes and Tribes). He was followed by Parshu Narayan Chaudhari, lately minister of education under the panchāyat regime. After welcoming the prime minister, he pointed out that the Tharu were the ādivāsi (indigenes) of Nepal. They were settled here even before the word *Nepal* had been applied to this country (applause). The Tharu, he said, were able only to do agriculture; they were ignorant of other skills and so became poorer and poorer. The Tharu of Dang (his home district) had been forced to emigrate to Banke, Bardiya, Kailali, and Kanchanpur, and even to India, because their circumstances were so desperate. The Tharu were poorly educated. His speech continued in this vein, cataloguing the perceived shortcomings in Tharu society, and ended by appealing to the prime minister to institute reservations in educational institutions for the Tharu. This has continued to be a principal motif in speeches made at the Sabha's meetings, as Ødegaard notes with respect to the fifteenth meeting in Bardiya (Ødegaard 1997: 123–124) and as I observed at the jubilee celebrations in Udaypur in 1999.

The prime minister's response was not encouraging. He criticized ethnic groups for voicing their individual group demands rather than speaking in collective terms of the whole Nepali nation. Rejecting the characterization of Tharus as being poor and exploited in the Nepali context, he said there were poor Brahmans and Chhetris in the mountains who till the land of rich Rais. What, he asked, does the Nepal Congress want? It wants to develop all Nepalese, whatever their *jāt*, to bring them into the mainstream. He called upon the Tharu Kalyankarini Sabha to carry out a social revolution *(samājik krānti)* within Tharu society, by which he meant a reform of "backward" practices.

While the various factions of the Communist Party have been receptive to varying degrees to this demand for reservations, put forward not only by the Tharu but by other janajāti groups, the Nepal Congress has been adamantly opposed to it (Hoftun, Raeper, and Whelpton 1999: 336). Nor do all Tharus in positions of leadership agree that such a policy is desirable; Padma Narayan Chaudhari, a Tharu leader in the Nepali Congress, observed in 1996, "It is very disappointing that some groups are demanding reservation rights for their community.... It will only divide the people and the nation. If there are reservations, they should be purely on an economic basis" (quoted in Hoftun, Raeper, and Whelpton 1999: 336).

After the opening ceremonies in Biratnagar, the meeting shifted to a Tharu village named Tetariya several kilometers away. The local village school served as both venue and dormitory for the delegates. There were more speeches here and a discussion of the various resolutions put forward, but on the final day, the undercurrent of opposition to the central committee on the part of younger men from the far-eastern districts, including Morang, burst into the open. It happened as R. P. Singh was making a speech introducing the new central committee, which had been selected by its predecessor and contained most of the old faces. Part of the way through he was interrupted by a small group of people from Morang, loudly insisting on a free vote. The meeting broke up into a number of groups engaged in vigorous argument. Soon

Ramanand Prasad Singh speaks at the 1991 Tharu national convention, Tetariya village, Morang.

thereafter, Ramanand Singh took up the microphone to challenge those critics of the central committee to put forward their own candidates, but no one came forward. After him, person after person came forward to take up the microphone and give their opinion of the situation. A young man from Jhapa told the assembly that he thought the candidates selected were good, but that they ought to be elected not selected. The last to speak was Parshu Narayan Chaudhari, who addressed himself to the task of pacifying the gathering. He appealed to reason and to parliamentary practice to resolve disputes. He defended the various members of the central committee, starting with Kewal Chaudhari ("the eyes of Tharu society") and ending with Ramdin Chaudhari of Chitwan, who had been selected president. He cited their services to the organization. He countered the opposition's view that only Tharus with educational qualifications should be made office bearers (Ramdin had none). He argued that the committee had been selected after much thought. If other people had other names to propose, they should submit them to the central committee and they would be carefully considered. But, he emphasized, the Tharu Kalyankarini Sabha was not a

Shanti Choudhary, the only woman in the Tharu Kalyankarini Sabha's central committee in 1991, talks to children and women in Tetariya during the Sabha's national convention.

political organization that had to have elections. Today, he ended, they were guests in Morang; if it had been any other district, they would have "gone to fight," but how could they quarrel with their hosts? It was a consummate performance, and it silenced, at least for the time being, the opposition.

More generally, the incident demonstrates the power of the central committee in the affairs of the organization; opposition to it, such as it is, is generally localized and can thus be isolated. In Tetariya, the opposition consisted of young men from Morang, Jhapa, and perhaps a few other eastern districts; most of the delegates from other areas of the Tarai watched the affray from the sidelines but did not participate.

While the men were engaged in the debates and discussions described above, Shanti Choudhary, the only woman on the central committee, was engaged in a different sort of activity, "motivating" local Tharu women to improve their lot. I was not there to record what went on, but my wife accompanied Choudhary during our stay in Tetariya and made the following notes:

I sat with Shanti Devi Choudhary and listened and watched her "motivate" some women here, telling them that it was necessary for them to get an education and to see to the education of their children so that they would be able to stand on their own feet (this is as close to the Tharu/Nepali idiom as I can get in English). She also showed photos of the things sold in her shop in Kathmandu and invited, in fact exhorted, the women to market their own things through the shop. There was considerable apparent interest in this proposal. As well as a lot of agreement with her rather passionate assertions of the pitiable lot of Tharu women and cries of "didi, dinus" [sister, please give] as she passed out her pink sheets detailing the problems of Tharu women. She gave these out to "pareko" [educated] women, urging them to read them and tell other women in their homes about the contents.

After showing her photos of her training in Nuwakot...and her photos of various Tharu handmade things, two women came to the front where Shanti was sitting, and with the help of the other women explained the younger woman's predicament: she had been left by her husband. He lives here in this village. She has returned to her *maiti* [natal home]. She wanted to know what could be done, and to enlist the help of some "*thulo manche*" [important person] on her behalf. Shanti took the name and address of her husband and said when she returned to Kathmandu she would send a notice. I asked her what would happen then. She said he would be summoned to court. There was also some discussion about whether he would beat her after receiving the summons.

The lack of women in leadership positions in the Tharu Kalyankarini Sabha has been another point of contention between the younger members of the organization and its older leadership (Ødegaard 1997: 119). Shanti Choudhary was no longer a member of the central committee when Ødegaard attended its fifteenth convention (the third since the success of the 1990 People's Movement). That meeting took place in April 1995 near Bhurigaon bazaar in Bardiya District, in the village of Baganaha, and was attended by Dilli Bahadur Chaudhari of BASE. The focus at this meeting, according to Ødegaard's account, was the need to "mobilize" and "teach" the Tharu of the west, as well as the desirability of registering as a nongovernmental organization.

With respect to the issue of mobilization, a consciousness of ethnic unity is weaker among the Tharu in the far west of Nepal than it is elsewhere. Ødegaard notes that "neither the Dangoras nor the Ranas" who lived in her research area "commonly refer to each other as Tharu" (1997: 52); moreover, she adds, "among the two main Tharu groups in the far west, the pan-Tharu message has so far gained very little support" (114). And with respect to the issue of registering as an NGO, the phenomenal success of BASE (described in chapter 4) is no doubt an example.

In fact the issue of bonded labor has been taken up by the Tharu Kalyankarini Sabha "as a political argument to use against the government in its claim for special treatment of the Tharus and in its attempts to mobilise and recruit Tharus in the far-western districts" (137). And as in Tetariya in 1991, the meeting was the occasion for a confrontation between the reform-minded youth and their more conservative elders (128).

The Tharu Kalyankarini Sabha celebrated its fiftieth anniversary in Hadiya village in Udaypur, under the chairmanship of Narendra Chaudhary, the former commissioner for the Bagmati Zone. He had become the Sabha's president since I had first seen him at Gaushala almost eight years earlier. Hadiya is not an easy village to get to; it is well off the main east-west highway and from Saptari is approachable only via an unpaved sandy road on uneven terrain. The difficulty of the journey did not prevent thousands of people from all over the Tarai attending the meeting; four busloads came from Kailali alone. The chief guest was Girija Prasad Koirala, and the speeches touched on the same topics that I have discussed above. One difference from 1991, however, was the cultural show that was performed in the evening, after the opening ceremonies were over and the prime minister had departed.

The show began at 10:15 P.M. and lasted into the small hours of the morning. Dance troupes of Tharus drawn from different Tarai districts performed dances peculiar to their areas in a variety of local folk costumes. The performances took place on the main podium, which was lit for the occasion by florescent lights powered by a generator (Hadiya village is not electrified) and the brilliant lights of a film crew. A crowd of between two and five thousand people was present. I watched troupes of dancers from Kailali, Kapilavastu, Mahottari, Chitwan, and Jhapa (whose dancing was a little "filmy"—that is, influenced by the style of Hindi movies—as my friend Man Kumar, who had accompanied me from Chitwan, observed). I did not stay to watch all the performances; I was told that each district was supposed to send at least one group, but many sent two and Kailali contributed four. Each group had two performances, a song and a dance. There were so many groups that all could not be accommodated in one evening, and I was told that the show would be carried over to the next night.

Such cultural performances, drawing on dance troupes from various districts, are becoming an increasingly popular way in which Tharu unity and identity is represented to the public, both Tharu and non-Tharu. Like the magazine *Thāru Saṁskṛti*, it is a demonstration of unity in diversity. The many different dance troupes, present and performing on the same stage, are there because they are all Tharu; that is the only reason that brings them together. There have been other such performances, one in Saptari in 1994, organized by the Tharu Culture Society, and another in Chitwan in 1998, organized as part of the Ministry of Tourism's "Visit Nepal 1998" year. The description of what happened was provided me by Man Kumar Chaudhary, an activist with NIDS, the Tharu NGO.

The Ministry of Tourism joined forces with the central committee of the Tharu Kalyankarini Sabha to sponsor a Tharu cultural performance in Sauraha. Dance troupes were invited from a number of different districts to perform. Amrit Khã of Rautahat, the secretary of the Sabha (who also happens to be Man Kumar's affinal relative), sent a letter to the Chitwan district committee asking them to organize the event. The letter went astray. Amrit Khã arrived in Chitwan sometime afterward to find out why there had been no response to his letter and discovered that nothing had been done to organize the event which had already been advertised and to which Tharu cultural troupes from other districts had been invited. With two days to go before the scheduled date, NIDS, feeling the honor of Chitwan was at stake, stepped into the breach. NIDS arranged accommodations for the visitors in various tourist lodges in Sauraha, the gateway to the national park and the venue for the performance, and even loaned the event 10,000 rupees. This was later reimbursed (in whole or in part) by the Ministry of Tourism. The event itself, which drew large crowds of local people and tourists, was a success and was videotaped in its entirety.

Man Kumar related this story to me during a conversation I was having with him and a Tharu forester whom I had met in Hadiya. The forester was being critical of what he saw as the Sabha's lack of organization; there was no one appointed to be a liaison with outsiders, no one to go to with a question. There were no facilities provided for the hundreds of people who had flocked to Hadiya (although I did see temporary eating arrangements set up in an adjacent field); nonetheless, he noted, the Sabha was looking after its own members.

Both the forester and Man Kumar thought that a great deal of money was being spent on this event to little constructive purpose. From their point of view, the money would have been better spent on education or development activities of some sort. All of the expenses (including the cost of souvenir briefcases and caps with logos) had been raised within the Tharu community. The forester pointed out that there were Tharus like him who had special skills and who would be willing to contribute their expertise to the Sabha, but the Sabha was unable or unwilling to harness their energy. His point was that at lower levels, people wanted to work on constructive activities, but at higher levels in the organization they were only interested in politics.

When Man Kumar also observed that the Sabha was unable to do anything constructive, I asked him why he and his friends, instead of founding NIDS, had not joined the local district committee of the Sabha and used it to work toward their goals of village development. He replied that they would not have enjoyed the same freedom that NIDS provides. They would have been subject to the constraints imposed by the central committee of the Sabha, whose approval they would need for their initiatives, and they would also have been required to send some of their revenues to the central committee.

Another opinion was given by a man from Saptari who used to be active in the Sabha. He felt it to be without direction and unable to properly utilize what he thought were the vast amount of funds flowing in from abroad to help the Tharu. This remark was probably inspired by the generous funding provided to BASE by various international donors, but he may have also meant that the Sabha was unable to tap into the flow of foreign funds that had benefited Tharu NGOs like BASE and NIDS. He attributed the problem to the leadership, which consisted of people who, despite being well educated, could not devote their full time to the Sabha. They were people affiliated with political parties who wanted to show "the king and the foreigners" that they were leaders with a large following. "People who should be leaders," he said, "are those who are not only well educated [or are intellectuals] but also committed to social work" (yesmā basne ko lāgi pivar [pure] "social worker" hunu parchhā ra "full academic worker" hunu parchhā). Even so, he felt that things were getting better, and he attributed this to the energy of the current president, Narendra Chaudhary, who was visiting every district, he said, to see for himself the problems Tharus faced.

Perhaps in response to such criticisms and in response to the criticisms of friends overseas like Tribhuwan Choudhary (2057), elite Tharus in Kathmandu have begun to be proactive in the area of promoting welfare. Shortly after the Hadiya convention, many of the prominent Tharus in Kathmandu set up an organization—the Sahakari Finance Corporation—to provide credit to Tharu entrepreneurs in the city. Despite some overlap in membership, this loan-making organization is not associated with the Tharu Kalyankarini Sabha. According to what I have been told by Tribhuwan Choudhary, about three hundred individuals have borrowed money from this corporation to start their own businesses. This credit organization was set up with funds of Rs 1.8 million available to it.

As of August 2001, it had a turnover of Rs 5.1 million with profits of Rs 300,000. Most of those who have benefited from its activities are apparently from the Eastern Tarai, from Parsa to Saptari. Following on this example, Tharus in Saptari established their own Finance Corporation; and much to everyone's surprise, Tribhuwan claimed, there have been no defaults so far.

THE VIEW FROM BELOW

One morning in late February, I noticed a gathering of about half a dozen men from the nearby village of Merauli, who were squatting on the verandah of my neighbor in Pipariya, the jimidār Ram Bahadur. In Rana times, Pipariya and Merauli together formed one maujā, or revenue village, and the affairs of Merauli fell within the jurisdiction of the jimidār of Pipariya. Merauli had no jimidār of its own. The men on my neighbor's verandah had with them a live chicken (its legs bound tightly together to prevent it from escaping) and a bottle of *raksi* (rice liquor). In accordance with custom, they had come to seek the jimidār's approval of an elopement (*uderi*) that had taken place. The jimidār's acceptance of the raksi and the chicken would signify his assent to it. Assent might be denied in cases where the elopement violated "caste law"—for example if the woman in question was of another jāt or if she were considered a "blood relation" of the man (consanguineal kin). If this assent were withheld, in former times a meeting (*pajani*) would have been called of all the jimidārs of that pragannā, to decide the fate of the woman. This is no longer the case. But even though the institution of jimidār has been abolished by the state, many Tharus still feel the necessity, when norms of proper social behavior are violated, to have the matter judged by some competent authority—in this case, by the personages who have been customarily invested with that authority.

In the present case, a man (who I will name Shanker) had eloped with his "mother's sister"—that is, a woman of his mother's lineage and generation—which made the marriage, in effect, incestuous. When the jimidār appeared, about half an hour after I had arrived on the scene, he refused to accept the raksi and the chicken. He said the matter would be referred to the local area committee of the Tharu Kalyankarini Sabha. They would have to wait for its decision.

Shortly after this incident, I had to leave for Kathmandu to renew my visa, a process that took me more than a month. Soon after my return, I asked the jimidār what had been the verdict on the elopement. He said that they had decided to allow it because the woman, although a member of her husband's mother's lineage, was not a close relative (i.e., she was her husband's mother's sister in a classificatory sense only). What he did not tell me was that the Sabha had charged the man's father five hundred rupees to hear the case, a fact which caused considerable resentment among many people in the village. Although I was nearing the end of my fieldwork, I had wanted to extend my stay in Pipariya to conduct a socioeconomic survey of the whole village. As a consequence of conducting the survey, however, I learned how nearly every Tharu family in Pipariya and Merauli felt about the case and its resolution.

The levying of this fee caused considerable resentment among many in the village, particularly in Merauli, where many in the population are bahāriyās (servants) or of bahāriyā descent. The chief cause of anger was that a fee had been levied simply to hear the case: "They say, come to us for advice, and when we do they charge us five hundred rupees!" People in general would have been willing to pay a fine if a violation had occurred. Although the jimidār and the Tharu Kalyankarini Sabha have no legal authority to exact a fine or penalty, custom and the realities of power relationships within the village make it unlikely that a member of one of the poorer families would refuse to pay. On the other hand, wealthier families can and do ignore the Sabha's judgments, a fact of which the village poor are well aware.

That the Sabha existed as an organized entity with the avowed aim of "uplifting" the Tharu was unknown to many of the men of bahariyā extraction interviewed in the course of the survey. Almost all of them had heard, however, of the committee that had raised the fines for elopement of married women from Rs 60 to Rs 1,000. The consensus was that the Sabha was an organization of the rich that cared little for the poor. One old man was blunt in his opinion: "Kām haine lagalai" [It's useless]. He observed that the Tharu Kalyankarini Sabha tries to make unimportant things (like the elopement of married women) important, but fails to do anything about things that matter, like lack of education among Tharus or the "upliftment" of their socioeconomic status. (This is an ironic observation given the Sabha's aims, but the Sabha has no solutions for the lack of education among the poor. Its policies and programs serve the interests of middle-status farmers and the well-to-do.) Another man observed, "They make this committee for the welfare of Tharus and say we must respect it and obey it. But after they get these posts, they just oppress us."

A former bahāriyā, who had acquired some land and was now doing reasonably well, was contemptuous of the Sabha. He claimed that if a peasant went to it, complained that his wife had eloped with another man, and asked it to collect the fine that custom and its own rules required that the other man should pay, it would first ask the plaintiff to deposit five hundred rupees with it. This sum would be returned to the plaintiff, he said, if the defendant paid the fine. If the fine were not paid, however, the money would not be returned.

Another man commented that while the Sabha has said many things about elevating the economic condition of Tharus, of improving their education, getting rid of "bad" customs, and of getting married with little expense, they have not been completely successful (purā rūpmāsaphal bhaeko chainā). The aims and purpose of the organization were good, it was just that it failed to live up to them. The Tharu Kalyankarini Sabha pays little heed to what the poor have to say; they listen only to the rich, the powerful and the educated; they do *their* work, not the work of the poor: "Hāmi jasto garīb sukumbhāsiko kurā uniharu sundai sundaina" [They just don't pay any attention at all to what poor landless people like us have to say].

Not all the village poor held negative opinions about the Tharu Kalyankarini Sabha. A kinsman of the jimidār, though not of the same lineage, felt it was important for Tharus because it discouraged great expenditure on festivals, hospitality, and so on. Some men approved of the idea that there should be an organization of Tharus to promote the general welfare. They held no strong opinions about the Sabha itself; it made mistakes, but overall it was a good thing. But even men who thought the organization had some saving graces (such as its efforts to eradicate "bad customs") were resentful over the matter of fines because it has not been applied to all Tharus equally. Even the jimidār's brother felt that the Sabha was too preoccupied with matters such as elopement (which he considered to be unimportant) and paid insufficient attention to more pressing needs, such as education.

The village poor unfavorably compared the response of the Sabha to their own complaints with the way it had responded to the problems of the village elite. They had in mind its handling of two similar cases, both of which involved the elopement of married women.

Thagamani Mahato of Merauli is the son of a cowherd, and holds a job in a local tourist hotel as a laborer; his brothers work as bahariyās. He had married a woman who subsequently eloped with a man from the neighboring Padampur panchāyat. Thagamani took the matter to the local area committee chairman of the Sabha, visiting him several times and pressing him to collect the fine. The Sabha did nothing on his behalf. Finally, Thagamani stopped going. He concluded that the Tharu

Kalyankarini Sabha acts according to the status of the supplicant: if he is rich, it will do something; if he is poor, it will not.

Villagers in Merauli contrasted this incident with that involving the daughter of Ram Chandra Chaudhari, a wealthy jimidār in a neighboring village. Ram Chandra was not only an important jimidār, he had also held local elective office under the former panchāyat government. His daughter eloped with another man after the feast, which sealed her betrothal to a man chosen by her father, had been eaten. In this case too, the intended bridegroom was from Padampur panchāyat. The jimidār refused to pay the fine when the pradhān panch of Padampur went to collect it. When her would-be husband, also a well-to-do Tharu, complained to the Sabha, it took up the matter with the jimidār. He continued to refuse to pay. It was a clear-cut case; by its own rules, they should have fined him five hundred rupees; but (in the opinion of the village poor) because he was rich, and one of the social circle of those who formed the local committee of the Sabha, the organization ended up doing nothing about it.

Before he approached the Sabha, Thagamani had tried himself to collect the fine from the family of the man who had eloped with his wife. He went with three of his kinsman to Padampur. The relatives of that man, who had heard of Ram Chandra's refusal to pay the fine for his daughter's elopement, told him to come back with the fine from Ram Chandra before they would consent to pay their own. All these matters were raised again when the Tharu Kalyankarini Sabha met to discuss Shanker's elopement with his mother's sister and the organization was publicly criticized. It promised it would try to do something about Thagamani's case, but as one Tharu villager observed to me, it always made promises and nothing ever came of them.

In order to get some statistical sense of how villagers felt about the Sabha, I included a question on the survey which asked respondents (the household heads) whether they felt the Tharu Kalyankarini Sabha to be very important for the welfare of Tharus, somewhat important, not important, or whether they had no opinion on it. The results are reproduced in table 8. When I posed the survey question to Ram Bahadur, who is a member of one of the Sabha's local committees, he chuckled and then remarked that he supposed he ought to answer "very important" but that I could put him down for "somewhat important" instead.

All household heads but one readily responded to the survey and expanded on their opinions in the way I have described above. The exception was Busaha, a man with little land of his own. Although he inveighed against the Tharu Kalyankarini Sabha, he seemed very reluctant or nervous about responding to the survey question. He said he was prepared to agree with whatever other villagers were saying about it. His wife, who was listening, criticized him for being afraid to give his opinion. His negative views of the Sabha derived from how it had dealt with his daughter's elopement. She had gone away with a Bantar Tharu (a Tharu jāt considered inferior to his own). According to custom, the man should have been fined and the girl returned to him. He went to the Sabha to ask it to take action, but they ignored his request and nothing happened about it. He was now very nervous about the "rich" people (Tharus) in the village; "We are poor people," he said explaining his refusal to tell us whether he thought the Sabha important or not, "the rich people can cause us trouble."

His account of what happened did not, however, appear to violate any of the Sabha's own rules, although from Busaha's point of view, it violated customary rules against marrying out of one's jāt. But the Sabha had decreed that such customary laws no longer applied where the other jāt in question was also Tharu (indeed, by definition, it would no longer be another jāt), nor was Busaha's daughter betrothed to any other man. It was a simple elopement, nothing more. But Busaha did not understand it that way, and felt he had been poorly treated.

Social norms and values that help people to evaluate behavior become rules of behavior only when they can be enforced. It might be a violation of a social norm or a value for a man to elope with a woman of different caste, but for such a value to become meaningful, it must be enforced, the offenders must be made to feel in some way the opprobrium of society. If someone can defy with impunity the values of his society, it suggests that that system of values has ceased to be relevant to its circumstances. For those whose thinking has not kept pace with the times,

Table 8. Opinions of Tharu household heads regarding
the Tharu Kalyankarini Sabha

Opinion	N	%
Very important	3	3.6
Somewhat important	19	22.9
Not important	17	20.5
Don't know/no opinion	6	7.2
Not heard of it	38	45.8
Total	83	100.0

Note: Of Tharus who had heard of the Tharu Kalyankarini Sabha, 6.7 percent thought it very important, 42.2 percent thought it somewhat important, and 37.8 percent did not think it important.

contradictions arise that must be resolved. When people confront what seems to be a violation of behavior they deem appropriate, they seek higher authority to resolve it, as they have been accustomed to (or compelled to) do in the past.

I asked the family and neighbors of the man who had eloped with his mother's sister why they took the matter of his elopement to the jimidār in the first place, since they were not legally obliged to do so nor subject to any other compulsion. Although they were angry at the way in which the Tharu Kalyankarini Sabha had dealt with the issue, they were nonplused by the question; an alternative course of action, such as dealing with the matter themselves, clearly had not occurred to them. If they had not done so, and if the jimidār had heard about the affair (as he was bound to) and had decided to intervene, and then they had publicly rejected his authority, a confrontation might have ensued. Even though the jimidār no longer has any formal authority (in the legal sense), he is still the largest landowner, and poor men cannot afford to alienate him. From the jimidār's point of view, unless he is economically a very powerful individual (which is the case with the jimidārs of Sultana, but not of Pipariya), he might prefer to let sleeping dogs lie, rather than precipitate a confrontation that might affect his standing in the village. I suspect this is what Ram Bahadur would have preferred, as he is an easygoing and tolerant man. In this case, the situation was so bizarre that the man's family instinctively turned to the customary higher authority to resolve something that they felt to be beyond them. And despite their condemnation of the Sabha for charging a fee of five hundred rupees simply to hear the case, they paid it.[14]

The incident of the elopement described above, which occurred a few months before the election, accentuated a general feeling shared by Pipariya's poor: the local Tharu elites were interested only in promoting the interests of the well-to-do. This negatively affected the perception that villagers had of the political causes that the elites espoused. That the Tharu did not follow the lead of their elites in this one locality (and doubtless in others) does not necessarily mean that poor Tharus are more class-conscious than ethnie-conscious. Indeed, poor Tharus are critical of Brahmans in general, and the villain of the piece in stories of how Tharus lost land is typically the impecunious Brahman who exploits Tharu generosity. Both the rhetoric of the Tharu elite and the experience of the Tharu poor suggest that Tharus as a category are poor and exploited. Yet, to the poor, the Tharu elite seems incapable of addressing those issues. Furthermore, its own activities (such as the levying of a five-hundred-rupee fee to adjudicate disputes) were seen as a participation in that exploitation. The Tharu poor in Pipariya turned to the Communist Party because the communists presented themselves successfully as representing the interests of the landless and the impoverished.

What the Sabha Has and Has Not Achieved

In terms of its stated goals—the economic betterment and "upliftment" of Tharus and the eradication of what are seen as backward social customs like the consumption of alcohol—the record of the Tharu Kalyankarini Sabha has been mixed. BASE, for instance, has done much more in a far shorter time to improve the economic status of the very poorest Tharus than the Sabha has been able to accomplish in its fifty years. In Chitwan the recent campaign against liquor has been organized not by the Tharu Kalyankarini Sabha (which appears to have had very little impact on liquor consumption by Tharus in the district) but by ordinary men and women of all ethnic groups, Brahman, Chhetri, and Tharu. But the Sabha has been successful in putting an end to child marriage, and it can probably take some credit for facilitating education at least for Tharus of middle and elite status, particularly in the east.

All this does not mean that the Tharu Kalyankarini Sabha is ineffective as a vehicle of ethnic identity formation, however. It has been ineffective as a vehicle through which significant improvement can be brought about in the lives of the poor. Although it sees itself as a social service organization, its constituency is not the very poor but the middle and upper strata of Tharu society, those with some education and the hope and expectation of a life free from the drudgery of agricultural work. The Tharu elite cannot be compared here to the Maithili Brahmans and Kayasthas, however, whose attempts to create a Maithili identity failed to generate much support among other Maithili speakers. In that case the problem was bringing a number of different, historically separate ethnic groups (Brahmans, Kayasthas, Yadavs, etc.) under the umbrella of an all-encompassing identity: being Maithil. In the matter discussed in the last section above, however, the Tharu of Pipariya are divided by class, not ethnicity. There are then two issues to keep distinct, because they have different outcomes: development and ethnicity. On the first, the Tharu poor, as we have seen, are critical of the Sabha; on the issue of the ethnic unity of the Tharu, in two years of fieldwork in Chitwan and the Tarai, I heard no voices raised in dissent—except perhaps for Busaha's. Similarly, the criticisms leveled at the central committee by younger Tharus, including the Sabha's own activists, does not call into question the wider project of Tharu unity; at most it challenges the way the Sabha sets about achieving it. The idea that the Tharu are a single jāt is on its way to becoming more or less universally accepted by Tharus, particularly those in the east (which in this instance refers to those districts to the east of Dang-Deokhuri). Such holdouts as there are appear to be in far-western Nepal. This state of affairs did not just happen, it came about through the active cultural production of the Tharu Kalyankarini Sabha and the supporting activities of smaller local organizations.

My purpose is not to evaluate the Tharu Kalyankarini Sabha's performance as a social service organization but to show how it has been a catalyst for the emergence of a shared ethnic identity among a widely disparate population. Indeed, as this chapter shows, it has played a centrally important role in crafting such an identity and in imbuing the idea of being Tharu with new meanings. From the point of view of ordinary Tharus, there is no contradiction in being critical of the Sabha for its class bias while accepting its message of Tharu ethnic unity. A measure of the Sabha's success and its appeal to a large segment of the Tharu population is that it has survived and prospered for over fifty years. During that period it has expanded from its base in the Bara and Rautahat districts to encompass every district in the Tarai, and in all of them it has created district organizations that allow it (in principle if not always in fact) to reach down to the village level. Its successful national conventions, especially the impressive event put on at Hadiya, demonstrate that the organization is capable of mobilizing thousands of people for its purposes from all over the Tarai. Whatever the tensions within the organization and the criticisms to which it is subject from within and without, a significant support base exists for the Sabha.

The activists who established the organization more than fifty years ago could have accepted the received definition of their jāt identity and focused their efforts on the Kochila of Bara, Rautahat, Sarlahi, and perhaps other eastern Tarai districts. A Kochila ethnic identity would have been a much easier thing to produce. That they chose to cast their net wider must be understood in terms of the changing configuration of their political and economic environment, which made such a course both logical and necessary.

CHAPTER SEVEN

Conclusion

The task of the various social sciences [is] to lay out the structural conditions for various forms of conscious action.
                                        Roy Bhaskar, *Reclaiming Reality*

I have argued in this book that a system of shared symbols is not a necessary precondition or basis for the development of a common ethnic identity. The shaping of an ethnic identity is cultural labor, but not one that requires a preexisting shared symbol around which that labor is organized. Tharu identity has emerged through a complex engagement with the praxis of the Nepali state over two centuries. The state itself has provided both the reasons for and the means through which those sharing the ethnic label *Tharu* could imagine a new kind of identity. The centralizing state—first of Gorkha and then of modern Nepal—shaped the conditions to which Tharu societies had to adapt. The cultural production of identity is not simply a matter of selecting one cultural symbol or another as the basis on which to organize an identity, as the Maithil Brahmans found out to their cost. Culture gives meaning to experience, and because the Maithili-speaking people of North Bihar lacked this shared experience, the identity promoted by the Maithili-speaking elite garnered few followers outside their own caste groups. The imagination does not work in an experiential vacuum, "in the realm of pure thought," as Marx said of German philosophy, but in relation to life experience. The process of identity formation described in this book requires what P. Berger and S. Pullberg call the *objectivication* of social and cultural life: "the moment in the process of objectivation in which man establishes distance from his producing and its product, such that he can take cognizance of it and make of it an object of his consciousness" (quoted in Bhaskar 1989: 76).

Culture may be understood as a system of symbols through which the world is apprehended and organized. These symbolic forms are shaped and transformed by the specific circumstances in which people find themselves and the ways in which they engage those circumstances to reproduce themselves as social beings. Circumstance in this context refers to the political, economic, and social conditions—as well as the strictly ecological—in which human beings must act, circumstances that are themselves shaped by other human beings acting according to very different logics. The organizing context for these conditions, in the instances described in this book, is the state. It is culture understood in this way that explains how Tharus, in their imagination as well as in that of most others, have come to be a single ethnic group.

My understanding of the process whereby culture and society are fashioned owes something to Marx and, more proximately, to the British philosopher Roy Bhaskar and the French sociologist Pierre Bourdieu. Culture and society are emergent forms. They are always in the process of becoming, shaped through the activity of conscious human agents who both reproduce and transform the cultural systems and social structures they inherit at birth, which in turn provide the necessary conditions for their activity. Society (and culture, a term Bhaskar does not explicitly discuss but to which his ideas can be extended) are relations, practices, and symbolic systems that preexist any individual human being but exist only by virtue of the conscious activity that human beings engage in. Bhaskar puts it thus:

> Conscious human activity, consists of work on *given* objects, and cannot be conceived as taking place in their absence. These objects may be material or ideational. And they may be regarded as the results of prior objectivations. Now this suggests a radically different conception of social activity, an essentially Aristotelian one: the paradigm being that of a sculptor at work, fashioning a product out of the material and with the tools available to him or her. (1989: 78)

Bhaskar calls this the transformational model of social activity. Such a model is in my view critical to understanding how Tharus negotiated or transcended their received social and cultural structures to transform, rather than simply reproduce, their received practices. Bhaskar's model is formulated in opposition to the two principal ways in which the relationship between social structure and human agency has been conceptualized in the social sciences, Weberian individualism and Durkheimian collectivism. Social structure, which consists of sets of relations among persons, preexist us but they exist in virtue of our everyday activities which reproduce or transform them. The same is true of culture, which consists of the relations that obtain among symbols, values, and ideas. Provided that the conditions of life remain stable, culture may be reproduced in relatively unproblematic fashion. However, when something happens in everyday life that is out of the ordinary, it is not simply accommodated or interpreted in terms of preexisting cultural structures. The process of integrating historical facts into those structures, of placing them in some kind of context so that they may be understood, is in itself a profoundly transformative act, transformative that is of the symbolic system into which they are integrated. To put it another way, culture may set the limits on what can be thought, but it does not determine it. The first proposition opens up the possibility of human agency and creativity as human beings engage the circumstances of their life; the second negates it.

The stability of social and cultural forms is predicated on what Bourdieu calls *doxa*: "a quasi-perfect correspondence between the objective order and the subjective principles of organization [that makes] the natural and social world [appear] as self-evident" (1977a: 164); it is belief without awareness or recognition that alternate truths may exist. The more stable the objective order, the more completely is the symbolic order—the subjective principles of organization—reproduced, and "the greater the extent of the field of doxa" (166).

Related to the concept of doxa is that of *habitus*, which Bourdieu conceives of as a system of dispositions mediating between structure and practice, delineating the (unconscious) boundaries within which the human subject carries out strategies. These strategies are the range of choices determined by habitus: what the actor regards both as possible and, in a loose sense, permissible. Thus habitus endows agents produced by a particular structure (the social and symbolic structure into which a person is born) with a system of predispositions, which engender practice, which in turn is adapted to the structure and serves to reproduce it (1977b: 487).

The "natural" character of social facts, hitherto accepted as part of the given order, becomes subject to critique when an objective crisis brings some aspect of doxa into question. The recognition of alternative possibilities engendered by crisis produces orthodoxy; of the various alternatives, only one is to be treated as a legitimate or possible choice. To treat culture in this way helps us better understand the process of identity formation described in this book.

Let us start with the border that demarcates Nepal from India. Rana Nepal is often described as a hermit kingdom or as being isolated from the rest of the world. This is not entirely true, and the border was far from being a hermetic seal. The Tharu, as a border people, were in intimate contact with social and cultural process on the other side, and the sons of the influential and wealthy among them were, as we have seen, educated in India. The transformations being wrought by colonialism on Indian society and culture are one aspect of the overall dynamic structure of social and cultural relations with which the Tharu had to contend and which inevitably shaped their praxis.

The other set of transformations, also originating outside of Tharu society, came about in post-Rana Nepal, that is, during the second half of the twentieth century. The relations between the state and the people were themselves fundamentally transformed during this period, and the result of these transformations was to facilitate or enable the objectivication (to use Berger and Pullberg's term) of Tharu identity.

Ethnicity was not an adequate or sufficient basis for political action in premodern Nepal. Prithvi Narayan Shah, when he set out to conquer what would become the modern state of Nepal, ruled over a polity consisting of different linguistic and cultural groups. It was a polity of "caste-Hindus" and "tribes," all of which participated in his enterprise. Insofar as they participated at all in the affairs of the polity, it was on the basis of a structured, codified inequality. The salient forms of identity were those of the local community (a village or a cluster of villages) and, beyond that, the group within which people could contract socially approved marriages. People identified, in other words, with their local units of social reproduction. Tharus did not view Tharus in other areas of the Tarai as being the same kind of people until modern times. Ethnic labels that were once simply "a convenient status summation...readily and incontestably claimed by anyone (except untouchables) who wants it" (Fisher 1986: 3)[1] are today becoming reified as something more enduring. They are not simply a summation of status but a description of the very essence of one's particular humanity.

There was no reason in agrarian societies such as Nepal for lateral "ethnic" integration of similar groups occupying adjacent or even discontinuous territories, organized around key symbols of one sort or another, to occur. What made that possible was the establishment of unified polities by centralizing states. The political unification of various Himalayan principalities in the eighteenth and early nineteenth century laid the basis for such ethnic integration in Nepal. The many different groups and categories of people living in this newly unified polity were brought into specific relationships both with one another and to a new source of power based in Kathmandu.

The circumstances enabling these different groups of people to coalesce or organize themselves into the ethnic categories we see today in Nepal is similar to those that brought forth caste (and ethnic) categories in India. They include political unification, the establishment of electoral politics, the development of the infrastructure of communication, and the adoption by the state of the rhetoric of equality (the idea that all citizens of the state are entitled to the same rights and privileges). These have all made it possible and even desirable that local groups seek out others like themselves in some way with whom to ally, in order to buttress their relative position in the polity.

Much of the writing on elite-led identity formation has noted, correctly, that elites do not start off with a cultural tabula rasa on which they inscribe the particularities of the identity they wish to promote. There are elements or symbols in preexisting cultures that elites use as the basis for fashioning new identities. The point is that these identities are in some fundamental sense new, and not merely extensions into contemporary times of an older cultural identity. Sometimes these attempts succeed, and sometimes, as Brass has pointed out with respect to the Maithili movement, they fail. What is interesting about the Tharu is that such preexisting symbols are absent; what these groups shared was a common ethnonym and a region characterized by a particular name (the Tarai). That was the extent of the received cultural raw materials from the past that Tharu ethnic activists had to work with. Neither of these facts need necessarily lead to any particular outcome; in premodern times the Tharu unproblematically thought of themselves as belonging to very different social orders. Indeed, they were unaware of the existence of many of the groups sharing the same ethnonym, and rejected the idea of consociality with those groups with whom they were in fact acquainted. And as we saw, the two facts mentioned above—the shared ethnonym and territory—have led to two separate outcomes for people sharing this ethnonym in Nepal and in India—outcomes shaped by the particular state structure in which they find themselves.

The shaping of ethnic identity and consciousness among the Tharu, their awareness of themselves as a distinct group with certain common interests, and their claim to a common identity with similar groups throughout the Tarai region with whom formerly they had no connection—all have developed out of transformations in the economic and social organization of lowland Nepal during the last forty years. These transformations constituted a series of crises affecting Tharu society that brought into question certain assumed truths about the social and symbolic order and functioned as a catalyst for the emergence of a new orthodoxy, a new way of thinking about themselves and their place in the wider polity of Nepal. The most significant crisis was the transfer of population from the surrounding hills (and earlier from India) on a scale so vast that it has reduced the Tharu to minority status almost everywhere. Along with the change in population have come the agents and institutions of the state, which have sought to bind the Tarai more closely to the Nepali state and its economy.

Three aspects of this process are of special importance. The first was the creation of a school system in Nepal that made education available to a broader spectrum of the population. Among other things, education made possible a shared language—whether Nepali or Hindi—in which to communicate. The idea of education itself, as a necessary good in a modernizing society, also helped shape the understanding Tharus have of their place in the polity. The identification of Tharus as a backward group, illiterate and therefore underprivileged, is an important organizing symbol of their identity.

The second was the establishment of a network of roads that bound the Tarai together more effectively and thoroughly than it was possible to do for the hills. While the road network greatly facilitated contact among the various Tharu groups (consider for example the impossibility of organizing an event like the jubilee meeting in Hadiya in the absence of good communications), it also facilitated widespread immigration into the Tarai, creating conditions that encouraged such linkages. Young men who had gone to school and college first in India and then, in greatly increasing numbers, in the institutions that sprang up in the Tarai towns after Rana rule ended, played an important role in creating the Tharu Kalyankarini Sabha. What gave their activities force and relevance was the issue of land.

The fundamental transformation that took place in the relation of Tharus to their land (itself the outcome of transformations in their relations to other Nepalese and to the state) is the third important factor shaping the cultural changes that this book describes. Local Tharu leaders had historically been important intermediaries between the state and village populations in the Tarai (Krauskopff and Meyer 2000). Their position was increasingly threatened first by immigrants from India and later, after the malaria eradication program, by the influx of settlers from the hills whose presence helped to change the economic and social structure of the region.

Land is both a symbol of identity (for the Tharu see themselves as the indigenous people of the Tarai, in contrast to the recently arrived immigrant groups) and the root factor in the development of ethnic consciousness. But it is not a symbol in the same way that religion or language or a myth of origin is a symbol. A particular religion or a particular language and their associated practices can lend themselves to boundary formation. What is at issue here is land as an abstract concept, the land necessary for a farming people to reproduce their existence. The important question is how Tharus think about the land and their relationship to it. Prior to modern times (which in Nepal can be said to date from the end of Rana rule), Tharus had no particular attachment to any given piece of land. Land was relatively plentiful and, because of labor scarcity, could be had for the asking. This is no longer the case. The intensive settlement of the Tarai, the clearing of forest and woodland, and the cultivation of pastureland closed off the land frontier. The agrarian reform failed to benefit most Tharus because they did not understand the significance of registration of land. Lastly, many of them lost some or all of their lands to immigrants through chicanery and fraud. Correspondingly, the way the Tharu think about land has changed; it has become something that was once theirs but then lost. Tharus have been reduced fairly precipitately from a situation in which land was not an issue into one in which it is. With the land frontier closed off and the population increasing, almost all Tharus are faced with the prospect of diminishing land and limited opportunities outside the agrarian economy. Tharus tend to attribute this impoverishment not to market forces or the capitalist world system but to the hill people (and in the eastern Tarai to Indian immigrants also) who have settled among them, occupying land formerly cultivated by Tharus. This experience is at the heart of Tharu consciousness; shared by all Tharu communities in the Tarai, it has facilitated the emergence of a shared ethnic identity. What binds them is this shared sense of loss.

While I have emphasized in this book the role that elites have played in the shaping of a Tharu identity, it should be apparent that elites are not a homogeneous group with a singular vision of what they wish to achieve. Indeed, an elite may be divided on the question of the essential nature of the identity it seeks to promote or fashion.[2] Among the Tharu of Nepal, there are at least two major organizations of ethnic identity formation. The first, the Tharu Kalyankarini Sabha, is the vehicle of the Tharu establishment. The second, Backward Society Education (BASE), is rooted more firmly among ordinary Tharu villagers but limited in its immediate impact to the Western Tarai. The membership of the first is largely drawn from the traditional elite: the descendants of jimidārs and large landowners, their numbers supplemented by those from the middle strata of Tharu society who have found success in the new economy. The leadership of the second group has emerged in one generation from the grassroots. They were, for the most part, impoverished share-croppers and tenant farmers of Parbatiya landlords who, by skill, deter-mination, and the financial support of foreign organizations, succeeded in forging a strong social movement firmly rooted in the Tharu commu-nity but also beginning to reach outside it to other marginalized groups.

While the Tharu were in contact with the populations of both the hills and the plains, and while they were an important source of labor power for the economic exploitation of the Tarai's resources, they were politi-cally marginal. They were not a warlike people and posed no military threat to their neighbors. On the contrary, the colonial accounts over the last two centuries suggest that they withdrew in the face of encroach-ment. It was probably this relative political unimportance that led to their becoming the only significant ethnic category (other than the Tamang) to be made enslaveable under the old *Muluki Ain*. It is note-worthy that most of the ethnic groups placed in the category of nonenslaveable liquor drinker were all involved, with the exception of the Newars, in the military. The caste hierarchy in nineteenth century Nepal had as much to do with the relative political importance of the various groups ordered within it as it had to do with attributes of purity and pollution. The Ranas never recruited the Tharu into the military, nor did the British recruit them into the ranks of their Gurkha mercenaries.

Given that theories of ethnicity tend to stress cultural unity of some sort in the formation of ethnic identities, or at least common symbols such as religion or language, it is instructive to consider what lies at the heart of Tharu ethnicity. Despite the insistence of the Tharu elite on the idea of a common language, the Tharu share no common symbols such as religion, language, or myth of origin, certainly none that they do not also share with numerous other ethnic groups. Insofar as Tharus are similar to one another in terms of their culture or their cosmology (and such similarities are limited), it is because they are part of a larger fabric of North Indian civilization. The *bramathān*, for example, was sometimes cited to me by Tharus as a cultural feature all Tharus had in common. A bramathān is a shrine to village deities, usually located by an imposing tree of some kind. Bramathāns are found in Tharu villages in Chitwan and throughout the eastern Tarai, but they are also a phenomenon of village religion in North India generally, and in that context are by no means peculiar to Tharus. On the other hand, Tharus share symbols (such as language) with other ethnic groups around them, but not with other Tharus. What draws Tharus together is not an a priori cultural principle but a material force: the issue of land and their identification with a particular territory, the Tarai.

The bramathān in Pipariya, a red-silk cotton tree where the village deities reside. Tharu villages in much of the Tarai have bramathāns, which are also a feature of North Indian villages.

While ethnic identities are defined against other ethnic identities, not all of the identities in the universe of possible contrasts are equally salient. Tharu identity is defined in opposition to that of immigrants into the Tarai who have displaced them as the region's primary landholders. More precisely, Tharu identity is defined in opposition to that of those social groups who pose the most immediate challenge to Tharu control of the cultural and material resources required for the social reproduction of Tharu society. In Bourdieu's terms, this is a crisis affecting doxa; the conscious activity that Tharus engage in to deal with this state of affairs shapes both their symbolic and their social structure.

The politically significant ethnic identity is the pan-Tharu one: the identity that subsumes all Tharus in Nepal. Other Nepalese tend to treat Tharus as a uniform group, not distinguishing between different local communities. Feeding into this pan-Tharu identity is a "confrontation" between local Tharu groups (in Chitwan, Dang, and elsewhere) and hill immigrants, which generates the consciousness on which the more inclusive Tharu identity can be based. There has been no forging of class unity between poor Tharus and poor Brahmans for a number of reasons, including the lack of social intercourse between them. One very important reason, however, is that Tharus see poor Brahmans as the ones who, through intelligence and cunning, robbed them of their land. The symbols of identity generated by their unhappy confrontation with Brahmans include the idea of being ādivāsi (the presence of preferably more successful later arrivals is required to make the first to arrive conscious of that status), and of being not only ādivāsi but dispossessed and exploited ādivāsi. These ideas, while they have helped unite Tharus, have the potential to forge links between Tharus and other ethnic groups espousing a similar set of ideas.

The various factors cited above affect Tharus of different class categories in different ways. The growth of communications and education, development programs, and the institution of the census are factors affecting the consciousness of elites. The elites are the segment of the population most likely to be oriented to participation in national political life, to achieve relatively high levels of education, and to travel outside their villages and local areas. The Tharu elite has worked to strengthen the links between its members in different districts through the Tharu Kalyankarini Sabha and through marriage alliances. But the poor, who have fewer resources and less freedom of movement, are much less likely to encounter their peers in other districts. They are also far more likely to be adversely affected by "development" (the monetization of the economy and the commodification of agrarian relations for example) than the elite. When measured in terms of food security, the standard of living for many poor Tharu peasants (particularly of the bahāriyā class) has not improved.

The significant contribution of dominant social groups in promoting and shaping ethnic identity is to stitch together—through material and symbolic acts including the establishment of ethnic associations, the widening of marriage relations, the rhetoric of ethnic unity, and so on—the various different traditionally endogamous groups sharing a common ethnonym in the Tarai. They are helped in this endeavor by the existence of a named category sanctioned by the state, which they can build upon as they organize themselves to meet the challenges of a polity undergoing rapid political and economic transformation. The point was explicitly made by Narendra Chaudhary, president of the Tharu Kalyankarini Sabha, in an interview with me in 1997, a few years after I had drafted the initial statement of the argument presented in this book. He had just observed that Tharus west of the Narayani (which forms the western border of Chitwan District) were "totally different" from those to the east. I responded by asking him how, then, they could be thought of as the same jāt. He replied,

Our culture is different, our dress is different, everything, you see. But we are all Tharus. So now we assume that we are all one. And let's be united and let's fight with the government so that we can get something for our people, because Tharus in totality, they are backward with the other communities. So our aim is...we have to fight against those people, we have to get our needs and whatever, you see, from the government. So we are backward in comparison to the other communities. So let us come [under] one umbrella and fight with the government so we can get the reservations, the political appointees, the government [offices].

While Tharu groups, despite having increasing contacts with one another as forests were cleared and communication networks were established, continued to reproduce themselves as separate societies and distinct moral communities, the elites began to reconstitute themselves as new sub-units of social reproduction. They established marriage ties with members of their own social class in other groups, they shared symbolic forms based on a common education and assimilation to Nepalese culture, and they shared a material culture and styles of consumption that diverged from that of the poorest strata within their local societies. Modernization, in other words, acted to homogenize the upper levels of Tharu society. The Tharu poor, with little or no land and confined to wage labor in agriculture, are unlikely to participate in these processes. They have little access to schools, and they are less likely (particularly the women) to be bilingual or Nepalized. Yet their relative economic deprivation reinforces their sense of being Tharu, for they are more likely than their better-off fellows to be treated with disdain and condescension by Brahman villagers. What the Brahmans disdain is not their poverty but their Tharuness (to which their poverty is sometimes attributed). Unlike the Rana Tharu of Naini Tal described by Srivastava (1958; 1999: 14–17), where certain sanskritizing Rana Tharu clans (*kuri*) reconstituted themselves as a jāt separate from and superior to other Rana Tharus, rejecting the name *Tharu* altogether and replacing it with *Thakur*, meaning "lord," the Nepali Tharu elite is unlikely to separate itself in the same way from the Tharu poor. The logic of status and improvement that motivates Tharus in Nepal is different from that which impelled the Rana Thakurs of Naini Tal to sanskritize.

Ethnicity has been a preoccupation for anthropology since the late sixties (Eriksen 1993: 1). Its increasing frequency in anthropological discourse reflects a growing awareness of the political salience of cultural identity in the modern world: the phenomenon of population groups constituting or reconstituting themselves on the basis of symbols inherited from the past or newly created to make demands of the state. Ethnicity is one way of expressing a relationship of alliance and unity with some in opposition to others. Modernization enables ethnic identity to come into being. Where communication is poorly developed (whether through lack of transport, illiteracy, or some other fact), identity tends to be parochial, concentrated on the local community or network of kin. Modernization, a project pursued by the state, enables such identities to expand to include others in response to the new circumstances that modernization brings into play.

Outsiders, as well as those who are part of it, often describe ethnic identity formation in terms of the play of cultural symbols. A common view is that ethnicity is a primordial attribute of the group; the symbols of group identity and the referent of the ethnonym have, supposedly, always been invested with the same set of meanings that one finds in the present. But if the ethnic identity of any given group is viewed as primordial and enduring, if the symbols that are meaningful today are supposed to have always been understood similarly, then culture loses much of its dynamism. In contrast to such views I have argued that although ethnicity presents itself to us as a cultural phenomenon (albeit one whose implications are political), its genesis and development must be sought in the material forces—such as class relationships, the state, and the process of modernization—that make it relevant as a principle of identity formation. Identities are formed and transformed as the circumstances in which individuals and societies find themselves change. The formation or enactment of identity and the attempts to act in terms of that identity is a way to address these circumstances and shape them. It is to those circumstances that we must attend.

Ethnic identity may then be thought of as the cultural expression, drawing on a symbolic repertoire inherited from the past, of these underlying systems of political, economic, and social relations. The particular form of cultural expression which has been termed ethnic identity is catalyzed by the competition between groups over resources—both material and symbolic—that are necessary for their social reproduction. When Tharus believe that some culturally defined group—not the rich but the Brahmans—benefit disproportionately or unfairly in the allocation of these resources, then ethnicity is likely to come into play as a "mask of confrontation" (Despres 1984; Vincent 1974).

Explaining ethnicity by reference to a shared culture does not adequately account for the emergence of identity. Sharing certain symbols does not necessarily lead to sharing an identity. Culture is like the water in which a fish swims. Normally we are unaware of culture; it is simply the way that we unreflexively *are* in the world. One's cosmology is accepted as natural and requires no justification; it just is. It is only when cosmologies or ways of being in the world threaten each other or come to be seen as a series of alternative possibilities (when they become denaturalized, in other words) that they rise to objective self-awareness and become the basis for a more self-conscious ethnic awareness. In such circumstances, cultural practices become "practices of collective identity," to use Talal Asad's phrase (Asad 1991: 323). In order to understand what generates those practices of collective identity, we need to focus on the underlying structures of political, economic, and social relationships that generate them. New forms of social structure arise from preexisting forms (they could not arise from anything else), but they do so through the active intervention of human agents. Those agents inherit certain ideas, a symbolic system, but those ideas are shaped and reshaped in light of the existing political and economic structures. These structures generate both activity (praxis) and discourse (see Bhaskar 1989). Praxis and discourse are shaped by the underlying reality even as they transform it. Practice is not determined, nor is it created through some process of free will. It is a strategy operating within limits set by the conditions of its production.

NOTES

Chapter One

1. "Mechi dekhi mahakāli sammā hamro jāt eutāi ho." The rivers referred to form the eastern and western borders of Nepal and are about eight hundred kilometers apart. According to Christian McDonaugh (1989: 201), the same sentiment is found in books in the Dangaura Tharu language published by the Tharu elite in the Dang Valley.

2. The earliest reference to the Tharu appears to be by Al Biruni in the eleventh century (Sachau 1910: 201) He describes the inhabitants of Tilwat, a country on the border of "Naipal" as "*Tarû*, people of very black colour and flat-nosed like the Turks."

3. Nepalization refers to the process by which members of other ethnic communities in Nepal adopt the language, religion, and other cultural practices of the country's dominant Brahman-Chhetri ethnic groups. These practices are the cultural template for a Nepali national identity.

4. Smith (1986: 26) cites language, religion, customs, institutions, laws, folklore, architecture, dress, food, music, arts, color, and physique—culture as a laundry list of traits.

5. In Gellner's usage, "entropic" cultural and social traits are those that have the capacity to become evenly distributed within the society at large, thus enabling those who bear them to become assimilated into the general population. If a particular social group is characterized by a trait that precludes it from being assimilated into the society at large, that trait is considered to be entropy resistant, or as Gellner puts it, a trait is entropy resistant if it does not become dispersed in the general population with the passage of time. Thus, in the construction of the racial category "white" in American culture, religion is entropic while skin color is not. From the point of view of the shaping of a sense of Tharu peoplehood, untouchability is an entropy-resistant cultural trait. Thus the

Musaher, an untouchable caste who share language and many cultural practices with the Chitwan Tharu, cannot be assimilated into the Tharu ethnic category. See Gellner 1983: 63–87 for a full discussion.

6. With reference to Nepal, this fluidity and its relationship to the state is discussed in a number of works: de Sales 1993, Fisher 1987, Guneratne 1994, Holmberg 1989, Levine 1987, Manzardo 1978, Ødegaard 1997, Oppitz 1974, and a number of papers in Gellner, Pfaff-Czarnecka, and Whelpton 1997.

7. See, for example, Charles Ramble's (1997) discussion of why the Tibetan-speaking people of Nepal (pejoratively referred to by other Nepalese as *bhotiyā*) never attempted a shaping of identity like the one described in this book.

Chapter Two

1. H. W. Gibson, deputy commissioner of Bahraich, to the deputy commissioner of Gonda, 23 February 1894, *Proceedings of the Government, North-Western Provinces and Oudh*, in the Revenue (Forests) Department, file 530A, May 1894, India Office Library (IOL).

2. As far as the Tarai around Champaran is concerned, Hamilton (1820: 277) suggested that its cultivation occurred only after the Tarai had been incorporated into the Gorkha state. The petty hill rajas who had ruled it earlier had been content to leave it under forest as security against their neighbors (a policy that the Gorkhas themselves would later follow in Chitwan and Makwanpur), and to draw from it only such revenue as was possible from the sale of timber, elephants, and pasturage rights.

3. Thus E. Gardner, agent to the governor-general, wrote to John Adams, secretary to the Government of India (Political Department) on 15 July 1815, on the progress of talks to end the Anglo-Nepal war: "They [the Nepalese] observed again, that the Terraie was the only valuable part of the Nepaul possessions: that deprived of that tract, the mere mountainous portion which would remain would not be worth the stipulating for; and that they would prefer to stand the chance of losing the whole, to voluntarily relinquishing the lowland." "Papers Respecting the Nepaul War," in *Papers Regarding the Administration of the Marquis of Hastings in India*, IOL.

4. These represent the administrative divisions in 1959.

5. It is possible, however, that many of these people did not remain permanently, as the estimated population figures for Nawalpur, Banke, and Bardiya (which would have received these immigrants) are not great enough to include a migration on the scale suggested by these numbers.

6. *Proceedings of the Government, North-Western Provinces and Oudh*, in the Revenue (Forests) Department, 1892; file 271A, January 1893, IOL.

7. In the Siraha District in the eastern Tarai, I once stayed with a Tharu family that belonged to a clan (*gotra*) known as *Tikedār*. The word means "broker." During the time of British rule in India, this family's ancestors, who had been the local jimidārs or revenue collectors, had acted as brokers or contractors in supplying timber to the Indian market. The term had come to be applied as the clan name of the lineage itself.

8. Despite the land reform, a dominant large landowning class still exists in Nepal (Blaikie, Cameron, and Seddon 1980).

9. Between 1961 and 1971 there was a net migration of 400,000 from the Hills to the Tarai (Ojha 1983: 33, citing the 1971 census). The 1971 census of Nepal gives a total population of 11,555,983, of which 4.29 percent were Tharu (His Majesty's Government 1987: 82–83).

10. Nineteenth-century British writers used the term indiscriminately and interchangeably with caste to refer to population groups in India. For example, Elliott describes the Bhuinhar as "a tribe of Hindús…The Maharaja of Benares is of this caste" (1869: 20–21). Elsewhere he refers to a "Rajput tribe" and to the "ten tribes of Brahmans" (102; cf. also Sherring 1872).

11. The *Muluki Ain* of 1854 uses the term *jāt* to refer to peoples variously described by anthropologists as castes, tribes, and ethnic groups (Höfer 1979: 46). Béteille argues that tribes, as a people separate from Hindu civilization, have been historically recognized in India, and described by the indigenous term *jana*. He notes also that the distinction between *jana* and *jāti* was probably less clear in ancient times than the distinction between caste and tribe is today. Nor is it easy to determine the precise connotation of *jana* in its historical usage (Béteille 1986: 308). In any case, I never heard Tharus in Chitwan use *jana* to describe themselves; their categories of choice were *jāt,* caste (borrowed from English), *samāj* (society, very rarely used), and *ādivāsi*. For a discussion of the concept of *jana,* see Singh 1985.

12. The constitution of India nowhere clearly defines a Scheduled Tribe; in practice, under article 342, the president of India has the power to specify which groups may be included in this category (cf. Atal 1963: 16–17).

13. My source for this information is Panishyam Tharu of Sunsari, who is himself a Rajghariya. The eastern Tarai, ethnographically speaking, is largely undocumented.

14. Stebbing describes the Gujars as a forest tribe, herding buffaloes and selling milk and butter to make a living (1926: 172). The Gujars occupy a different niche than do the Tharu, who are primarily cultivators and not herdsmen. Ibbetson noted that "in the Peshawar district almost any herdsman is called a Gújar, and it may be that some of those…are not true Gújars by race." But he adds that elsewhere in the Punjab large numbers of true Gujars are to be found, and that these share a common language distinct from the Panjabi or Pushtu spoken around them (Ibbetson 1974: 138). He also describes the Gujars as seminomadic pastoralists in the hills, practicing a form of transhumance, and it is only in the plains that they practice agriculture. In some parts of the plains, the Gujars have become a dominant caste (Raheja 1988a: 1–5).

15. I am indebted to Asif Agha for this information. The French Orientalist Sylvain Levi translated this as "the country of the Tharus," but Chattopadyaya, who translated Taranatha's history into English, rendered it as "the frontier country" (Krauskopff 1990: 34; Chimpu and Chattopadhyaya 1970). V. P. Vasil'ev, who translated Taranatha's text into Russian in 1869, rendered the phrase as "belonging to the Tharu tribe," noting as he did so that the earlier German translation by Schiefner in 1868 rendered it as "the border land" (Chimpu and Chattopadhyaya 1970).

16. Bharatiya Tharu Kalyan Mahasangh, *Saṁsodhik saṁvidhān evaṁ thāru vivāha saṁhitā* (Revised Constitution and Compendium on Tharu Marriages), 1984–85.

17. About the Tharu of Champaran, Hunter noted in 1877 that "the Tharus themselves say they were originally Ahirs, Rajputs, Kurmis, and Gareris; and that they fled from their homes in Rajputana when the Emperor of Delhi tried to convert them to Muhammadanism" (1877: 246).

18. The reader should consult Mahesh Regmi (1976, 1984) for a discussion of the revenue system in general during the nineteenth and twentieth centuries. Krauskopff and Meyer (2000) discuss the role the Tharu elite played in the revenue system in general, and my own work (Guneratne 1996) discusses the topic with specific reference to Chitwan District.

19. Makwanpur, the original seat of the Sen kings in eastern Nepal, was subdivided into the kingdoms of Makwanpur, Chaudandi, and Vijayapur. However, the rulers of all three kingdoms continued to be addressed as *makwāni*, which would explain the reference in Pratap Singh's *lāl mohar* (Krauskopff and Shrestha 2000: 119).

20. A land grant made to an individual on a tax-exempt basis and usually inheritable. Birta tenure was abolished in 1959 (Regmi 1976: 42–43).

21. See also *Regmi Research Series* 1 (1): 14.

22. Secret letter from Bengal to the East India Company, 21 June 1815, on matters pertaining to the Gorakhpur frontier. "Papers Respecting the Nepaul War," in *Papers Regarding the Administration of the Marquis of Hastings in India*, 625–626.

23. *India and Bengal Despatches*, vol. 72, 6–27 August 1851, 579–591.

24. *Proceedings of the Government, North-Western Provinces and Oudh*, in the Revenue (Forests) Department, file 530A, May 1894.

25. Ibid.

26. Ibid.

27. Interview with Prem Singh, a Thakuri landlord with an estate in Kanchanpur. His father acquired this estate in the early 1930s and encouraged Tharus from Dang to come to Kanchanpur by telling them that they would be given land and food would also be provided until they harvested their first crop. These Tharus worked for their landlord under the *trikut* system: they kept two-thirds of the crop, the landlord received the rest.

Chapter Three

1. The 1981 census gave the numbers of Buxa speakers in India as 20,000, and of Rana Tharu speakers as 64,000 (Grimes 1996).

2. A popular uprising in the early part of 1990, led by the Congress Party and the Communist Party, ended thirty years of monarchical rule ("panchāyat" government), legalized political parties, and reintroduced a multiparty democratic political system to the country.

3. For another view of the reasons why hill people were unwilling to settle the Tarai, see Ojha 1983.

4. From 80 to 90 percent of the people in these districts still regard Maithili and Bhojpuri as their mother tongues, and it is in these areas that support for the

Sadbhavana Party, which claims to represent the interests of Tarai people vis-à-vis the center, is strongest. Even so, it should be noted, to gauge from the electoral returns of 1991, the Sadbhavana Party had much less support in these areas than either the Congress or the Communists.

5. It still does; according to the 1991 census, 93 percent of the population were directly or indirectly dependent on agriculture.

6. The Sunuwars are a small population, less than 14,000 at the time of the 1961 census, who live in eastern Nepal. They are thought by some to be related to the ethnic category Magar (Bista 1972: 69).

7. The Rana Tharu, for example, were characterized in the Oudh Gazetteer as people who "will on no account take service as soldiers" and as "a cowardly race" (*Gazetteer of the Province of Oudh* 1877: 2:208–209).

8. Gurung states that over 70 percent of the signatories of the *Ain* were Brahmins, Chhetris, and Thakuris (1992: 19); according to Höfer, over 100 of 219 members of the Court Council which drafted the law were Chhetris (1979: 42).

9. The *Muluki Ain* uses the single term *jāt* to refer to the various groups that Western social scientists describe by terms such as caste, ethnic group, or tribe (Höfer 1979: 46).

10. The *Muluki Ain* does not itself distinguish between Hindus and "tribals"; minority groups such as the Rais, Limbus, Gurungs, and also Buddhists were subsumed under the category of Hindu. Non-Hindus were principally the Moslems (who form a tiny minority in Nepal) and Europeans (Sharma 1978: 4).

11. In caste systems generally and in Nepal in particular, some form of hypergamy was recognized.

12. Thus the Indian constitution recognizes the categories *Scheduled Caste* and *Scheduled Tribe*, which entail that groups so labeled have been socially, economically, and politically discriminated against in the past, and that specific measures need to be taken to reverse this discrimination.

13. Nor is this phenomenon peculiar to Chitwan; Upreti (1975) has noted it in Eastern Nepal as well, and Adhikary (1995) discusses a similar situation in the western hills. There are anti-alcohol movements in the Tarai, but these (certainly where Chitwan is concerned) should not be confused with sanskritizing movements. In Chitwan, the anti-alcohol movement was a multiethnic movement comprising both Brahmans and Tharus, mostly women, who wanted to put a stop to alcohol consumption in the village because public drunkenness was disturbing the peace. Whereas offering alcohol to guests was a norm of Tharu hospitality during my initial fieldwork in 1989–91, in subsequent visits beginning in 1997, I was rarely offered liquor, and that only furtively. Villagers attributed this change to the impact of the local anti-alcohol movement. But it had nothing to do with status concerns.

14. The category of *pichhaṛi* or "backward" is explicitly recognized in the 1990 Nepali Constitution in article 11 (under "Fundamental Rights"); the provision reads "special provisions may be made by law to protect or promote the interests of . . . people who belong to a class which is economically, socially, and educationally backward" (from the translation of the constitution published in 1991 in the Nepali *International Forum* 5 (1): 2).

Chapter Four

1. According to the 1991 census of Nepal, Tharu language speakers comprised 29.6 percent of the population of Dang (His Majesty's Government 1999); in 1971 they constituted 43.2 percent of the population (Aryal, Regmi, and Rimal 1982).
2. A bighā equals 0.68 hectares.
3. A report in the newspaper *Rising Nepal* (February 7, 1991) claimed that ten thousand families in Kailali and Kanchanpur districts alone were living in debt-bondage. The incidence of bonded labor has declined in Dang since the rise of the Tharu social movement known as Backward Society Education or BASE.
4. Birtā was a land grant made to individuals, often on a tax-exempt basis; jagir was land given to government officials in lieu of salary. Jagir tenure was abolished in 1952. The holders of such land grants seldom lived on their estates and depended on village level intermediaries to collect the revenue owed them (Regmi 1978: 70–72).
5. "Introduction of Backward Society Education (BASE)." Pamphlet published by BASE (no date).
6. Freedom Nepal, "Chronology of Kamaiya Movement." http://www.freedom nepal.org/kamaiyachronology.html.
7. Regmi Research Project, #2004. "Report on the Land Problems of Dang, Deokhuri and Salyan," by Shri Kewal Choudhury, member, Land Reform Commission, 1954 (Goodall Papers, box 5, folder 60, Honnold Library, Claremont, Calif.).
8. See note 3.
9. Personal communication from Ramanand Prasad Singh, then editor of *Tharu Saṃskṛti,* a magazine irregularly published by the Tharu Welfare Association. The article was never published.
10. An account of the emergence of BASE may be found in Ødegaard 1999 and in Cox 1995.
11. Each member of BASE pays an annual fee of one rupee.
12. This description is based on Internet sources (http://www.freedomnepal .org/kamaiyachronology.html), email bulletins from the listserv kamaiya@ yahoogroups.com, and telephone conversations with Dilli Bahadur Chaudhary.
13. Article 20 of the *Constitution of the Kingdom of Nepal* prohibits "traffic in human beings, slavery, serfdom or forced labor in any form."
14. Similar attitudes toward land have been noted by Pandey (1987: 11) of the Tharu of Nawal Parasi.
15. The title *jimidār* continues to be used as an honorific for the descendants of the former revenue collectors.
16. Bhikna Thori, on the Indian side of the border with Champaran, was a small market town and the terminus of a railway.
17. A mīt is someone with whom one has established a ritual friendship solemnized by a special ceremony.
18. I had given three copies of my dissertation (Guneratne 1994) to those people in the village who had been most closely associated with my work; the story of Devkota appears in it.

19. In making this calculation I have excluded the two largest landowning house-holds, which together owned twenty-four hectares (Guneratne 1994: 164).

20. Other matters that had become election issues and were discussed at this meeting included, inter alia, the agreement between Nepal and India on the use of Narayani River water, the policies of the Congress Party as opposed to that of the Communists, the use of jeeps imported from India by the Congress for electioneering, and the shape of Indo-Nepal relations under a Congress government.

21. According to Bhandari, in 1955, just prior to the commencement of the Malaria Eradication Project, only 2,500 bighās were cultivated in Chitwan. By 1985 the figure had grown to 40,000 (Bhandari 1985: 13).

22. My last visit to Dang was in 1997, shortly after the insurgency began in 1996 but before it had spread to Dang, and I have no information of my own with which to discuss this question.

Chapter Five

1. R. P. Singh's nephew Girish Kumar Singh asserts that no Tharus are landless in Saptari; there were no Tharu *sukumbāsi* (squatters). Most Tharu in the district, he claimed, owned a few bighā and some had between 20–40 bighās; he placed his uncle in this category. A few (he named three or four individuals, including an important politician in the neighboring district of Siraha) owned 300–700 bighās.

2. Chiranjivi Chaudhary uses the word *demān* to refer to these people; the word means "minister," but in this context it probably refers to individuals holding powerful and important offices locally, like Amar Bahadur himself.

3. This is a reference to the political reforms introduced by Padma Shamsher and halfheartedly implemented by his successor, Mohan Shamsher. These reforms provided among other things for a bicameral legislature—what Govinda Chaudhari refers to as a "mock" parliament (2052: 46)—while retaining all power in the hands of the Ranas (see Shaha 1990: 184–188). Shaha approvingly cites a contemporary British criticism of Padma Shamsher's constitution, which described it as "eyewash to disarm criticism from progressives while retaining powers firmly in the hands of the Rana family" (188). This parliament met only once, on September 22, 1950.

4. The Tharu of Naini Tal and those of Champaran both have their own organizations. That of Naini Tal is the Tharu Rana Parishad; in Champaran, it is the Bharatiya Tharu Kalyan Maha Sangh, founded in 1971.

5. Shambhu Oja, personal communication.

6. "Tharu Mahadhiveshan" (The Tharu Convention), a photocopied page from a magazine or pamphlet (title and place of publication unknown) similar to those published by Tharu organizations in different districts in the Tarai, given to me by Ram Sagar Chaudhary of Sunsari. He had sought me out at the convention held in Tetariya, Morang, to give me a sheaf of photocopied articles on the Tharu in Nepali and local languages. This particular article is an account of what took place at the Tharu convention in 1979.

7. The discussion of the district-level organization of the Tharu Kalyankarini Sabha is based primarily on the written constitution of the Chitwan District branch of the organization.
8. He is the author of the poem discussed on page 171.

Chapter Six

1. I was able to follow only those discussions that were carried on in Nepali and Hindi and to some extent in various Tharu languages, and I had no one to interpret for me.
2. In a similar vein Tej Narayan Panjiar is critical of Mahesh Regmi, the preeminent economic historian of Nepal, because his extensive writings on landownership and taxation in Nepal makes no reference to Tharus.
3. An interesting footnote to Singh's views is an observation of Edwin Atkinson's on the Tharu:

> There is evidence at the present time of a religious movement among the Tharus. They appear dissatisfied with the teaching of the Brahmans and are seeking information regarding other creeds. The Christian religion is not acceptable chiefly because it seems to bring with it expenses they are unable to incur; the creed of Islam, as authorizing the killing of kine, is altogether unacceptable; and were but a teacher of the tenets of Buddhism to appear, it is highly probable that the Tharus would become converts to that form of religion. (Atkinson 1886: 705)

4. In support of his contention that the Mauryas were Tharu, he cites Sylvain Lévi (in *Ancient Nepal*, nos. 59–60 [1980]). He adds, "Tharus today don't know that Ashok[a] [the Mauryan emperor of India] belonged to their community; they have forgotten their history." See also Chimpu and Chattopadhyaya 1970.
5. About four hundred years prior to the *Muluki Ain*, introduced in 1854, King Jayasthiti Malla, who ruled over the Kathmandu Valley, introduced a legal code which also laid down a caste hierarchy for the population, but it was confined to the social context of the valley only (Höfer 1979: 41). In doing so, he was doubtless formalizing and regulating an existing state of affairs.
6. The same point is emphasized (but with reference specifically to the Dangaura Tharu language) by the editors of the books published in Dang in the Dangaura language in the 1970s and 1980s. See McDonaugh 1989: 201.
7. According to Whelpton, while questions on caste/ethnic affiliation have been included in previous censuses, the results were never released prior to the census of 1991 because of their potential sensitivity (1997: 51). The 1991 census is the first to make those numbers available.
8. The languages used were Tamang, Tharu, Rai-Bantawa, Limbu, Magar, Gurung, Bhojpuri, and Awadhi. Hindi, Newari, and Maithili broadcasts had begun earlier (Sonntag 1995: 7).
9. In an article in *Thāru Saṁskṛti* (2057: 41), Tribhuwan Choudhary criticizes Radio Nepal for having advertisements in Tharu read by a non-Tharu (a Pahari). He recounts that he was in his home in Kathmandu when an advertisement was

broadcast in the Tharu language of Kailali. A Kailali Tharu woman who was present could not understand completely what was being said—presumably because of the Pahari's accent or intonation. He urges his readers to demand of Radio Nepal that it provide native Tharu speakers to read Tharu ads. His rationale is that benefits intended for Tharus are appropriated by non-Tharus, something I have heard other Tharus say as well.

10. A shaman employed by a household.
11. An uncastrated goat or *bokā*.
12. The clan deity.
13. I am reminded of an observation made by a well-to-do Thakuri landowner with a large estate in western Nepal. When one of his Tharu workers made a mistake, he remarked, the worker would excuse himself by saying, "I am only a stupid ox." The worker in this case was probably playing on his master's prejudices to save himself from chastisement.
14. Money collected in this way is placed in the district committee's treasury and used to fund its activities.

Chapter Seven

1. The reference is to the ethnic label *Magar*.
2. See, for example, Fox 1990, particularly the chapters by Verdery and Dominguez.

GLOSSARY

ādivāsi	An original inhabitant; indigenous person.
adhiyā̃	Sharecropping on a fifty-fifty basis.
bahāriyā	A servant who lives and works in his or her master's home on a yearly contract.
begārī	Corvée or forced labor.
bighā	A variable unit of land measure in the Tarai; in Chitwan, it equals about .68 hectares.
Baisākh	The first month of the Nepali (bikram sambat) calendar; April–May.
bādh	Dam across a stream; a barrier.
banavāsī	A forest dweller; uncivilized.
bhārādār	A counselor to the king.
bhāsā	Language.
birtā	A tax-free grant of land made by the state to one of its officials as compensation for services; *birtā* grants were inheritable.
boksā, boksī	A witch.
bramathān	An area, usually on the outskirts of a Tharu village, consecrated to the village deities.
chaudhari	Revenue collector in the Tarai responsible for a revenue unit known as a *pragannā*.
chaurāsi	Lit., eighty-four; name given to a large administrative unit in the eastern Tarai (perhaps a unit of eighty-four villages?). *Chaurāsi* was also a punishment imposed by

213

jimidārs for various offences: the offender was compelled to provide a feast to which all the *jimidārs* of the *chaurāsi* would be invited.

ḍaini	Witch (Chitwan Th.).
demān	A minister.
dhāmi	A traditional healer, a shaman.
ḍhāth	A gate for a cattle enclosure; obstacle.
dūn	Inner Tarai valley.
gotyār	A patrilineal and exogamous kin group among the Dangaura Tharu that serves primarily to structure marriage relations.
itihās	History, tradition.
jagir	Tax-exempt land grants made to government servants in lieu of salaries; unlike *birtā*, a *jagir* was not inheritable.
jajmānī	A system of patron-client relations linking a number of castes to a jajmān or patron.
janajāti	A term used in Nepal to describe the so-called tribal groups.
janti	The procession in which a Nepali Hindu groom goes to the bride's house for the wedding ceremony.
jāt	Refers to the notion of kind or species, and glossed in English as tribe, nation, caste, ethnic group, etc.
jhārā-begāri	Forced labor.
jimidār	Revenue collector, responsible for revenue collection and agricultural development in a *maujā*.
kalyāṇ	Welfare, good fortune.
kamaiyā	Traditionally, a laborer working for a farmer under a contract; in return for the *kamaiyā*'s labor, the farmer provided food, shelter and clothing. Also refers to someone who is in a relation of debt peonage.
kisān	A farmer or peasant.
kul	A clan.
kurī (kurie)	A clan among the Rana Tharu.
lākh	One hundred thousand.
lāl mohar	A royal edict granting some privilege to a subject; the name derives from the red seal (*lāl mohar*) stamped on it.
lohotā	A metal gourd, commonly used a drinking vessel throughout North India and Nepal.
mades	The Tarai; the plains of India.
mahato	Village headman.
makwāni	A term of address for the rulers of Makwanpur.

matwāli	Ethnic groups for whom liquor is of social and ritual importance; these are considered clean castes of middle rank in the Muluki Ain.
maujā	Subunit for revenue collection of a *pragannā,* comprising one or more villages.
melā	Fair or festival.
pad	Rank, title, profession, occupation.
pahāṛ	Hill, mountain.
pahāṛiyā	Someone from the hills (*pahaṛ*), usually referring to a Brahman or member of the Chhetri caste. See also *parbatiyā.*
panchāyat	The smallest unit of local administration during the period of monarchical rule in the post-Rana period. Since 1990, these administrative units have been called Village Development Boards (*gaun bikash samiti*).
parbatiyā	Someone from the hills.
phaujdār	A village official responsible for maintaining law and order and in helping to collect taxes.
pichhaṛi	The condition of "backwardness"; suffering from social, political and economic disadvantages.
pradhān panch	The chief elected official of a *panchāyat.*
pragannā	A revenue unit in the Tarai.
raiti	Landholding peasants subject to taxation.
raksi	Homemade liquor distilled from rice or sugar cane.
sāno	Small.
saṁskār	Tradition.
saṁskṛti	Culture.
sawāri	A royal procession; a tour by an important personage.
subbā	The chief administrator of a district; district governor.
sukumbāsi	Someone with no apparent means of livelihood; landless person, squatter.
tāgādhāri	A wearer of the sacred thread; twice-born castes.
talukā	A large landed estate.
talukdār	A person invested with authority; headman in charge of a large estate.
thar	A subcaste; a fictive patrilineage, which assumes that all those sharing the same last name are related, even though the relationship may not be traceable.
thūlo mānchhe	Important or powerful person, a person of high rank.
uderi	Elopement (Chitwan Th.).
zamindār	A landlord.

BIBLIOGRAPHY

Nepali and Tharu Languages

(dates are given in Bikram Sambat, with approximate Common Era dates in parentheses)

Chaudhari, Baburam. 2047 (1991). "Thāru kalyāṇ kāriṇi sabhā (dosro?) mahā-sammelan 2012 sālko chhoto smaraṇ" (A brief recollection of the [second?] convention of the Tharu Kalyankarini Sabha in 2012). *Smārikā* ([Convention] Souvenir). Biratnagar: Morang District Committee, Tharu Kalyankarini Sabha.

Chaudhari, Govinda. 2052 (1995/96). "Shri Kewal Chaudhariko jīwanī" (The life of Kewal Chaudhari). *Thāru Saṁskṛti* 2052, 46–47.

Chaudhari, Mahesh. n.d. "Bahusaṁkhyā thāru jātiko bhāsā alpasaṁkhyā rūpmā" (The majority Tharu language treated as a minority one). Mimeo.

Chaudhary, Chiranjivi Prasad. 2055 (1999). "Thāru kalyāṇkāriṇi sabhāko parichaya" (An introduction to the Tharu Kalyankarini Sabha). *Thāru Saṁskṛti*, 2–3.

Chaudhary, Prabhunarayan. 2045 (1988). "Thāruke chaurāsi dhāth, bādh" (The Tharus' [system of] chaurasi: A barrier and obstacle [to progress]). *Thāru Saṁskār*, 50–54.

Chaudhary "Tharu," Lekhnath. 2055 (1999). *Thāru tathyāṅka*. Dang-Deokhuri: Sarita Swechha Prakāshan.

Tharu, Chandra. 2054. "Thāru Kalyāṇkāriṇī Sabhāke janmakālse hāl takke itihās" (The history of the Tharu Kalyankarini Sabha from its origins to the present day). *Thāru Saṁskṛti*: 5-8.

Tharu Kalyankarini Sabha. 2055 (1999). *Thāru Saṁskṛti* (Tharu culture). Kathmandu.

Western Languages

Adhikary, Kamal R. 1995. "The Fruits of Panchayat Development." *Himalayan Research Bulletin* 15 (2): 12–24.

Alexander, E. B. 1881. "Gorakhpur." In *Statistical, Descriptive, and Historical Account of the North-Western Provinces of India*, vol. 6, *Cawnpore, Gorakhpur and Basti*, ed. Edwin T. Atkinson, 271–550. Allahabad: North-Western Provinces and Oudh Government Press.

Anderson, Benedict. 1991. *Imagined Communities: Reflections on the Origin and Spread of Nationalism*. 2d. ed. London: Verso.

Armstrong, John A. 1982. *Nations before Nationalism*. Chapel Hill: University of North Carolina Press.

Aryal, Deepak, Rabindra Regmi, and Nirmal Rimal, eds. 1982. *Nepal District Profile. A Districtwise Socio-techno-economic Profile of Nepal*. Kathmandu: National Research Associates.

Asad, Talal. 1991. "Afterword: From the History of Colonial Anthropology to the Anthropology of Western Hegemony." In *Colonial Situations: Essays on the Contextualization of Ethnographic Knowledge*, ed. George Stocking. Madison: University of Wisconsin Press.

Atal, Yogesh. 1963. "The Tribe-Caste Question." *Bulletin of the Bihar Tribal Research Institute* 5 (1):1–23.

Atkinson, Edwin T. 1886. *The Himalayan Districts of the North-Western Provinces of India*. Vol. 3 (Vol. 12 of the Gazetteer, N.W.P.). Allahabad: North-Western Provinces and Oudh Government Press.

Bailey, F. G. 1961. "; 'Tribe' and 'Caste' in India." *Contributions to Indian Sociology* 5:7–19.

Barth, Fredrik. 1969. "Introduction." In *Ethnic Groups and Boundaries: The Social Organization of Cultural Difference*, ed. Fredrik Barth. Oslo: Universitetsforlaget.

BASE 1994. *Kamaiya Report 2051 (1994)*. Tulsipur, Dang.

Benett, W. C. 1878. *The Final Settlement Report on the Gonda District*. Allahabad: North-Western Provinces and Oudh Government Press.

Béteille, Andre. 1986. "The Concept of Tribe with Special Reference to India." *European Journal of Sociology* 27 (2):297–318.

Bhandari, Bhishnu. 1985. "Landownership and Social Inequality in the Rural Terai Area of Nepal." Ph.D. diss., University of Wisconsin, Madison.

Bhaskar, Roy. 1989. "On the Possibility of Social Scientific Knowledge and the Limits of Naturalism." In *Reclaiming Reality: A Critical Introduction to Contemporary Philosophy*. London: Verso.

Bista, Dor Bahadur. 1969. "The Forgotten People of Dang Valley." *Vasudha* 12 (10):10–14.

———. 1972. *People of Nepal*. 2d. ed. Kathmandu: Ratna Pustak Bhandar.

———. 1982. "The Process of Nepalization." In *Anthropological and Linguistic Studies of the Gandaki Area in Nepal*, ed. Dor Bahadur Bista et al. Monumenta Serindica, no. 10. Tokyo: Institute for the Study of Languages and Cultures of Asia and Africa.

Blaikie, Piers, John Cameron, and David Seddon. 1980. *Nepal in Crisis: Growth and Stagnation at the Periphery*. Delhi: Oxford University Press.

Blunt, E. A. H. 1912. *Census of India 1911*. Vol. 15. *United Provinces of Agra and Oudh*. Pt. 1. Report. Allahabad: Government Press.

Blyth, W. D. 1892. *Report on the Census of the District of Champaran, 1891*. District Census Report.

Bourdieu, Pierre. 1977a. *Outline of a Theory of Practice*. Cambridge: Cambridge University Press.

———. 1977b. "Cultural Reproduction and Social Reproduction." In *Power and Ideology in Education*, ed. Jerome Karabel and A. H. Halsey. New York: Oxford University Press.

Brass, Paul R. 1974. *Language, Religion and Politics in North India*. Cambridge: Cambridge University Press.

———. 1985. *Ethnic Groups and the State*. London: Croom Helm.

———. 1991. *Ethnicity and Nationalism: Theory and Comparison*. New Delhi: Sage Publications.

Breuilly, John. 1982. *Nationalism and the State*. Manchester: Manchester University Press.

Buchanan, Francis. 1928. *An Account of the District of Purnea in 1809–10*. Patna: Bihar and Orissa Research Society.

Burghart, Richard. 1984. "The Formation of the Concept of Nation-State in Nepal." *Journal of Asian Studies* 44 (1):101–125.

Cameron, Mary M. 1998. *On the Edge of the Auspicious: Gender and Caste in Nepal*. Urbana: University of Illinois Press.

Campbell, A. 1851. "Papers on the Sikhim Morung." In *Selections from the Records of the Bengal Government*, no. 5. Calcutta: F. Carbery, Military Orphan Press.

Caplan, Lionel. 1967. "Some Political Consequences of State Land Policy in East Nepal." *Man*, n.s., 2 (1):107–114.

———. 1970. *Land and Social Change in East Nepal: A Study of Hindu-Tribal Relations*. Berkeley: University of California Press.

———. 1990. "'Tribes' in the Ethnography of Nepal: Some Comments on a Debate." *Contributions to Nepalese Studies* 17 (2):129–145.

———. 1991. "From Tribe to Peasant? The Limbus and the Nepalese State." *Journal of Peasant Studies* 18 (2):305–321.

Cavenagh, Orfeur. 1851. *Rough Notes on the State of Nepal, Its Government, Army and Resources*. Calcutta: W. Palmer, Military Orphan Press.

Chand, Geeta, et al. 1975. *Studies in Bilingualism in Nepal: A Survey of Bilingualism and Primary Education in Bara and Chitwan Districts of Narayani Zone, Nepal. Report on Pilot Project No. 2*. Kathmandu: Institute of Nepal and Asian Studies, Tribhuvan University.

Chimpu, Lama, and Alaka Chattopadhyaya, trans. 1970. *Taranatha's History of Buddhism in India*. Simla: Indian Institute of Advanced Studies.

Choudhary, Shanti. 1990. *My Own Story*. Kathmandu: Creative Development Centre. Mimeographed.

Choudhary, Tribhuwan. 2057. "Some Tips and Hints from U.S.A." *Thāru Saṁskṛti*, 50–51.

Clark, Edgar Gibson, and Henry Scott Boys. 1873. *Report on the Revision of Settlement of the Bahraich District, Oudh, 1865–1872*. Lucknow: Oudh Government Press.

Cohn, Bernard S. 1987. "The Census, Social Structure and Objectification in South Asia." In *An Anthropologist Among the Historians and Other Essays*. Delhi: Oxford University Press.

Comaroff, John L. 1987. "Of Totemism and Ethnicity: Consciousness, Practice and the Signs of Inequality." *Ethnos* 52 (3–4):301–323.

Connor, Walker. 1978. "A Nation Is a Nation, Is a State, Is an Ethnic Group, Is a..." *Ethnic and Racial Studies* 1 (4):377–400.

Constitution of the Kingdom of Nepal. 1991. *International Forum* (Nepal) 5 (1):1–20

Conway, Dennis, and Nanda R. Shrestha. 1981. *Causes and Consequences of Rural-to-Rural Migration in Nepal.* Indiana University Monograph Series, no. 6. Bloomington, Indiana.

Cox, Thomas. 1990a. *The Vegetable, Fruit and Cash Crop Program in the Dang Valley.* Unpublished report to USAID.

——. 1990b. "Land Rights and Ethnic Conflict in Nepal". *Economic and Political Weekly* 25:1318–1320.

——. 1995. "Backward Society Education: The Development of a Grassroots Movement." Unpublished.

Crooke, W. 1896. *The Tribes and Castes of the North-Western Provinces and Oudh.* Vol. 4. Calcutta: Superintendent of Government Printing.

Cruickshank, A. W. 1891. *Final Report on the Settlement in the Gorakhpur District, North-Western Provinces.* Pt. 1. Allahabad: North-Western Provinces and Oudh Government Press.

Dahal, Dilli Ram. 1983. "Economic Development through Indigenous Means: A Case of Indian Migration in the Nepal Terai." *Contributions to Nepalese Studies* 11 (1):1–20.

——. 1992. "Grasping the Tarai Identity." *Himal* 5 (3):17–18.

de Sales, Anne. 1993. "When the Miners Came to Light: The Chantel of Dhaulagiri." In *Nepal, Past and Present*, ed. Gerard Toffin. Paris: CNRS Editions.

Des Chene, Mary. 1993. "Soldiers, Sovereignty and Silences: Gorkhas as Diplomatic Currency." *South Asia Bulletin* 13 (1–2):67–80.

Despres, Leo E. 1984. "Ethnicity: What Data and Theory Portend for Plural Societies." In *The Prospects for Plural Societies: 1982 Proceedings of the American Ethnological Society*, ed. David Maybury-Lewis. Washington, D.C.: American Ethnological Society.

Devkota, Bharat M. 2000. *A Status Report on the Situation of the Kamaiyas in Kanchanpur, Kailali, and Bardia Districts.* Unpublished.

District Gazetteer of the United Provinces of Agra and Oudh. 1925. *Supplementary Notes and Statistics.* Vol. 32. *Gorakhpur District.* Allahabad.

District Political Profile of Chitwan. 1991. Kathmandu: Himalayan Center for Applied Economic Research.

Diwakar, R. R., ed. 1959. *Bihar through the Ages.* Bombay: Orient Longmans.

Egerton, Francis. 1852. *Journal of a Winter's Tour in India with a Visit to the Court of Nepal.* 2 vols. London: John Murray.

Elder, Joseph W., et al. 1976. *Planned Resettlement in Nepal's Terai: A Social Analysis of the Khajura/Bardia Punarvas Projects.* Kathmandu: Institute of Nepal and Asian Studies; Madison: Department of Sociology, University of Wisconsin.

Elliott, H. M. 1869. *Memoirs on the History, Folk-lore, and Distribution of the Races of the North Western Provinces of India.* Vol. 1. London: Trübner.

Elliott, J. H. 1959. *Guide to Nepal.* Calcutta: W. Newman.

Eriksen, Thomas Hylland. 1993. *Ethnicity and Nationalism: Anthropological Perspectives.* London: Pluto Press.

Fayrer, Joseph. 1900. *Recollections of My Life.* London: William Blackwood and Sons.

Fisher, James F. 1985. "The Historic Development of Himalayan Anthropology." *Mountain Research and Development* 5 (1):99–111.

——.1986. *Trans-Himalayan Traders: Economy, Society and Culture in Northwest Nepal.* Berkeley: University of California Press.

Fisher, William F. 1987. "The Re-creation of Tradition: Ethnicity, Migration and Social Change among the Thakalis of Central Nepal." Ph.D. diss., Columbia University.

——. 1993. "Nationalism and the Janajati." *Himal* 6 (2): 11–14.

Fox, Richard G., ed. 1990. *Nationalist Ideologies and the Production of National Culture.* Washington, D.C.: American Anthropological Association.

Fürer-Haimendorf, Christoph von. 1966. "Unity and Diversity in the Chetri Caste of Nepal." In *Caste and Kin in Nepal, India and Ceylon*, ed. C. von Fürer-Haimendorf. London: Asia Publishing House.

Furnivall, J. S. 1956. *Colonial Policy and Practice: A Comparative Study of Burma and Netherlands India.* New York: New York University Press.

Gaige, Frederick H. 1975. *Regionalism and National Unity in Nepal.* Berkeley: University of California Press.

Galanter, Marc. 1989. "Pursuing Equality in the Land of Hierarchy: An Assessment of India's Policies of Compensatory Discrimination for Historically Disadvantaged Groups." In *Law and Society in Modern India.* Delhi: Oxford University Press.

Gazetteer of the Province of Oudh. 1877. 2 Vols. Lucknow: Oudh Government Press.

Gellner, David N., Joanna Pfaff-Czarnecka, and John Whelpton, eds. 1997. *Nationalism and Ethnicity in a Hindu Kingdom: The Politics of Culture in Contemporary Nepal.* Amsterdam: Harwood.

Gellner, Ernest. 1983. *Nations and Nationalism.* Ithaca, N.Y.: Cornell University Press.

Ghurye, G. S. 1980. *The Scheduled Tribes of India.* New Brunswick, N.J.: Transaction Books.

Glazer, Nathan, and Daniel P. Moynihan. 1975. "Introduction." In *Ethnicity: Theory and Experience*, ed. Nathan Glazer and Daniel P. Moynihan. Cambridge: Harvard University Press.

Grimes, Barbara F., ed. 2001. *Ethnologue: Languages of the World*, 14th ed. Dallas: Summer Institute of Linguistics (Internet ed.: http://www.ethnologue.com/web.asp).

Guha, Ranajit. 1989. "Dominance without Hegemony and Its Historiography." In Ranajit Guha, ed., *Subaltern Studies 6: Writings on South Asian History and Society.* Delhi: Oxford University Press.

Guneratne, Arjun. 1994. "The Tharus of Chitwan: Ethnicity, Class and the State in Nepal." Ph.D. diss., University of Chicago.

——. 1996. "The Tax-Man Cometh: Revenue Collection and Subsistence Strategies in Chitwan Tharu Society." *Studies in Nepali History and Society* 1 (1):5–35.

——. 1999. "The Shaman and the Priest: Ghosts, Death and Ritual Specialists in Tharu Society." *Himalayan Research Bulletin* 19 (2):1–12.

Gurung, Harka. 1992. "Representing an Ethnic Mosaic." *Himal* 5 (3):19–21.

Hachhenthu, Krishna. 2000. "Nepal: Maoist Challenge." Paper presented to the Harvard University Conflict Prevention Initiative—Nepal Web Conference, January–February 2001.

Hamilton, Walter. 1820. *A Geographical, Statistical and Historical Description of Hindostan and the Adjacent Countries.* Vol. 1. London: John Murray.

Hardgrave, Robert L. 1969. *The Nadars of Tamilnad: The Political Culture of a Community in Change*. Berkeley: University of California Press.

Hasan, Amir 1979. *The Buxas of the Tarai: A Study of Their Socio-economic Disintegration*. Delhi: B. R. Publishing Corp.

——. 1993. *Affairs of an Indian Tribe: The Story of My Tharu Relatives*. Lucknow: New Royal Book Co.

His Majesty's Government. 1984. *Population Census—1981. Social Characteristics Tables*. Vol. 1, pt. 3. Kathmandu: Central Bureau of Statistics.

——. 1987. *Population Monograph of Nepal*. Kathmandu: Central Bureau of Statistics.

——. 1990. *Support to District Agricultural Planning. Agricultural Plan for Chitwan (1990–2000)*. Kathmandu: Ministry of Agriculture, FAO/UNDP.

——. 1993a. *Statistical Yearbook of Nepal*. Kathmandu.

——. 1993b. *Population Census 1991, Nepal*. Kathmandu: Central Bureau of Statistics.

——. 1999. *Statistical Year Book of Nepal*, 7th ed. Kathmandu: Central Bureau of Statistics.

Höfer, Andras. 1979. "The Caste Hierarchy and the State in Nepal: A Study of the Muluki Ain of 1854." *Khumbu Himal* 13 / 2. Innsbruck: Universitätsverlag Wagner.

Hoftun, Martin, William Raeper, and John Whelpton. 1999. *People, Politics and Ideology: Democracy and Social Change in Nepal*. Kathmandu: Mandala Book Point.

Holmberg, David H. 1989. *Order in Paradox: Myth, Ritual and Exchange among Nepal's Tamang*. Ithaca, N.Y.: Cornell University Press.

——. 2000. "Ethnic Movements in Contemporary Nepal." *Himalayan Research Bulletin* 20 (1–2): 13–14.

Hunter, W. W. 1877. *A Statistical Account of Bengal*. Vol. 13. *Tirhut and Champaran*. London: Trübner.

Ibbetson, Denzil. 1974. *Punjab Castes*. Lahore: Sh. Mubarak Ali. Reprint of "The Races, Castes and Tribes of the People" from the Punjab Census Report 1881 (Lahore, 1882).

Imperial Gazetteer of India. 1908. Vol. 7. Oxford: Clarendon Press.

Isaacs, Harold. 1989. *Idols of the Tribe: Group Identity and Political Change*. Cambridge: Harvard University Press.

Joshi, Bhuwan Lal, and Leo E. Rose. 1966. *Democratic Innovations in Nepal: A Case Study of Political Acculturation*. Berkeley: University of California Press.

Khare, R. S. 1970. *The Changing Brahmins: Associations and Elites among the Kanya-Kubjas of North India*. Chicago: University of Chicago Press.

Kirkpatrick, William. 1996. *Account of the Kingdom of Nepal*. 1811. Reprint, New Delhi: Asian Educational Series.

Knowles, S. 1889. *The gospel in Gonda: being a narrative of events inconnection with the preaching of the gospel in the trans-Ghaghra country*. Lucknow: Methodist Publishing House.

Kochar, V. K. 1963. "Size and Composition of Families in a Tharu Village." *Vanyajati* 11: 99–106.

Kothari, R., ed. 1970. *Caste in Indian Politics*. New Delhi: Orient Longmans.

Krauskopff, Gisèle. 1987. "Des paysans dans la jungle: Le piégeage dans le rapport des Tharu au monde de la forêt." *Études Rurales* 107–108:27–42.

——. 1989. *Maîtres et possédés: Les rites et l'ordre social chez les Tharu (Nepal)*. Paris: Éditions du CNRS.

——. 1990. "Les Tharu et le royaume hindou de Dang." *L'Homme* 116 (4):30–54.

——. 1999. "Corvées in Dang: Ethno-historical Notes." In *Nepal: Tharu and Tarai Neighbours*, ed. Harald O. Skar. Kathmandu: EMR.

——. 2000. "From Jungle to Farms: A Look at Tharu History." In *The Kings of Nepal and the Tharu of the Tarai*, ed. Gisèle Krauskopff and Pamela Deuel Meyer. Los Angeles: Rusca Press; Kirtipur: Centre for Nepal and Asian Studies.

Krauskopff, Gisèle, and Pamela Deuel Meyer, eds., 2000. *The Kings of Nepal and the Tharu of the Tarai*. Los Angeles: Rusca Press; Kirtipur: Centre for Nepal and Asian Studies.

Krauskopff, Gisèle, and Tek Bahadur Shrestha. 2000. "Translation of Royal Documents with Commentary." In *The Kings of Nepal and the Tharu of the Tarai*, ed. Gisèle Krauskopff and Pamela Deuel Meyer. Los Angeles: Rusca Press; Kirtipur: Centre for Nepal and Asian Studies.

Lévi, Sylvain. 1980. "Nepal." *Ancient Nepal* 59–60:1–40.

Levine, Nancy E. 1987. "Caste, State, and Ethnic Boundaries in Nepal." *Journal of Asian Studies* 46 (1):71–88.

Maheshwari, J. K., K. K. Singh, and S. Saha. 1981. *The Ethnobotany of the Tharus of Kheri District Uttar Pradesh*. Lucknow: Economic Botany Information Service, National Botanical Research Institute.

Majumdar, D. N. 1937. "Some Aspects of the Economic Life of the Bhoksas and Tharus of Nainital Tarai." *Journal of the Anthropological Society of Bombay*, Jubilee Volume, 133–135.

——. 1944. *The Fortunes of Primitive Tribes*. Lucknow: Universal Publishers.

Malla, Kamal P. 1992. "Bahunvada: Myth or Reality?" *Himal* 5 (3):22–24.

Manzardo, A. E., 1978. "To be Kings of the North: Community Adaptation and Impression Management in the Thakalis of Western Nepal." Ph.D. diss., University of Wisconsin.

Marriott, McKim. 1955. "Little Communities in an Indigenous Civilization." In *Village India: Studies in the Little Community*, ed. McKim Marriott. Chicago: University of Chicago Press.

Marriott, McKim, and Ronald B. Inden. 1974. "Caste Systems." *Encyclopaedia Brittanica*, macropaedia 3:982–91

Marx, Karl. 1970. *The German Ideology*. Ed. C. J. Arthur. New York: International Publishers.

McDonaugh, Christian E. J. S. 1984. "The Tharus of Dang: A Study of Social Organization, Myth and Ritual in West Nepal." Ph.D. diss., Oxford University.

——. 1989. "The Mythology of the Tharu: Aspects of Cultural Identity in Dang, West Nepal," *Kailash* 15 (3–4):191–206.

——. 1997. "Losing Ground, Gaining Ground: Land and Change in a Tharu Community in Dang, West Nepal." In *Nationalism and Ethnicity in a Hindu Kingdom: The Politics of Culture in Contemporary Nepal*, ed. David N. Gellner, Joanna Pfaff-Czarnecka, and John Whelpton. Amsterdam: Harwood.

Modiano, G., et al. 1991. Protection against Malaria Morbidity—Near Fixation of the Alpha Thalassemia Gene in a Nepalese Population." *American Journal of Human Genetics* 48 (2): 390–397.

Nepal Trading Corporation. 1959. *Nepal Trade Directory*. New Delhi.

Nesfield, John C. 1885. "The Tharus and Bhogshas of Upper India." *Calcutta Review* 80 (159):1–46.

Nevill, H. R. 1905. *Gonda: A Gazetteer, being Volume XLIV of the District Gazetteers of the United Provinces of Agra and Oudh.* Naini Tal: Government Press, United Provinces.

Northey, W. Brook, and C. J. Morris. 1928. *The Gurkhas: Their Manners, Customs and Country.* London: John Lane, The Bodley Head.

Ødegaard, Sigrun Eide. 1997. "From Castes to Ethnic Group? Modernisation and Forms of Social Identification among the Tharus of the Nepalese Tarai." Ph.D. diss., University of Oslo.

———. 1999. "Base and the Role of NGOs in the Process of Local and Regional Change." In *Nepal: Tharu and Tarai Neighbors*, ed. Harald O. Skar. Kathmandu: EMR.

Ojha, Durga P. 1983. "History of Land Settlement in Nepal Tarai." *Contributions to Nepalese Studies* 11 (1):21–44.

Oldfield, H. Ambrose. 1974. *Sketches from Nepal.* Vol. 1. 1880. Reprint, New Delhi: Cosmo Publications.

Onta, Pratyoush. 2000. "The Politics of Knowledge." *Kathmandu Post,* June 30.

Oppitz, Michael. 1974. "Myths and Facts: Reconsidering Some Data concerning the Clan History of the Sherpa." In *Contributions to the Anthropology of Nepal*, ed. Christoph von Fürer-Haimendorf. Warminster, England: Aris and Phillips.

PACT-Nepal. 1993. "An Evaluation of Backward Society Education (BASE) Conducted for the Royal Danish Embassy, Kathmandu, Nepal." Unpublished report.

Pandey, Tulsi Ram. 1987. *The Subsistence Farmers and Workers of Sunwal Village Panchayat, Nawal Parasi District.* Rural Poverty Research Paper Series, no. 12. HMG-USAID-GTZ-IDRC-Ford-Winrock Project.

Panjiar, Tej Narayan. 1993. "Faceless in History." *Himal* 6 (4):20-21.

———. 2000. "In My Own Words: In Search of the Tharu Past." In *The Kings of Nepal and the Tharu of the Tarai*, ed. Gisèle Krauskopff and Pamela Deuel Meyer. Los Angeles: Rusca Press; Kirtipur: Centre for Nepal and Asian Studies.

Pyakuryal, Kailash Nath. 1982. "Ethnicity and Rural Development: A Sociological Study of Four Tharu villages." Ph.D. diss., Michigan State University.

Quigley, Declan. 1993. *The Interpretation of Caste.* Delhi: Oxford University Press.

Ragsdale, Tod A. 1989. *Once a Hermit Kingdom: Ethnicity, Education and National Integration in Nepal.* Kathmandu: Ratna Pustak Bhandar.

Raheja, Gloria Goodwin. 1988a. *The Poison in the Gift: Ritual, Prestation, and the Dominant Caste in a North Indian Village.* Chicago: University of Chicago Press.

———. 1988b. "India: Caste, Kingship, and Dominance Reconsidered." *Annual Reviews in Anthropology* 17:497–522.

Rajaure, Drone Prasad 1981. "Tharus of Dang: The People and the Social Context." *Kailash* 8 (3–4):155–82.

———. 1982a. "Tharus of Dang: Tharu Religion." *Kailash* 9 (1):61–96.

———. 1982b. "Tharus of Dang: Rites de Passage and Festivals." *Kailash* 9 (2–3):177–258.

Ramble, Charles, 1997. "Tibetan Pride of Place; Or, Why Nepal's Bhotiyas Are Not an Ethnic Group." In *Nationalism and Ethnicity in a Hindu Kingdom: The Politics of Culture in Contemporary Nepal*, ed. David N. Gellner, Joanna Pfaff-Czarnecka, and John Whelpton. Amsterdam: Harwood.

Rana, Pashupati J. B. 1969. "Towards an Integrated Policy of National Integration." *Vasudha* 12 (8):7–14.

Rankin, Katharine. 1999. "Kamaiya Practices in Western Nepal: Perspectives on Debt Bondage." In *Nepal: Tharu and Tarai Neighbours*, ed. Harald O. Skar. Kathmandu: EMR.

Regmi, Mahesh C. 1976. *Landownership in Nepal*. Berkeley: University of California Press.

——. 1978. *Thatched Huts and Stucco Palaces: Peasants and Landlords in 19th Century Nepal*. New Delhi: Vikas Publishing House.

——. 1984. *The State and Economic Surplus: Production, Trade and Resource Mobilization in Early 19th Century Nepal*. Varanasi: Nath Publishing House.

Risley, H. H. 1892. *The Tribes and Castes of Bengal*. Vol. 2. Calcutta: Bengal Secretariat Press.

Robertson, Adam, and Shisham Mishra. 1997. *Forced to Plough: Bonded Labor in Nepal's Agricultural Economy*. London: Anti-Slavery International; Kathmandu: Informal Sector Service Center.

Rose, Leo E., and Margaret W. Fisher. 1970. *The Politics of Nepal*. Ithaca, N.Y.: Cornell University Press.

Roy Choudhuri, P. C. 1952. "The Tharus." *Man in India* 32:246–250.

Rudolph, Lloyd I., and Susanne Hoeber Rudolph. 1960. "The Political Role of India's Caste Associations." *Pacific Affairs* 33 (1):5–22.

Sachau, E. C. 1910. *Alberuni's India*. London: Kegan Paul, Trench, Trübner.

Shafey, Omar. 1997. "Medical Pluralism among the Tharu People of Far West Nepal: The Logic of Shamanism at the Jungle Frontier." Ph.D. diss., University of California–San Francisco and Berkeley.

Shaha, Rishikesh. 1982. "Political Elites of Nepal: Their Identity, Role and Character." In *The Nepalese Elite*. Occasional Papers, ser. 2. Varanasi: Center for the Study of Nepal, Banaras Hindu University.

——. 1990. *Modern Nepal: A Political History 1869–1955*. Vol. 1. Riverdale, Md.: The Riverdale Company.

Sharma, Prayag Raj. 1977. "Caste, Social Mobility and Sanskritization: A Study of Nepal's Old Legal Code." *Kailash* 5 (4): 277–299.

——. 1978. "Nepal: Hindu-Tribal Interface." *Contributions to Nepalese Studies* 6 (1):1–14.

——. 1992. "How to Tend This Garden?" *Himal* 5 (3):7–9.

——. 1997. "Nation-Building, Multi-Ethnicity, and the Hindu State." In *Nationalism and Ethnicity in a Hindu Kingdom: The Politics of Culture in Contemporary Nepal*, ed. David N. Gellner, Joanna Pfaff-Czarnecka, and John Whelpton. Amsterdam: Harwood.

Sharma, R. C. 1965. *Village Bankati (Tahsil Nighasan, District Kheri)*. Village Survey Monograph 11. Census of India 1961, vol. 15, pt. 6. Delhi: Manager of Publications.

Sherring, M. A. 1872. *Hindu Tribes and Castes, as Represented in Benares*. London: Trübner.

Shils, Edward. 1957. "Primordial, Personal, Sacred and Civil Ties." *British Journal of Sociology* 8:130–145.

Shrestha, Manesh. 1994. "Broadcasting Tongue Twister." *Himal* 7 (5):32.

Singh, K. S. 1985. *Tribal Society in India*. Delhi: Manohar.

Singh, Ramanand Prasad. 1988. *The Real Story of the Tharus*. Kathmandu: The Tharu Samskriti.

Sinha, Surajit. 1962. "State Formation and Rajput Myth in Tribal Central India." *Man in India* 42 (1):35–80.

——. 1973. "Re-thinking about Tribes and Indian Civilization." *Journal of the Indian Anthropological Society* 8:99–108.

Skar, Harald O. 1995. "Myths of Origin: The Janajati Movement, Local Traditions, Nationalism and Identities in Nepal." *Contributions to Nepalese Studies* 22 (1):31–42.

——. 1999. "Becoming Rana: Identity and Regional Self-Ascription in Lowland Nepal." In *Nepal: Tharu and Tarai Neighbors*, ed. Harald O. Skar. Kathmandu: EMR.

Skaria, Ajay. 1999. *Hybrid Histories : Forests, Frontiers and Wildness in Western India*. Delhi: Oxford University Press.

Skerry, Christa A., Kerry Moran, and Kay M. Calavan. 1991. *Four Decades of Development: The History of U.S. Assistance to Nepal, 1951–1991*. Kathmandu: USAID.

Smith, Anthony D. 1986. *The Ethnic Origins of Nations*. Oxford: Basil Blackwell.

Smith, Raymond T. 1966. "People and Change." In *New World: Guyana Independence Issue*. Demerara, Guyana.

Smith, Thomas. 1852. *Narrative of a Five Years' Residence at Nepaul*. 2 vols. London: Colburn.

Sonntag, Selma K. 1995. "Ethnolinguistic Identity and Language Policy in Nepal." *Nationalism and Ethnic Politics* 1 (4):108–120.

Srivastava, S. K. 1958. *The Tharus: A Study in Culture Dynamics*. Agra: Agra University Press.

——. 1999. "Culture Dynamics among the Rana Tharus: The Past in the Present." In *Nepal: Tharu and Tarai Neighbours*, ed. Harald O. Skar. Kathmandu: EMR.

Stebbing, E. P. 1926. *The Forests of India*. Vol. 3. London: John Lane, The Bodley Head.

Stevenson-Moore, C. J. 1900. *Final Report on the Survey and Settlement Operations in the Champaran District, 1892–1899*. Calcutta: Bengal Secretariat Press.

Stewart, J. L. 1865. "Notes of Observations on the Boksas of the Bijnour District." *Journal of the Asiatic Society of Bengal* 34, pt. 2 (3):147–173.

Stiller, Ludwig F. 1976. *The Rise of the House of Gorkha: A Study in the Unification of Nepal (1768–1816)*. New Delhi: Manjusri Publishing House.

Swinton, Alan. 1862[?] *Manual of the Statistics of the District of Goruckpore*. Allahabad: Government Press.

Takaya, Yoshikazu. 1977. "The Agriculture of Nepal: Its Ecology and Historical Development." In *Changing Aspects of Modern Nepal*, ed. Shigeru Iijima. Monumenta Serindica, no. 1. Tokyo: Institute for the Study of Languages and Culture of Asia and Africa.

Terrenato, L., et al. 1988. "Decreased Malaria Morbidity in the Tharu People Compared to Sympatric Populations in Nepal." *Annals of Tropical Medicine and Parasitology* 82:1–11.

Thompson, Richard H. 1989. *Theories of Ethnicity: A Critical Appraisal*. New York: Greenwood Press.

Tiwari, Ashutosh, 2001. "Ex-Kamaiyas' Act of Peaceful Civil Disobedience." *Nepali Times*, 26 January–1 February.

Trevor, C. G., and E. A. Smythies. 1923. *Practical Forest Management. A Handbook with*

Special Reference to the United Provinces of Agra and Oudh. Allahabad: Government Press, United Provinces.

Turner, Ralph Lilley. 1980. *A Comparative and Etymological Dictionary of the Nepali Language.* New Delhi: Allied Publishers.

Turner, Terence. 1991. "Representing, Resisting, Rethinking: Historical Transformations of Kayapo Culture and Anthropological Consciousness." In *Colonial Situations: Essays on the Contextualization of Ethnographic Knowledge,* ed. George Stocking. Madison: University of Wisconsin Press.

Upreti, Bedh Prakash. 1975. "Analysis of Change in Limbu-Brahmin Interrelationships in Limbuwan, Nepal." Ph.D. diss., University of Wisconsin, Madison.

Van den Berghe, Pierre L. 1981. *The Ethnic Phenomenon.* New York: Elsevier.

Vansittart, Eden. 1894. "The Tribes, Clans and Castes of Nepāl." *Journal of the Asiatic Society of Bengal* 63, pt. 1 (4):213–249.

Vincent, Joan. 1974. "The Structuring of Ethnicity." *Human Organization* 33:375–379.

Webber, Thomas W. 1902. *The Forests of Upper India.* London: Edward Arnold.

Weber, Eugen. 1976. *Peasants into Frenchmen: The Modernization of Rural France, 1870–1914.* Stanford, Calif.: Stanford University Press.

Weiss, Mark L., and Alan E. Mann. 1990. *Human Biology and Behavior: An Anthropological Perspective.* Glenview, Ill.: Scott, Foresman / Little Brown Higher Education.

Whelpton, John. 1997. "Political Identity in Nepal: State, Nation, and Community." In *Nationalism and Ethnicity in a Hindu Kingdom: The Politics of Culture in Contemporary Nepal,* ed. David N. Gellner, Joanna Pfaff-Czarnecka, and John Whelpton. Amsterdam: Harwood.

Wyatt, A. n.d. *Statistics of the District of Sarun, Consisting of Sircars Sarun and Chumparun.* Calcutta: Military Orphan Press.

INDEX

Note: Page numbers with an *f* indicate figures; those with a *t* indicate tables.